The Big Collection Of Teacher Tips

Book 2

Editors:
Lori Bruce
Grace Buonocore
Jill Champion
Lynn Coble
Irving Crump
Sheryl Miller
Kathy Wolf

Artists:
Pam Crane
Teresa Davidson
Susan Hodnett
Rebecca Saunders
Barry Slate
Jennifer Tipton

Cover Design:
Pam Crane

THE
EDUCATION
CENTER
INCORPORATED

The Big Collection Of Teacher Tips

Book 2

About This Book

In this follow-up volume to our popular *Big Collection Of Teacher Tips,* we've compiled more of the best teacher-tested ideas featured in *The Mailbox* magazines during the past few years. As an added bonus, we've included hundreds of never-before-published ideas from our subscribers—who now number over a quarter of a million! These ideas were sent to The Education Center from elementary teachers from all over the United States and Canada.

Many of the ideas in this book come from regular features in the three editions of *The Mailbox,* including "Lifesavers" and "Our Readers Write." In addition, there are hundreds of other timesaving teacher-tested tips to help make your teaching easier and more creative.

How To Use This Book

The ideas in this resource are arranged so that you can refer to a topic quickly and choose just the idea you need. In each section, you'll find creative ways to teach a skill, management tips, or activities to fill in a few extra minutes of the teaching day. Most of the ideas are adaptable to any grade level.

Look in several sections for ideas to suit your individual needs. For example, if you're looking for a game idea for a classroom birthday party, be sure to look in both the games and the birthdays sections. We're sure that you'll find many new ideas within these pages that will add to your teaching success!

About *The Mailbox*

If you're not already a subscriber to *The Mailbox,* we invite *you* to become a member of our family of teachers. We're sure you'll find *The Mailbox* to be the most practical teacher magazine around—loaded with thematic units, appealing reproducible student activities and projects, teaching activities to use with children's literature, bulletin board ideas and patterns, learning center activities, ready-to-use games and manipulatives, and lots, lots more!

The Mailbox is available in the following three grade-specific editions:

Pre/K (Preschool/Kindergarten)
Primary (Grades 1–3)
Intermediate (Grades 4–6)

Table Of Contents

Fluff And Stuff

Before school begins in the fall, mail a letter to each new student, welcoming him to your class. So he'll be able to locate the room easily, tell him to look for the stuffed animal by your door. Then make a lasting impression by displaying a huge or particularly eye-catching toy.

Mary Daubersmith
Ketchikan, AK

Stuffed Teddy Bear

At the beginning of each year, I buy a stuffed teddy bear. The bear goes home with a different child each Friday to spend the weekend. The bear has a notebook that goes with it, and the child and his parents must write down everything the bear does with them. One bear even traveled to California on an airplane! The students love taking the bear home, and writing in the notebook is a nice way for the family to spend time together.

Kim Brown
Ellendale, ND

WANTED: New Students

Welcome your new crew with fact-filled "WANTED" posters. Write important information about each student (gathered from school records or last year's teachers) on a duplicated "WANTED" poster. Place the posters on a large bulletin board. Students will enjoy reading about each other on the first day of school. Have students add photos from home and other pertinent information about themselves as the week progresses.

Melissa Matusevich
Blacksburg, VA

Wind Chimes

At my new school, all the buildings and sidewalks look alike to my first graders. To help them quickly identify my room, I hang wind chimes outside the door. The children enjoy keeping a "gauge" on the weather too!

Sheilah Broughton
Mayo, FL

Flower Finders

At the beginning of each school year, very young students need a lot of assistance in the cafeteria. I put bouquets of paper flowers on our assigned lunch tables so that the children will know where to sit. This frees me to help the children in the lunch line with their trays and thus avoid a lot of confusion.

Sheila R. Chapman
Decatur, AL

The ABCs Of Me

Here's a great back-to-school center that promotes self-esteem and confidence. Label the inside of a file folder with the letters of the alphabet and laminate. Using a wipe-off marker, the student writes things he likes that begin with each alphabet letter. Provide time for students to share their favorites with their teacher or class.

Carolyn Barwick
Madison Heights, MI

The ABCs Of Me!

A-apple
B-balls
C-Cats

1. Write the letters of the alphabet on a sheet of paper.
2. After each letter, write something that you like that begins with that letter.

WANTED
Jeremy Jones

Height: 4'9"
Hair: Blonde
Eyes: Blue
Address: 110 Wade Avenue
Last seen in Mrs. Smith's 4th grade class.

Now's The Time To Plant!

Give your classroom a warm, homey feeling by filling it with plants. Ask students to collect unwanted seeds and clippings from friends' and relatives' plants. Put the children in charge of caring for the plants. At the end of the year, let each child take one home.

Rebecca Gibson Calton
Auburn, AL

Then And Now

"Before-and-after" papers make an instant year-end bulletin board. File away student papers at the beginning of the school year. About a month before the end of the year, pull them out. Post a September and May paper for each student on a bulletin board, and connect the pairs with colored yarn. Students are thrilled to see their progress, and your last bulletin board is a big hit!

Annette Mathias
Partridge, KS

Class Yearbook

During the school year, I have my students work on a class yearbook. I divide them into committees and have them collect pictures, photos, news clippings, and program bulletins. After field trips and other special events, we write descriptive paragraphs to add to our yearbook. The project helps students to make decisions, work in groups, and create a finished product. We proudly display our book at the end of the year in the school library or office.

Sandra Reynolds
Ooltewah, TN

Spelling Test Booklets

Get a jump on spelling work for the year. Make a spelling test booklet for each child. Include the number of pages he'll need for weekly tests in one grading period. Have the children take the booklets home along with their report cards. Parents can easily see their child's grades and progress.

Pam Pease
Keystone Heights, FL

Do You Remember When...?

During the school year, I keep a list of class anecdotes about individual students. For example, "Donna was chosen by the magician to assist him during the assembly," and "Ray wore different-colored socks to school." At the end of the year, I type the anecdotes on a ditto, leaving out the students' names ("_____ wore different-colored socks to school."). Seeing which student can fill in the most correct names is a fun way to recap the school year. I always include some of my own mishaps too!

Mary Jo Bailin
Toledo, OH

Grumpy Bear

At the beginning of the year, I set up a Grumpy Bear chair. I tell students when they are feeling grumpy or sad they can sit in Grumpy's chair, and he'll take their blues away. The chair stays in place all year long.

Jana Jensen
Gelette, WY

Slide Show Presentation

Throughout the year, take slides of your students involved in daily activities, special events, field trips, and programs. Toward the end of the year or at a PTA meeting, invite parents to your class for a slide show to be followed by refreshments. To accompany the slide show, play some special songs, such as "Greatest Love Of All," by Whitney Houston; "You Are The Sunshine Of My Life," by Stevie Wonder; "You Are So Beautiful," by Kenny Rankin; or "We Are The World, We Are The Children." Have boxes of tissues handy, as there are sure to be tears of love at this event!

Mary Dinneen, Bristol, CT

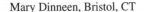

5

LIZA

Helpers Chart

When preparing a helpers chart, I take a picture of each student. I mount each photo on construction paper, label it with the child's name, and put the date on the back. The cards are then laminated. The children love seeing their pictures, and it's easy for a substitute to match the names and faces. At the end of the year, I have a lovely reminder of each student.

Lynn E. Teague
Charlotte, NC

Magnetic Nametags

Are you tired of fussing with nametags all year long? Try this! Glue a magnet to the back of each nametag. Display tags from the metal fronts of desks until names are learned. Then simply remove and store the tags. When a special guest or a substitute arrives, the tags can quickly be placed on the desks again.

Carol L. Wojtecki
St. Francis, WI

Freddy

Promoting Class Unity

Promote good feelings and unity in your class with these beginning-of-the-year activities. First have your students decide on a class mascot. If possible, find a stuffed animal or other item that can represent the mascot. Then when someone does something special or a new student arrives, allow that student to keep the mascot on his desk for the day. Make class T-shirts that include the mascot by using sponges and fabric paints. Wear the T-shirts to school assemblies, on field trips, on field day, or on any day to show class pride. Also have students incorporate their mascot in a class banner and cheer.

Dawn Helton
Silsbee, TX

Lasting Nametags

Do you make nametags many times a year? Try cutting shapes out of vinyl place mats for durable nametags you make only once.

Connie Thompson

Laminated Tags

Make unusual nametags with shape notepads (available from The Education Center). Label and laminate one page for each child. My kids love them!

Gail Cross
Bluff City, TN

Derrick

Stamp Collecting

For a year-long classroom project, I turned my first graders on to the hobby of stamp collecting. We invited two guest speakers (postmasters) to help us kick off our project. Photo albums—the kind with adhesive pages covered with plastic—were used to store stamps. A decorated box was placed in our post office so that local citizens could donate stamps. We also created our own stamps and collected reward stickers on a ditto designed to look like a blank stamp. In May, students wrote thank-you letters to all the people who helped with the project. Our local postmaster decorated the post office with letters he received. Photographs that I took during our stamp-collecting time were posted along with the letters. Parents were very pleased that the children now had a fun hobby that could be continued for years to come.

Deborah Paouncic
Slickville, PA

Name Badges

At the beginning of the year, have students design badges with their names on them. Laminate the badges or use the Badge-It kits to make professional-looking pins. After the first week of school, collect the badges and store them to use with student teachers, substitute teachers, chaperones on field trips, or visitors. Pass out the badges so all students can be called by name.

Jan Drehmel
Chippewa Falls, WI

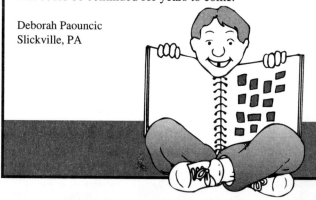

Donations, Please!

In my monthly newsletter to parents, I always include a paragraph that begins, "Donations are now being accepted for...." I include such goodies as stickers, old game markers, and dice for making centers; bookmarks for prizes; and whatever else is needed for that month. Parents are very generous once they're aware of specific needs.

Mary Anne T. Haffner
Waynesboro, PA

Wall Of Fame

Induct your new students into a "Wall Of Fame." Divide a large bulletin board into sections, one for each student. During the first week of school, let each child decorate his section with personal items—baby pictures, hobby items, family snapshots, original drawings. Classmates will be amazed at how much they can learn about their old and new friends from this attractive display.

Video Memories

Before school begins each fall, I purchase a new videotape and label it with my name, grade, and the upcoming year. I begin videotaping my class in September, with "back-to-school" pictures of each student. Then each month I videotape the students in action, including special events such as Halloween, Thanksgiving, Christmas, Valentine's Day, special PTA programs, Awards Day, and so on. We view the tape periodically throughout the year; the students love to see themselves! At the end of the year, I send a note to each child's parents informing them about the tape. Each parent who would like a copy sends me a blank tape, and a volunteer makes copies for me. What a way to remember a child's school year!

Brenda Hancock
Columbus, GA
Barbara Gump
Little Rock, AR

"Dear Me"

Begin and end the year with this thought-provoking activity. Have each child bring in stationery and a stamped envelope. Discuss setting goals, sharing some of your own goals for the year. Next have each student write a letter to himself stating five goals he'd like to meet during the year. The student addresses the envelope to himself, places the finished letter inside, and returns it unsealed to you. Store the envelopes in a safe place. At the end of the year, place a brief letter or "Thanks for being in my class" note in each envelope before mailing. Students will enjoy reflecting on their goals and receiving a personal note from you.

The Joy Of Giving

At the beginning of the school year, I send letters to my students' parents asking them not to send me personal gifts for Christmas, Valentine's Day, or Teacher Appreciation Week. Instead, I suggest they send something that the children can enjoy. The parents generously give stickers, reward certificates, pencils, flash cards, and puzzles. The children love these surprises!

Lea Holton
Louisville, KY

Scrapbook In A Box

For a different way to store memorabilia, have your students make scrapbooks in boxes. First measure the inside length and width of a box. Then accordion-fold a long piece of paper to fit inside. Paste the first and last pages to the inside top and inside bottom of the box. You may extend the pages of this scrapbook for display.

Quick Classroom Money

Looking for a great way to earn money for school supplies? Ask parents to donate items to be sold at a well-advertised class garage sale. I always send a note home afterward advising parents of how the money was used and the ways their children benefited.

Sr. Margaret Ann Wooden
Martinsburg, WV

First-Day Friends

For a welcome warm-up on the first day of school, cut squares from colored paper. Then cut each square into two irregular shapes. As you greet each child, ask him to choose a shape. After everyone has arrived, have the children find the person with the shape that completes his square. Then let the "new friends" get acquainted for a few minutes. Try this for a few days until everyone has met.

Annette Mathias
Partridge, KS

Introductory Letter

Parents and students are always curious about their new teachers. The first day or week of school, send home a letter stating who you are and where you live and your educational background, teaching experience, family life, and hobbies. Students and parents will feel they know the teacher a little better after reading this letter. You may learn you have some things in common!

Sheila Smith
Templeton, PA

H-E-L-L-O

Break the ice on the first day of school with a bingo game of student names. Duplicate a blank bingo grid or cut one-inch graph paper to size. Students gather signatures from classmates until their grids are full; then they cover names with markers as they are called out. When a student covers a row vertically, horizontally, or diagonally, he calls out "Hello!"

Joanne Davis
Orlando, FL

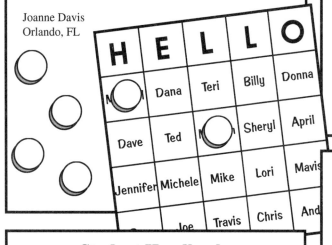

The Pledge

The first day of every school year, when we get ready to say "The Pledge Of Allegiance," I ask the children why we do it. In the many years I've been teaching, there have been only three years when someone could answer that question! I keep asking each morning until the class understands that the pledge is a promise of loyalty to our nation. Occasionally I ask the question again so students won't forget to love their country.

Mary Dinneen
Bristol, CT

Pair And Share

Take time on the first day back to school to introduce students to one another. Have children line up in order of their birthdates. Pair each student with a person standing next to him. Give the pairs five minutes to interview each other on the topics of their choice. When time is up, each student will introduce his partner to the class. Everyone will get to know at least one person a lot better. Be sure that you "pair and share" with someone too!

Student Handbooks

Design a student handbook especially for your class. Begin it with a short welcome and continue with pages outlining school and classroom rules, rewards and consequences, materials needed, your basic schedule, your name and phone number, and the room number. On the first day of school, give each student a handbook as he enters the classroom, providing something to read until everyone has arrived. The students can share the handbooks with their parents and will adjust more quickly since they can consult their booklets rather than asking you questions. An added bonus— as new students join the class during the year, the handbook will save you time going over the basics!

A Poem For Open House

On the first day of school, have students copy a poem for handwriting practice. Keep this first-day writing assignment. The week before Open House, ask children to copy the poem again. Attractively display both copies side by side to show handwriting improvement.

Julia K. Mozingo
Altus, OK

Getting-Acquainted Cards

Help new students get over the "first-day jitters" with this activity. Label a set of cards with statements such as "I was born in a foreign country" or "I have an unusual pet." In turn, read each card orally. Any student to which the card applies stands up and gives the class more information.

Sample cards

I am an only child.
I play on a Little League sports team.
My mother has an unusual job.
My father has an unusual job.
I have traveled outside this state.
I have met a famous person.
I read an interesting book this summer.

Getting To Know You

Try this "get acquainted" activity during the first week of school. Be sure all students have been introduced and are wearing nametags. In a small bag, place cards with directions such as "Find out John Smith's favorite game" and "Find out Mary Doe's least favorite subject." Have students sit in a circle and pass the bag while music plays in the background. When the music stops, the child holding the bag must pull out a card and follow its directions. By reading the cards orally, students become acquainted with their classmates more quickly.

Jeffrey Kuntz
Punxsutawney, PA

Back-To-School Raps

Older students enjoy listening to Top 40 tunes on the radio. Many of these include "rapping." Introduce your students to the year ahead with a toe-tapping, back-to-school rap. Begin by duplicating the following rap. Have several students recite it in unison, teaching it to the rest of the class. Then divide your class into groups. Give each group a textbook you will use during the year. Have each group review their book and write a rap describing its topics. Hold a "Rap Session" for groups to perform their raps for their classmates.

Back To School

Well, it's really cool
'Cause we're back in school.
We're going to study hard
So we won't be fools.
The subjects we'll learn just can't be beat,
and we'll always be sure our work is neat.
There'll be math, social studies,

Science and art,
Writing, spelling, and health
Will play a big part.
Music, reading, and English will be part of our day,
And when we're finished, we'll go out to play!
So we'd better get busy 'cause it's time to begin,
So we can be smarter when this year ends!

Welcome
Parents and Friends of

1.____ 8.____ 15.____
2.____ 9.____ 16.____
3.____ 10.____ 17.____
4.____ 11.____ 18.____
5.____ 12.____ 19.____
6.____ 13.____ 20.____
7.____ 14.____ 21.____

Welcome Parents And Friends

Hang a large sign outside your door to welcome visitors to Open House. Each child signs his name to welcome family members and friends to their special night at school.

Joan Holesko
North Tonawanda, NY

Sign Up, Please!

Looking for parent volunteers for field trips, class parties, and clerical tasks? Design a display they can't miss at Open House! Place an attractive booklet and several pens in an area of the classroom. Invite parents to sign up for the jobs they would like. It will save you countless hours on the telephone searching for last-minute help.

Paula K. Holdren
Chalfon, PA

Valentine's Day Party
Date: February 14
Time: 1:00
Cupcakes/Cookies ____
Drinks ____
Cups and Napkins ____

Classroom Newspaper
Date: October 15
Typing ____

Zoo Field Trip
Date: May 10
Time: 8:00-2:00

Classmate Scramble

Help classmates get acquainted with each other. Have students list several facts about themselves on index cards on the first day of school. Each day, scramble one student's name on the chalkboard, adding several clues to his identity (taken from his index card). Using the clues, students unscramble the letters to discover the mystery student's name. After he has been identified, the mystery student becomes the "star" pupil and is awarded a star or badge to wear throughout the day.

Brenda N. Dalton
Portsmouth, VA

Vae Dovasnid
-Has blonde hair
-Loves horses
-Has a friend named Kiesha

It's In The Bag!

Help your students get to know one another with an interviewing activity. Write each child's name on a small paper bag. Staple the bags to a bulletin board with the title "___ Grade—It's In The Bag!" Place the name of a classmate inside each bag. Have a few students at a time remove their bags from the board. Each child pulls the name from his bag and spends a few minutes interviewing that classmate. Set aside time for each student to "introduce" the interviewee to the rest of the class. On the board, write a list of good questions to ask:

- Where were you born?
- What are your hobbies?
- What is your favorite movie?
- Who are the other members of your family?
- How do you like to spend a Saturday afternoon?
- What is the most interesting place you've ever visited?

Learning Favorites

Set out some of the students' favorite learning centers for parents to view. Open House is also a good time to show some centers for skills that students will be working on later in the year.

Connie Connely
Catoosa, OK

Parents And Students Are Winners!

As the parents enter the classroom for Open House, have them sign up for a door prize to be given the next day in class. The prize can be a flower, book, plaque, or other inexpensive item. The parents enjoy it, and the children are excited to see who wins.

Sr. Margaret Ann Wooden
Martinsburg, WV

Open House Invitation

Write an invitation to Open House on the board. Use it as a handwriting assignment. Children will do their best when they know it's going home to Mom and Dad!

Kathy Beard
Keystone Heights, FL

Open House Checklist

Post a "Welcome To Open House" checklist on each child's desk. The child checks off each item he shares with his family. In this way, special projects and labs are less likely to be overlooked. For a colorful way for guests to sign in, cover a table with bright butcher paper. Provide colored markers for parents to sign their names, write comments, and add drawings. Sharing the messages the following day is a great opener!

Barbara Hosek
Valencia, CA

Welcome to Open House!
Mrs. Conley —Third Grade—Room 2B
Check each item that you show your family.
Have fun!
Parent Sign-In Sheet
Daily Schedule
Homeroom seat and desk ....□
Reading seat and reading book ....□
Spelling seat and spelling teacher ...□
Math seat and math book ....□
Computer Lab ....□
Our Room
Class creed, rules ....□
Homework chart ....□
Super Student awards ....□
Poetry bulletin board ....□
Telescope with constellations ....□
Science table ....□
Reading is a Treasure ....□
Don't Forget
Introduce parents to Mrs. Conley .....□

All About Me

As they present these books to parents at Open House, children can proudly say, "Here's a book all about me!" Watch as children and parents sit down to turn the pages together. Have students begin work on their books on the first day of school. Each day, hand out pages for children to fill in with information about themselves. Topics may include: Interests, Favorites, Special Feelings, Dreams, Things That Bug Me, My Autobiography, Family Tree, Places I Have Lived, Places I Have Visited, Family, School, and Weekends. Bind each student's pages together to make a unique book and a special gift that is sure to impress parents.

Julia K. Mozingo
Altus, OK

Dear Mom and Dad,
Welcome to my desk. Look inside and see all of my books. Would you like to sit at my desk?
Love,
Jill

Welcome To My Desk

Each child has his or her own space in the classroom. Each has a special view of school from that space. Have children write notes to their parents telling about their spaces or their desks. Students will take a fresh look at their surroundings as they use their best handwriting skills.

Sr. Margaret Ann Wooden

A Welcoming Committee Of One

If your Open House comes in the fall, a scarecrow may be just the thing to welcome family and friends to your classroom. Students will have fun building a scarecrow from an old lamp stand and adding clothes stuffed with straw or newspaper. Let class-mates name their class mascot. Give him a sign, place him by the door to welcome guests, and add a few pumpkins at his feet. Visitors can't miss your classroom with this charming fellow to meet and greet them!

Lynda Holding
Blanchard, OK

WELCOME
To Mrs. Smith's Class

Class Pride

Show parents how proud you are of their children! Write five reasons you are proud of each student. Then before Open House night, tape the reasons to each child's desk so that parents can see at a glance why their son or daughter is special in the teacher's eyes.

5 Special Things About Matthew:

Me Mobiles

For Open House, decorate your classroom with "Me Mobiles" hanging from the ceiling. Each student writes his name on a piece of colored construction paper. Children slip the colored papers over their hangers and attach items that describe them-selves or things that they enjoy.

Paula K. Holdren
Chalfont, PA

Parent-Child Artwork

Be prepared to have parents and children create works of art together. Save scraps of paper, yarn, cloth, stickers, and other materials from a cleanup day in June. Put the bits and scraps into paper lunch bags for your new students. When parents and children come to school, give each family a paper bag of materials, and let them create pictures together. You not only end up with artwork to display, you also get to meet parents in an informal, relaxed atmosphere.

Marie Wiseman
Flower's Cove, Newfoundland, Canada

Student Dummies?

Welcome parents to Open House with a classroom full of student dummies! Have each child lie down on a piece of butcher paper. Trace around him, and let him color and cut out his outline. Put each outlined form in the child's desk. Will parents be able to find their child's place?

Kathy Beard
Keystone Heights, FL

Silhouette Riddles

A display of classroom silhouettes will attract parents' attention at Open House. Use an overhead projector to create each child's silhouette on black paper. Cut out and mount these on white paper. Have each child write a riddle about himself. Mount riddles beside cutouts. Parents will have fun finding their child's like-ness by shape and riddle.

Clara Presutti
Wheeling, WV

I have blue eyes.

My hair is brown.

I like pizza for dinner.

I have a pet named Crocket.

Who am I?

Who Am I?

Here's an intriguing way to get parents involved at Open House. It also helps students to get acquainted. Put student names in a hat, and have classmates draw names. Each child then sketches his classmate and writes five clues to his or her identity. Post the drawings with clues on the bulletin board, and hide the name of each student subject under a flap. Parents will have fun guessing which child is theirs!

Paula K. Holdren

BIRTHDAYS

Birthday Caterpillar

I use a Birthday Worm to help children remember their birthdates. On green poster board, I trace a 33rpm record for his head and a 45rpm record for his 12 body sections, one for each month. From pink construction paper, I cut caterpillar feet and label one for each child's birthday. The feet are taped to the appropriate month. Students can see the sequence of the months of the year and whose birthday is coming up next.

Linda Owens
Danville, AL

Jan. Gerard 1-17, Nichlaus 1-30 — 17, 30
Feb. Janet 2-6 — 6
Mar. Joshua 3-10 — 10
April Rose 4-5 — 5
May David 5-11, Keri 5-20 — 11, 20
June Elizabeth 6-28 — 28
July Maggie 7-12, Danielle 7-12 — 12, 12
Aug. Katie 8-4, Caroline 8-9, Stacie 8-21 — 4, 9, 21
Sept. Leon 9-5, Jacob 9-10 — 5, 10
Oct. Benny 10-3, Allie 10-4, Ian 10-16 — 3, 4, 16
Nov. David 11-6, Corey 11-18 — 6
Dec. Tad 12-?

Bear Birthday Chart

Keep up with your students' birthdays with an adorable birthday reminder. Make a dozen bear cutouts. On each bear's tummy, glue a construction-paper symbol for that month. Laminate the bears and use a permanent marker to write students' birthdates.

Beth Fleming
Rainsville, AL

Colorful Birthdays

This birthday bulletin board is a hit with my children! To make, I purchase crayon box invitations and fill one out for each child. I post all invitations on the bulletin board displaying each child's name and birthday. On the day of a child's birthday, the invitation is taken down in the morning and read to the class. That afternoon there is a party in honor of the birthday child.

Jana Jensen
Gillette, WY

 Jacob Jan. 8
 Jill Mar. 14
 Raji May 10
 Pam Feb. 12
 Miriam April 5
Elizabeth June 28

It's a party!
for: David
date: Nov. 6
time: 2:45
place: Rm 3
given by: Mrs. Jones's class

Chocolate-Chip Birthday

A giant chocolate-chip cookie can make a birthday celebration a simple matter! Spread the contents of two packages of refrigerator cookie dough onto a pizza pan, and bake. Break the cookie into pieces and have a chocolate-chip birthday.

Mary Larson, Bristol, CT

Forget-Me-Not Birthdays

Having trouble keeping up with students' birthdays? Put colorful birthday stickers on the appropriate dates on your calendar desk blotter to represent student birthdays. Beside each sticker write the name of the student born on that date. Each time you refer to your calendar, you'll be reminded of approaching birthdays.

Sue Ireland, Waynesboro, PA

Hear Ye! Hear Ye!

Let everyone know about your special birthday student. Make a sign that can be laminated for use the whole year, on which announcements of birthdays can be made. Hang the sign up outside your door. If your school has morning or afternoon announcements, you might ask the principal to include birthday wishes one day each week. Children always get a special feeling when their names are announced on the intercom!

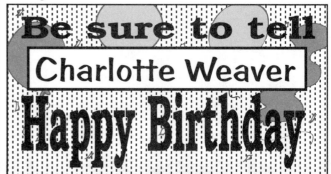

Be sure to tell **Charlotte Weaver** Happy Birthday

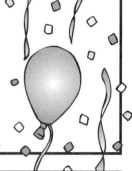

Un-birthday Parties

Children with summer birthdays will feel special when you give them "un-birthday" parties. During the last full month of school, celebrate children's birthdays on the matching dates in that month. For example, if Andy's birthday is July 22, celebrate his "un-birthday" on the 22nd. Proceed as usual with special birthday activities, and watch the happiness grow.

Sue Ireland
Waynesboro, PA

Summer Birthdays

Children with summer birthdays miss celebrating with their classmates. During the final week of school, surprise them with computer-made cards signed by the class. Bring in plain cupcakes, cans of frosting, and cake decorations so each child may fix his treat.

Mary Anne Haffner
Waynesboro, PA

This Certifies…

Give a birthday child a birthday gift certificate. Give the gift of no homework, extra recess, or a choice of game. Make the presentation a special time— let everyone join in a rousing chorus of "Happy Birthday" as you present it!

This certifies that

Has no homework because of a **Birthday!**

Choose Me!

It's always nice for the birthday child to have special privileges on his day, but many teachers have "job charts" already in place. Have some different "tasks" reserved for birthday people. For example, let the birthday boy or girl be the one who gets to choose a story for you to read to the class, or let him be your assistant in planning an art activity that week.

Happy Birthday

To say "Happy Birthday" to a student on his special day, pass out 4" x 4 1/2" pieces of construction paper in various colors. Each student cuts or tears his paper to look like a scoop of ice cream and then prints his name on it. The teacher staples the scoops to a large paper cone. Students and parents love this special remembrance from the class.

Sherry Newton
Wendell, ID

Half Birthdays

Here's a way that everyone can have a birthday celebration during the school year. If a student has a summer birthday, celebrate his half birthday. (A June 1 birthday would be celebrated on December 1.) No one will feel left out!

Kim Zimmerman
Cleveland, MS

"All About Me" Ribbon!

Make a special birthday ribbon from construction paper for your birthday child to wear on his day! On the day before, ask each of his classmates to write an adjective describing him on the ribbon.

BIRTHDAYS

Birthday Cards

Send each child in your class a birthday card through the mail. The time and money are well worth it when you see your students' happy faces. It's a real ego booster!

Joyce Hodge
Orange Park, FL

Birthday Balloons

When a student has a birthday, I write his name on a colorful paper balloon and attach the balloon's string to the appropriate date on our class calendar. The balloon can be presented to the student on his special day.

Kendra Atkinson
Myrtle Beach, SC

Computer Printout Birthday Banners

Make each student's birthday a big event with computer printout banners. Using your school's computer and software, make a big banner that says "Happy Birthday." Laminate it so it will last through many uses. Also make a banner with each child's name and a cute picture for the child to take home and color. On a student's birthday, use your "Happy Birthday" banner with the banner bearing the birthday person's name. Post the banner before school on birthdays so children will see it as they arrive.

Connie Luginsland
Waverly, KS

Birthday Place Mats

Make your students' birthdays extra special with festive, laminated place mats. On a child's birthday, a place mat is put on his desk so everyone knows that it is his special day. At the end of the day, the place mat is put away for the next birthday.

Sr. Margaret Ann Wooden
Martinsburg, WV

Free Birthday Assignment

I give each of my students a "Birthday Assignment" during the month of his birthday (May or September for summer birthdays). The student may choose not to complete one class assignment, as a birthday gift from me. It makes a great gift, and the kids love it!

Beverly Carlson
DePere, WI

Special Recognition

I make my students' birthdays extraspecial by setting a toy clown on their desks for the day. The clown holds a sign that says "Birthday Kid." My students know that the clown will be watching for their extraspecial birthday work all day long!

Sandra Anderson
Montevideo, MN

Birthday Bear Pencils

Birthday pencils from The Education Center become cuddly critters to brighten up everyone's birthday! Glue four pom-poms and a pair of wiggly eyes to the eraser end of each pencil. Give each child a pencil on his birthday. Hold a special celebration for summer birthday people.

Lois Cooper
Beckley, WV

Calendar Cards

When putting up the calendar for the new month, I always fill out a birthday card for each child born that month. I then staple the card directly to the date. The children look forward to the day when each card is opened, and I never miss a birthday!

Ann E. Fausnight
Canton, OH

Carry-In Breakfast

We have a small school district and like to let our janitors know that we truly appreciate their work. On each of their birthdays, we have a carry-in breakfast. Our day starts a bit earlier than usual, but it's become a traditional way of telling our custodial staff thanks.

Millie Kelly
Pleasant Hill, IL

Birthday Poster

For a quick and easy keepsake, I make a poster for each student's birthday. Along with "Happy Birthday!" the poster includes signatures and short messages from the rest of the students to the birthday person. The child gets to take home something special that also serves as a remembrance of the members of the class.

Susan Graham
Merion Station, PA

Birthday Bar Graph

A simple bar graph can be made by compiling students' birthdays beside each month. It also serves as a visible reminder to all. Use the information for a lesson on making graphs, too. Have students fill in the graph on a duplicated worksheet.

Debbie Wiggins
Myrtle Beach, SC

Remembering Birthdays

At the beginning of the year, I put each child's name and birthdate in a bag with that month's calendar pieces. When I get ready to put up the calendar, I will be reminded which birthdays are in that month. I also make a dozen cupcakes at a time and store them in the school freezer. On the morning of a child's birthday, I take one cupcake out, and it is thawed in time for his lunch.

Becky Williams
Roanoke, VA

A Bar Graph Showing Our Birthdays!

January	13 Robin		
February	2 Ricki	15 Tom	20 Betsy
March	17 Ron	19 Karen	
April	3 Ben	18 Mary	
May	16 Lynette	25 Sherry	26 Sue
June	5 Bud	12 Kay	

Helping Kids Feel Special

Under The Rainbow

Join hands together and display a rainbow of friendship on your classroom wall. Have each child trace and cut out a handprint for each color of the rainbow. Have each student color, paint, or finger paint each of his handprints a different color. Children may write a "friendship word" on each handprint also. Develop a list of friendship words so that students have many to choose from. Each morning let a student share a special thought while standing under the rainbow.

Friendship Clap And Rap

Setting aside a special time each week for a Friendship Clap and Rap session can help children to sort out their feelings and make new friends. Invite a neighboring class to join you. Gather in a large circle to discuss a recent topic or film; to share a book, poem, or class story; or to demonstrate a craft. At the beginning and end of the session, clap or rap this fun chant. (This chant works well with "Pat-a-Cake," finger snapping, or rapping to your own beat.)

To be a friend	We like each other
Is a special thing to be.	But we don't always agree,
I like you and	As you are you
You like me.	And I am me.

Mirror Magic

Over my sink, I placed a large mirror and these words…
Mirror, mirror on the wall
Who's the nicest kid of all?
At hand-washing time, it's a real ego booster!

Kathleen Baily
Avon, CT

Rays Of Sunshine

Let children earn rays of sunshine by displaying good friendship qualities. When a student shares with a friend, waits his turn, or makes a positive remark, present him with a ray of sunshine. Students add rays to smiling paper sun cutouts mounted on their desks. Rays may be given by classmates or the teacher.

Swapping Shoes

"Walking in someone else's shoes" can help children to understand the effects of their behavior and help them to make better behavior choices. Duplicate two copies of an athletic shoe outline for each child. Have him decorate his shoe; then join his pair with a long piece of yarn. After exchanging shoes with a classmate, have youngsters role-play various classroom situations such as name calling, excluding others from play, or teasing. Encourage ideas and suggestions for different outcomes that would avoid negative feelings.

Grandparents' Day

Help your youngsters take pride in their family heritages by celebrating a "Grandparents' Day." Write letters to grandparents inviting them to the celebration. Ask each guest to bring something from his childhood to share with the class: a baby dress, a photo album, and even amusing stories of the past. Afterward, have students compare their childhood with those of the guests.

Nancy Fish
Weaverville, NC

Autobiographies

To increase self-awareness, have students write autobiographical sketches. Ask them to pair up to share their sketches. Keep the autobiographies so the exercise can be repeated with a new partner.

Dr. Rebecca Graves, Burlington, NC
Dr. Fritz Mengert, Greensboro, NC

Good Job!

Special Buddies

Encourage young students to make new friends. Have each girl draw a girl's name and each boy draw a boy's name. The student pairs become "Special Buddies of the Week," sitting beside each other at lunch and helping one another with art projects. Draw new names the following week.

Carol Coler
Hastings, NE

Special Student

My Special Student of the Week is in charge of the "Good Work" bulletin board. I put checked papers in a basket on an old teacher's desk that the Special Student sits at for the week. That student is in charge of putting complimentary stamps or stickers on the sheets and displaying them on the board.

Jan Drehmel
Chippewa Falls, WI

Book Buddies

Build responsibility, confidence, and reading skills in your students by sponsoring a "Book Buddy" reading program. Choose interested readers to select and read books to children in lower grades. Have your readers practice the stories at home before reading them to the younger children. Everyone's excited when the Book Buddies come to visit!

Kathy Goldstein
Coral Springs, FL

Bicycle Buddies

Help children to realize that, although we are all different, we can all work together. Duplicate a bicycle wheel as shown for each student. Using the code below to answer eight questions of your choice, children color the sections between the spokes.

Some sample questions are:
1. Do you like spaghetti?
2. Do you have a sister?
3. Do you think school is fun?

red = yes
blue = sometimes
yellow = no

When the wheels are complete, display them and discuss how each wheel is unique. Then discuss how two students might work together to complete a common task as you introduce the idea of cooperation and teamwork.

Little Brothers And Sisters

Each of my fifth graders chose a little brother or sister from the kindergarten class at our school. After a brief visit, we returned to our classroom and made personalized place mats for our new family members. They were laminated and delivered. The room came alive with smiles!

Rebecca Gibson Calton, Auburn, AL

Student Thoughts

During the afternoon, I write a "thought question" on the board. At the end of the day, I ask the students what their answers to the thought question might be. Some of the questions I have used are "What is your favorite subject?" and "What is your favorite sport, and why?" It's a great way to discover hidden interests and talents of your students.

Becky Berg
Jefferson, SD

Help Wanted!

Need help coloring centers or drawing bulletin board figures? I invite fifth and sixth graders who are former students of mine to help me out. Markers and other supplies are kept in plastic shopping bags so students can easily take work home and return it. At the end of the year, I have a pizza party to thank my helpers for the work they have done.

Mary Anne Haffner
Waynesboro, PA

Helping Kids Feel Special

Good Job!

Students Needed

Here's an idea that will let you use your student helpers and their talents effectively. Post a notice announcing the jobs available (making games, centers, bulletin boards, etc.). Ask each applicant to provide one sample of his work. Assign your helpers to specific jobs according to their talents (coloring, lettering, drawing). I received plenty of help!

Mary Anne Haffner
Waynesboro, PA

Student Artists

Utilize students' talents to help make your worksheets more appealing. The next time you make your own worksheet, ask a student to add some original artwork. Be sure to have him sign and date it. The artist will feel especially proud when his worksheet is duplicated for the entire class. The worksheet will also be special since it will be used by others in years to come.

Mary Dinneen
Bristol, CT

Puttin' On The Hits

A popular TV show, "Puttin' On The Hits," invites contestants to choose a favorite record and imitate the singer or group while the record plays. Use this idea to build self-confidence and perk up the next rainy day. Let small groups of children play a favorite recording and lip-sync to it as it plays. The only noise will be the record! Students will have fun while they practice being in front of a group.

Rebecca Gibson Calton
Auburn, AL

Bear Hugs

Keep a box of felt wristbands decorated with small felt bears in a prominent place. When a student is having a bad day or needs extra attention, he or she puts on a wristband. This alerts the class to give that student some Tender Loving Care. The wristband helps minimize bad behavior because the student receives positive attention before resorting to a temper tantrum or outburst.

Diana West
Big Horn, WY

Group Captain

This method of organizing the classroom builds a sense of responsibility and encourages good citizenship. Divide the class into groups of four or five students. Make sure there is a wide range of ability among students in each group. The groups should arrange their desks together. Each group has a captain who alternates every week. The captain's responsibilities are:

1. Writing down and compiling work for absent students in the group;
2. Collecting assignments;
3. Reporting any student who doesn't complete an assignment;
4. Encouraging the group to work quietly;
5. Making sure the area around the group is clean.

Linda Rookstool
Beavercreek, OH

Guest Teachers

Encourage individual differences and talents by allowing your students to become guest teachers. Set aside a special period each week for a student to teach a lesson about one of his interests. Lessons can be taught on painting, dancing, pet care, or practically anything. It's a great way to build self-esteem and learn more about your students.

Sr. Margaret Ann Wooden
Martinsburg, WV

Potpourri

Keep a bunch of potpourri in your desk drawer. When students come to your desk, they'll enjoy smelling the fragrance.

Mary Dinneen

Welcome Note

Greet your newcomers with a rebus greeting written on your door.

I'm happy to see you!

Wendy Brunker
Sauk City, WI

Comforting Coughers

Especially during the winter, coughing can be "contagious." To ease the coughing before it becomes epidemic, keep a supply of small, disposable cups on hand. Whenever a student has a coughing spell, allow him to fill one of the cups with water and take it to his desk. He can sip on the water when he feels the need to cough and you can continue your lesson with fewer interruptions.

Mary Dinneen
Bristol, CT

Congratulations Poster

Recognize student achievements on a congratulations poster displayed outside your classroom door. Laminate the poster and list student accomplishments with an overhead-marking pen. Use a damp cloth to keep the list up to date. Students will glow with pride!

Debbie Wiggins
Myrtle Beach, SC

☆ Congratulations

TO: FOR:

Stacie Hodnett   Winning the "Best Essay" contest

Nichlaus Prellwitz Second Place in the Science Fair

Something Good Happened Today

With all of the criticism of the education system today, it's easy for teachers to begin to doubt themselves. To combat this, purchase an inexpensive blank book, found in most bookstores. On the front or inside cover, write "Something good happened today." At the end of each day, write at least one nice thing that happened. It might be as simple as "Mary Jones brought me a rose," or as exciting as "Everyone finally understands fractions!" When you're feeling low, read through these pages, and you'll feel better about the year. You may also wish to have your students take turns writing nice things in a book for the class to share.

Jan Hodgin
High Point, NC

Something Good Happened Today!

Personalized Sentences

When putting sentences on the board for children to copy, write their names instead of those in the book. It will keep their attention and draw out the correct answers. "David Ragsdale discovered America, right?"

Rebecca Gibson Calton
Auburn, AL

Person Of The Week

On the first day of school, each of my students fills out an information sheet (favorites, family and pet information, hobbies, etc.). I choose one sheet each week and copy the information onto a large piece of construction paper. This is posted on a "Person Of The Week" bulletin board. The chosen student wears a special button, leads the class line, and enjoys other special privileges. My fifth graders rush to the room on Monday morning to see who the special person will be.

Ginny Lichlyter
Hanover, IN

Spotlight On Students

Give your students special keepsakes. When one of your students is featured in a local or school newspaper, laminate the article and present it to him. He'll be pleased that you noted his accomplishment, and the article is sure to become a prized momento.

Rebecca Gibson Calton

Helping Kids Feel Special

Show-offs

Let your students display their favorite work on a show-off bulletin board. Each child selects one paper from his weekly work to be exhibited. At the bottom of this assignment he adds a sentence sharing why he feels good about this particular paper. This sentence is informative for the teacher and parents, and lets the student express his feelings about his achievement.

Mary Anne Haffner
Waynesboro, PA

"Ask Me" Badge

One of your students made a major breakthrough today. You'd love to write his parents so they could share in the excitement..., but... there simply isn't time to write a note. No problem! Have him wear the "Ask Me" Badge home so that he will be invited to tell about his day. Use these badges sparingly, and they will add excitement and create parent involvement.

Rebecca Gibson Calton
Auburn, AL

Taking Attendance

When I call roll, I ask the students questions such as "What is your favorite color of the leaves?" or "What do you like to do in the fall?" Instead of responding, "Here," the student answers my question. We've learned a lot about one another this way.

Bobbie Hallman
Merced, CA

A Real Lifesaver

To make a clever thank-you note, attach a miniroll of Lifesavers candy to the middle of an unlined index card. Under the candy, tell the recipient why you think he was a "real lifesaver."

Chris Christensen
Las Vegas, NV

You're a "Real Lifesaver"

Thank you for your help in class. Mrs. Jones

Tooth Tree

I have a "tooth tree" in my classroom. When a child loses a tooth, we add a paper "tooth" to its branches. The tree will be covered before the year ends.

Mrs. W. R. Jeffery
Chesterland, OH

The Golden Chair

Treat your students to a place of honor. Spray a chair gold. Children are thrilled to sit in the "Golden Chair" on their birthdays or as a reward for good behavior or other achievements.

Jenny Kieswetler
Bowling Green, KY

Sunshine Quilt

Spread a little sunshine to a child who is sick for an extended period. Give each student a piece of construction paper folded in fourths. Each child traces over the folds and makes crayon "stitches" on the lines and around the edges. He draws simple pictures in the boxes to illustrate friendship, happy thoughts, or best wishes. Then he writes and signs a message on the back. Tape all of the papers together to make one large quilt, or punch holes around the edges and lace them together. Send the "quilt" home in a decorated basket.

Mary Lafser Via
Vinton, VA

Positive Profiles

Make a construction-paper silhouette of each child. Mount each silhouette on tagboard and label. Then have each student say one positive comment about that child. Write the comments around that child's silhouette. Laminate and display.

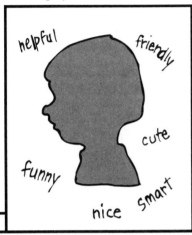

ABC Feeling Book

Help youngsters develop a larger "feeling vocabulary" by making ABC Feeling Books. Each day, use a different letter and discuss "feeling" words that start with that letter. Then act out situations involving the feelings. Each child then picks a word to include in his book, writes a sentence using the word, and illustrates it. Bind the books when they are completed so the children can keep them and refer to them as needed. Some words to use are: angry, bored, cranky, dreadful, excited, frustrated, generous, happy, involved, jumpy, kooky, loving, mad, naughty, ornery, peaceful, queer, robust, special, tearful, understanding, violent, wonderful, Xeroxed (kid-coined term meaning to feel ordinary, not special), yearning, and zealous.

Linda Crissman
Dayton, OH

Class Meetings

We have a class meeting once a week. At the meeting, my students and I discuss problems picked from the Suggestion Box and plan class events.

Douglas K. Dillon
Cincinnati, OH

Ego-boosting Poetry

Use oral poetry presentations to boost students' self-esteem. Divide students into groups. Have each student memorize two to three lines of a poem by Shel Silverstein, Jack Prelutsky, or other popular children's poets. When groups have memorized their poems, invite them to share them with their classmates. As confidence increases, you may find your students memorizing and sharing poems of their own choosing.

Marilyn Borden, Bomoseen, VT

Circle Session Sharing

Once a week, a parent volunteer and I each take half of the class. We spend 30 minutes sitting in a circle on the floor sharing our feelings about certain topics (My Favorite Place, When Someone Teases Me, etc.). Students know there are to be no interruptions or judging, and that everything shared is confidential. The children learn a lot about themselves and their classmates.

Sr. Joanne Francis

Feelings-Go-Round

See students' responses at a glance and get to the heart of the issue. Instruct students to make a "feelings-go-round." Each child will need a poster board circle, a marker, a brad, a piece of construction paper, glue, and scissors. Have each student draw five faces on the circle as shown. Then instruct each student to make a construction-paper arrow, and attach it to the circle with a brad. Students use their feelings-go-rounds to indicate how they feel about topics that you mention.

Beverly Brannon
Hattiesburg, MS

Mood Circles

When the children arrive in my classroom, they pick up a "mood" circle. On one side is a "smiley" face; on the other is a sad face. Children place the circle side that matches their moods that day on their desks. We then discuss everyone's mood and talk about why we feel the way we do. This gets the day off to a good start—good moods or bad!

Sr. Margaret Ann Wooden
Martinsburg, WV

Helping Kids Feel Special

Positive Messages

Help students focus on the positive points of their classmates with this activity. After each student makes a booklet of blank pages, pass them out. Have students write positive messages inside the books about their owners. Collect the books and repeat this procedure daily or weekly until every student has written in each book. Later each child will receive a book full of positive messages about himself. Be sure to make a book yourself and participate in the writings.

Mary Anne Haffner
Waynesboro, PA

Emotions And Feelings

Have each student put his name at the top of a blank sheet of paper and number the paper to equal the number of students in the class. Next have students exchange papers with their neighbors. Each student must write a true, positive statement about the person whose name is at the top of the paper. Exchange papers every 60–90 seconds until all of them are completed. Each student will have a page full of positive comments which will help boost self-esteem. This also helps children think about one another in a positive manner.

Ginny Lichlyter
Hanover, IN

Student Questionnaire

To alleviate preconference jitters, I have my students answer certain questions on a piece of paper. The questionnaire asks questions such as "What will the teacher say at your conference?"; "How do you think you have worked and behaved in each subject area?"; and "What do you need to work on?" This gives students a chance to express their opinions and evaluate how they have performed in class.

Dr. Rebecca Webster Graves
Burlington, NC

Good News Box

To help children see positive behavior, I have a Good News Box. All day students make it a point to write on slips of paper any positive or kind behavior they see on the playground or in the classroom. They place the slips in the box, signing their names if they wish. Two children read the slips at the end of the day. If it was a good day, sometimes I'll have treats (cookies) available. This idea emphasizes the good things and helps children not to tattle.

Marie Brost
Gladstone, ND

"Hurt Cream"

Little ones often need a little extra tender loving care. Here's a simple way to spread warm feelings. Label a bottle of hand lotion "Hurt Cream." Whenever a child has a "hurt" (real or imagined), have him apply a small amount of the Hurt Cream to the affected area. It works great for small bumps, bruises, and hurt feelings. This little bit of extra attention can often do wonders!

Sarah Arnold
Martinsville, VA

Recognizing Patrol Members

Every year, we emphasize how important our patrol members are by taking individual snapshots of each patrol. The photos are then placed on a bulletin board by the patrol schedules. Children enjoy seeing their names and faces displayed.

Pat Weinand
Sioux Falls, SD

Warm Fuzzies

Spread warm feelings with these "warm fuzzies." Using construction paper, duplicate copies of the pattern shown. To make a warm fuzzy, glue colored cotton balls in the space around the face. Students can write a special message on the back of their warm fuzzies and give them to someone in need of a perk.

Mary Slaba, Vermillion, SD

No More Boo-Hoos

Decorate plain Band-Aids with smiley faces, flowers, or seasonal shapes using an indelible marker. You are sure to receive a smile for your efforts.

Katie Bailey
Avon, CT

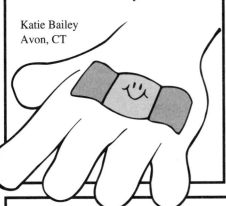

Sunshine Box

To cheer up a student in the hospital, the class can make a Sunshine Box for him which contains a contribution from each child. Examples: a book they've read, a candy bar, a piece of fruit, a homemade crossword puzzle or maze. Cover the box with bright paper and glue yellow sun cutouts all over it.

Cynthia Albright
Tyrone, PA

Warm Fuzzy Pom-Poms

As an incentive for earnest efforts or encouragement to get through a bad day, I reward students with "Warm Fuzzy" companions to wear for the day. Use round, fuzzy pom-poms (usually found in fabric stores) and attach two wiggly eyes to each one. I loop a piece of masking tape, attach it to the pom-pom, and stick it to the deserving student's shirt. Students love these little creatures and feel very special when wearing them.

Kari King
Westminster, CO

Youth Group Support

Because I live in the community where I work, I support various youth group activities by buying numerous cookies, candy, pancake supper tickets, etc. I've hit upon a method of deciding who to buy from that satisfies everyone. If ten of my girls are selling cookies, for example, I have each one put her name into a jar. I pick one name, and that's the person who gets my business. The kids think it's fun, and they understand why it's impossible for me to buy from everyone.

Gail Kostka
Palatine, IL

Good luck in your new school!!

Good Luck In Your New School

When a student moves during the school year, my class presents him or her with an autograph book entitled "Good Luck In Your New School." The book contains signatures and brief messages from members of the class. The idea is appealing to students and parents.

Wilhelmina Burress
Bowie, MD

Get-Well Calls

My class found that a get-well phone call can bring lots of cheer! Last year one of my students was hospitalized. In addition to sending cards, two or three different students went to the office each day to make a quick call just to say hi. The hospitalized student looked forward to his phone call that came at the same time each day.

Kim Zimmerman
Tulsa, OK

Keeping In Touch

When a student is ill for an extended period, have the class send a weekly tape to update him on school happenings. Students love talking into the microphone, and it's great medicine for the absentee. Keep a copy of the tapes for a permanent record of the year's activities.

Caren Hobbs
Summerfield, NC

Motivating Kids To Do Their BEST

Assertive Discipline Plan

Each of my students has a library card pocket taped to my desk. Using the idea of the stoplight, each pocket holds a green, yellow, and red index card. When a rule is broken, the child must replace his green card with the yellow card. At the second infraction, the date and the broken rule are written on the yellow card. The third time, the red card "stops" the student from continuing his activity. Again I note the date and broken rule on the red card. Smiley faces are drawn on all green cards which remain at the end of the day. On Friday, all cards are taken home as a weekly behavior report. Those students earning five smiley faces for the week earn a special reward.

Nedra Isenburg
Utica, NY

Lunchtime Restaurant

To encourage good table manners, turn a portion of your school lunchroom into a "delicatessen." Section off one area of the lunchroom with nice tables, centerpieces, low lighting, soft music, and special hostesses. Classes collect points each day for showing good table manners. On Friday, the class with the most points eats in the deli. Parent volunteers bring the lunch trays to the honored children. As they leave the deli, the students shake hands with the principal and hostesses. A chaotic lunchroom may suddenly become a pleasant eating place!

Michelle Martin James
Macon, GA

Super Kids Box

At the beginning of the day, I draw a box on the chalkboard labeled "Super Kids." (I sometimes label the box "Super Santas," "Super Bunnies," or other seasonal titles.) When a child is "caught" doing a good deed, he gets to write his name in colored chalk in the box. If he continues to follow class rules, his name stays up for the rest of the day. At the end of the day, he may choose one of our classroom awards. Students love writing their names on the board and work hard to receive the awards.

Randi Fields
Tampa, FL

★ SUPER KIDS ★

Ian
Katie
Spencer
Trish

Naptime Pillow

Help preschool and kindergarten children get ready for rest time with a seasonal incentive. Sew and stuff a prestamped pillow appropriate for each season. Offer the pillow to the first child who prepares himself for naptime quietly.

Luci Peabody
Rock Hill, SC

Behavior Cards

Behavior cards can help students make behavior improvements. Keep individual student cards in a file box. When a child misbehaves, he records the behavior and date on his file card. His teacher must also initial it. Behavior cards pinpoint areas of concern for the student, teacher, and parents.

Lona Hanner
Cape Girardeau, MO

Kevin
Running in the halls.
9-18-92 LH

Quiet As Mice

Your students will strive to keep quiet times quiet when you use mice cutouts with tails that "grow." Make and label a mouse cutout for each child. Using a paper clip, attach each mouse to a poster board with its tail curled up behind it. For each student who remains quiet, pull an inch of his mouse's tail from the paper clip. You may be surprised to see that your students can be as quiet as mice.

Ann Fausnight
Canton, OH

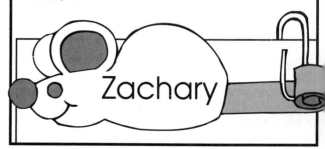

Zachary

Beat The Teacher

To encourage good behavior, use a scorekeeping chart titled "Beat The Teacher." Each time students are quiet or work well together, award them one point. If they begin to get noisy, give yourself a point. At the end of the day, the side with the most points wins a sticker. At the end of the week, if the students have more stickers, they receive a special treat.

Sr. Margaret Ann Wooden
Martinsburg, WV

Beat The Teacher	
Students	Teacher
JHT	II
Week Of:	

Laminated Incentive Chart

Use stars to promote positive behavior in your classroom. Make a laminated wipe-off chart as shown. Divide the class into five groups and assign each group a leader. During the week, stars are earned for positive behaviors. On Monday, members of the group with the most stars become the group leaders for the new week. Each group leader is given a number, and the remaining students draw numbers from a can for group assignments. Encourage students to reorganize quietly by awarding the first star of the week to the most deserving group.

Susan Kunda
Naknek, AK

Group Leader	M	T	W	Th	F
Michael	★★	★★	★	★★	★★★
Pam	★	★★★	★★	★	★★★
Bryon	★	★	★★★	★★★	★
Argeane	★★★	★★	★	★	★★
Karen	★★★	★	★★	★	★★

Earn While You Learn

Each year I hold a holiday bazaar just before the Christmas holidays. Each superior paper or display of outstanding conduct earns a holiday sticker and one point for the bazaar. Students use earned points to shop for discarded games and other goodies. Working for points keeps students working steadily at a distracting time of year.

Jane Cuba
Redford, MI

Motivating Good Behavior

Try this puzzle idea to reward your students for good behavior. Each week select an interesting picture or poster and laminate it. Cut it into puzzle pieces. One at a time, award puzzle pieces to students displaying good behavior. At the end of the week, the child with the most puzzle pieces wins the entire puzzle to take home.

Debbie Giamber
Annandale, VA

Kernel Quieter

Get a grip on class discipline with a popcorn surprise. Put a "frowny" face on a clear quart jar and fill the jar with unpopped popcorn. Label another quart jar with a happy face. When your class behaves well, transfer a handful of the popcorn to the happy jar. For undesirable behavior, move some corn from the happy jar back to the "sad" one. When all of the popcorn gets into the happy jar, reward your class with a well-deserved popcorn party!

Lisa Rae Anderson
Norfolk, NE

Student Behavior Charts

I encourage positive classroom behavior and student responsibility by having my students monitor their classroom behavior. Each student receives a behavior chart at the beginning of the week. The chart shows each day of the week, followed by five symbols. The goal of the students is to have all five symbols remaining at the end of each day. Whenever a child needs a reminder about classroom behavior, he must mark off one symbol for that day. My students look forward to taking their charts home at the end of the week, especially when I have added a positive comment. Students displaying perfect charts for the week are rewarded with ten minutes of extra reading or free time. If needed, behavior charts are helpful at conference time.

Kathy Quinlan
Lithia Springs, GA

Name	Beth				
Mon.	☺	☺	☺	☺	☺
Tues.	⊗	☺	☺	☺	☺
Wed.	⊗	⊗	☺	☺	☺
Thurs.	☺	☺	☺	☺	☺
Fri.	☺	☺	☺	☺	☺

Worth Framing

To recognize good papers or artwork in my classroom, I keep three picture frames on the wall. Work that is done neatly or creatively earns the right to be "framed" and hung on the wall for everyone to see.

Lia Buursma
Grand Rapids, MI

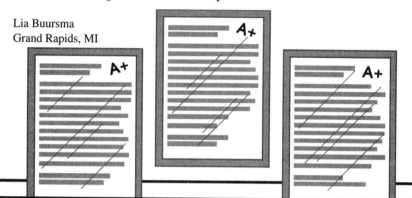

Lunch With The Teacher

In conjunction with my assertive discipline plan, my students have the opportunity to earn the privilege of eating lunch with me. Each student's name is placed on an incentive chart. At the end of the day, all students whose names have not been written on the board, receive stickers to place on the incentive chart. At the end of the month, the student with the most stickers enjoys a special lunch with me.

Jane Luzzo
Salem, NJ

Compliment Chart

Encourage good behavior with a compliment chart. Label a sheet of poster board "Our Compliment Chart." Each time another adult (another teacher, parent, visitor, etc.) compliments the class on its good behavior, record the compliment on the chart. After the class earns ten compliments, celebrate with a popcorn party or extra recess time.

Rebecca Abney
Richmond, KY

Sweet "In-scent-ives"

Save the cologne sample cards department stores often enclose in their mail. Surprise a student with an especially neat desk by slipping one of the perfumed cards in his desk. Since the cards come scented with both masculine and feminine fragrances, this reward is "scent-sational" for boys and girls.

Mary Dinneen
Bristol, CT

Student Of The Week Tablecloth

To reward good behavior throughout the school, have each teacher select a student of the week. Each Friday, cover a lunchroom table with a special vinyl tablecloth to designate a table for the honorees. Each student who earns the privilege of sitting at the special table uses a permanent marker to add his name to the tablecloth.

Diane Vogel
Macon, GA

A Jarful Of Good Works

To reward good behavior, place a clear plastic glass or jar on your desk. Each time the class follows a rule, drop a cookie in the jar. Keep a tally of the number of cookies and add some every day. When there is one cookie in the jar for each student, pass the jar around and start again. To vary, place marbles, jelly beans, or nuts in the jar. When a prearranged number of items is put in the jar, reward your class with extra recess, a snack, or free reading time.

Tina Palmer
Wolcott, CT

Put It In Writing

Recognize good deeds that might otherwise go unnoticed as you reduce the amount of tattling with this behavior modification system. Duplicate copies of a "good deed" form as shown. Encourage students to fill out a form whenever they see another student performing a good deed. Also duplicate copies of a "spout off" form similar to the one shown. Instead of tattling, have students fill out a form if they feel there is something that needs to be brought to your attention. At the end of the week, screen the "spout off" forms, selecting a few for class discussion if desired. Then share all of the good deeds from the week with the entire class.

Janice Bradley
Flossmoor, IL

Puzzle Awards

I mount calendar pictures on tagboard and cut them into puzzle pieces to make unusual rewards. Each student has an envelope in which to store his pieces. Children earn pieces of their puzzles for good behavior, finished assignments, and thoughtful deeds. When they earn all of their pieces, they have their own puzzles to keep!

Lia Buursma
Grand Rapids, MI

Cool-It Cubes

For a chilly treat on a hot school day, I give each of my students an ice cube outside after P.E. The children quietly suck on the ice, or rub it on their bodies while sitting under a tree. We've tied the ice cubes into a "mini" science lesson on melting, freezing, solids, liquids, body temperature, and evaporation—all in kindergarten!

Sandy Docca
Silver Spring, MD

Chicken Wire Reading Reward

Looking for a unique way to encourage reading or good behavior? Outline a seasonal shape on a 3' x 3' piece of chicken wire and hang it in a convenient place. For each 15 minutes read, or for good work or behavior, allow each child to fill in one hole in the design with tissue paper. The whole class will pitch in to finish this room decoration quickly!

Nicole Olmstead
East Bloomfield, NY

Quiet Award

Here's a reward that's sure to please! Place several stuffed animals on a table or in a laundry basket. Let each student who is working quietly select one of the toys to sit on his desk for the rest of the day. Use this same idea to recognize birthdays or as an award for a clean desk.

Pamela Myhowich
Selah, WA

Fruity Fillers

Fresh fruit treats are a healthy break from junk food rewards. Have children bring fruit to school. Cut it up, and serve it in paper cups. For special occasions, add a dallop of whipped topping to the fruit salad. Send extra cups of fruit to the principal, librarian, or secretary.

Lois Cooper

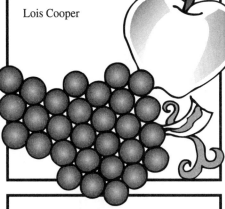

Diner's Club

Since my students must eat lunch in the classroom, I wanted to make lunchtime special. Every day, four children are chosen to be in the "Diner's Club." This entitles them to eat together at a back table which is set with place mats, paper plates, napkins, and place cards. There is even a "Diner's Club" sign on the wall. After eating, the children may play some quiet games chosen from the "Diner's Club" game box. Additionally, the "Diner's Club" experience helps teach good table manners and responsibility since students must clean the table and put everything away. They love it!

Rhonda Peterson
Baltimore, MD

Carrot Day

To perk up a "blah" day, I have children bring in bags of washed carrots. On "Carrot Day," the students may eat the carrots whenever they wish. The nutritious snacks add a fun twist to an ordinary day.

Nancy Lach
Mandan, ND

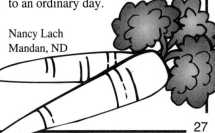

Motivating Kids To Do Their BEST

Student Of The Day

Place a sticker under one chair in your reading group area to promote good work. Each student who has a positive and productive reading period may check the bottom of his chair before leaving the area. The "Student of the Day" is the person whose chair has the sticker. That student receives a small treat. Mix up the chairs before calling another group.

Cathie Weaver
Springfield, GA

Sticker Bracelets

As an incentive, make attractive bracelets for students to wear. Laminate a sheet of construction paper. Cut into strips. Put colorful stickers on each strip. When a student deserves recognition, secure a bracelet around his wrist with tape.

Rebecca Gibson Calton
Auburn, AL

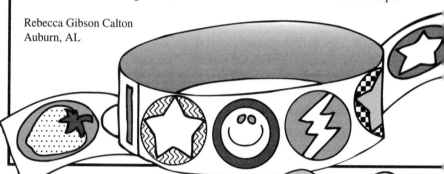

Crayon Molds

Use small candy molds to make inexpensive gifts to give children on various holidays. Save all of your old crayons at the end of the year. Peel off the paper and break crayons up, sorting colors into small jars. Melt the crayon pieces in a microwave. Pour into holiday candy molds. Place molds in the freezer for about five minutes or until hard. Pop crayon shapes out of the molds and you have instant gifts or awards for children.

Janet B. Vaughan
North Augusta, SC

See Me!

My children are thrilled when they find the words "See me!" stamped on their daily papers. That's because "See me!" indicates an exceptional paper and entitles the student to choose a special reward (sticker, pencil, etc.) from the treasure box on my desk.

Susan Winkel
Kokomo, IN

Plain Is Better!

My students love finding plain dot stickers on their outstanding papers. They look forward to creating their own stickers by adding funny faces or designs to the plain dots. Plain dot stickers can be purchased in a variety of colors at an economical price.

Kellie Newton
Raeford, NC

Motivation Stamps

Are you in the market for a quick and simple incentive for your students? Then try using rubber stamps. Stamp the backs of the hands of good listeners and hard workers. It's a great motivator and takes very little time.

Dee Camilotto
Fond du Lac, WI

Take Two A Day!

Every day I pass out two awards for good behavior. To be sure that I get around to each student, I fill out one certificate for each child in the class ahead of time. Then I just have to select two awards each day to present. When all awards are given out, I start over with a different award.

June Brantley
Robins AFB, GA

28

Shirt-With-A-Name

Here's a gift idea for anyone who has helped your class in a special way. Buy a sweatshirt or T-shirt. Write the person's name or title in big letters across the front of it using a laundry pen. Have each student draw a small picture and sign it. It would also be a great gift for a classmate who is moving or has been out a long period of time!

Mary Dinneen
Bristol, CT

Ready Rewards

There are many coloring and fun books that make great "reward" pages. After finding mazes and puzzles, I paste the pages onto construction paper, write the answers on the backs, and laminate. As children complete their work, they can do "reward" papers with wipe-off markers.

Sr. Margaret Ann Wooden
Martinsburg, WV

Secret Pal Award

Give each student an award with another student's name on it. During the day, students take note of the other person's academic or social success. After filling out the awards, they put them in a designated place. Awards can be posted. This helps students think positively about their classmates!

Mary Anne Haffner
Waynesboro, PA

Uses For Adhesive Dots

Press-on dots can be stuck on tops of desks passing inspection, stuck under chair seats to declare winners of door prizes during holiday parties, or affixed to small pieces of ribbon to make certificates very official looking. They're also great as smiley faces for students' papers.

Mary Anne Haffner

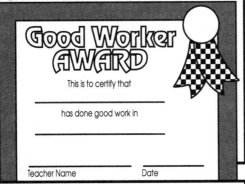

Toy Store Incentive

A classroom toy store promotes good behavior. Ask students to donate toys they don't use. Place these toys in a "toy store" area. At the end of the day, award a bean or token to each student who had good behavior. Students store the tokens in plastic containers in their desks. Students who have three tokens on Friday may visit the toy store and purchase a toy with the tokens. Let the children draw numbers to see who goes first, second, etc.

Suzanne White
Hopewell, VA

Work Awards

I use The Education Center's multipurpose cards as work awards. If a child satisfactorily completes all of his work, I write his name on the front of a card and the date on the back. Then I punch two holes in the top of the card and add a length of string to make a necklace. The student has an award he can wear proudly all day.

Kerrie L. Good, Sumter, SC

School-Spirit Pillow

Turn a school T-shirt into a school-spirit pillow. Simply sew the bottom and sleeves closed, stuff, and sew up the neckline. It's easy and inexpensive. Our school pillow is kept at the reading center and occasionally may be used in a student chair as a special treat.

Francine Reinel
Sarasota, FL

Lunch Rewards

Encourage good lunchroom behavior while helping students become better acquainted with the principal. Our principal awards prizes to classes who practice good cafeteria manners. The prizes are awarded monthly (or weekly) with the winning class selecting one of the following awards:

Mary Anne Haffner
Waynesboro, PA

- Ten minutes of extra recess
- Popcorn party with the principal
- Bingo party with the principal
- Neat Eaters' crowns (from fast-food restaurants)
- Neat Eaters' banner to display in the classroom

The 100-Percent Club

To encourage good study habits, I decorate a shoe box and cut a hole in the lid. Beside it, I place a large jar of gumdrops. Each time a student earns 100 percent on an assignment, he is entitled to guess the number of gumdrops by putting his estimate in the shoe box. At the end of the quarter, the person with the closest guess gets to go out to lunch with me, and the class shares the candy.

Chris Christensen
Las Vegas, NV

Winter Sunshine

"Bottled Sunshine," in the form of a jar of lemon drops, has become a winter must in my classroom. This jar of candy provides a quick reward for one student or the whole class. Lemon drops are also great nonmedicinal soothers for scratchy throats—yours and theirs!

Janice Scott, Rockport, TX

File-Folder Rewards

Extend the use of file-folder patterns from *The Mailbox*. When preparing the ready-to-go file folders, I duplicate extra copies of the cover sheet. I use them as rewards or certificates for students who successfully complete the activity.

Cathie Weaver
Springfield, GA

Super Reader Certificates

Encourage and reward reading accomplishments with computerized certificates. I record the number of books and pages each student reads and total them following each grading period. Using the school's computer equipment and the PRINT SHOP program, I create the format for the certificate and make a personalized copy for each of the five students who read the most pages. Also the top five readers may each select a prize from my prize bag. The prizes are all articles I have received free of charge, such as bonus books from book clubs and items purchased by redeeming proof-of-purchase coupons.

Kathy Peterson
Alpha, IL

Inexpensive Bookmarks

Use seasonal wrapping paper to create colorful and inexpensive rewards. Laminate gift wrap and cut it into small strips. Give the strips to students to be used as bookmarks. As students receive stickers for rewards, they may decorate their bookmarks with them.

Clarese Rehn
Lake Villa, IL

Treat Tree

Draw a tree on a bulletin board to provide your students with extra incentives. Cut leaves from construction paper, and program one side of each with a treat your students would enjoy. Staple the leaves on the tree so that the blank side of the leaf is visible. When your class earns a reward, have a student take a leaf from the tree to determine what the reward will be. Use seasonal shapes instead of leaves to vary the appearance of your tree.

Martha Herin
Hanover, IN

Lunch With The Teacher

Here's a positive reinforcement technique that encourages good behavior and responsibility. It also provides an opportunity for teachers to spend some time getting to know their students. On Fridays, students who have worked especially hard and have followed directions all week long earn stars on our star chart. Students who have earned four stars after five weeks are invited to eat lunch with the teacher. I write letters to parents, informing them of the child's accomplishment. The students select the menu, and we eat in the classroom. So far, pizza has been the most popular choice!

Ellen Muscato
Slaton, TX

Teddy Bear Kisses

Reward your youngsters with special kisses—chocolate ones, that is. Fill a small bag with chocolate kisses; then attach the bag to a teddy bear. Use monofilament line to suspend the bear from the ceiling, just out of youngsters' reach. Rewards will be close at hand whenever they're needed.

Betty Kobes
Kanawha, IA

Reward Coupons

Here's an inexpensive reward your students will love! In place of tangible rewards, present your students with "coupons." Duplicate copies of a coupon form as shown. Fill in the value, such as "one free homework assignment" or "five free math problems" and the student's name. Students will enjoy redeeming these "valuable" rewards.

Linda Warner
Akron, OH

| GOOD FOR:_____ |
| FREE _____ |
| Name |

Jewelry Rewards

Youngsters will love this jewel of a reward! Instead of throwing away old jewelry, use it as rewards. Decorate a small box to resemble a treasure chest and fill it with old jewelry. Instead of candy or stickers, let youngsters choose their rewards from the treasure chest.

Mary Dinneen
Bristol, CT

Reward Point Chart

When other rewards don't work, I use this point system with my class. I assign a point value to each letter grade: A=4 points, B=3, C=2, D=1, and F=0. For handwriting and conduct, I designate these point values: Satisfactory+ =3 points, Satisfactory=2, Satisfactory– =1, Unsatisfactory=0. Each student has his own chart with a list of points he needs and the rewards he is working toward. I total each student's points at the end of each day. On Friday, I add the daily totals and give out rewards based on the total number of points earned.

Kalen Inabinett
Meggett, SC

Purple Applesicles

Try this easy recipe for a special, nutritious treat. To make 24 treats, mix together six cups of applesauce and three cups of grape juice. Spoon the mixture into three-ounce cups. Freeze for one hour before inserting wooden Popsicle sticks. Continue freezing overnight. To serve, thaw for a few minutes; then remove Popsicles from cups.

Patsy Higdon
Arden, NC

Magic Mount Awards

Design your own awards to motivate students. Duplicate appealing designs on colorful construction paper. Decorate as desired and cut out. Attach a Magic Mount wall hanger to the back of each award. Peel the protective covering off the wall hanger and press the award onto a student's clothing.

Beverly Bippes
Humphrey, NE

	M	T	W	Th	F	
READING	2	3	3	2	3	
SPELLING	3	-	3	-	2	
BEHAVIOR	2	1	2	2	2	
Total	7	4	8	4	7	30

Sticker Saver

My students enjoy collecting the stickers they earn as rewards. For each student, I fold a 9" x 12" piece of tagboard in half before decorating and laminating it. Now my students have a special place in which to collect and display their stickers. They especially enjoy repositioning them as new ones are earned.

Eileen Carroll
Oak Lawn, IL

Choose An Award

Allow your students to select their own award certificates. Display several different awards. Give each child a sticky note; then have him choose his own award. Have him write the reasons why he is worthy of the award on his sticky note and attach it to the award. Screen each student's comments before transferring them to his award.

Mary Anne Haffner
Waynesboro, PA

"Work Fever"

Here's a great way to increase students' time on a task. Fill a jar with "Work Fever" pills (jelly beans, M&M's, etc.). Whenever an especially hardworking student is spotted, reward him with a "pill." Watch out! "Work Fever" is extremely contagious.

Annette Mathias
Mt. Hope, KS

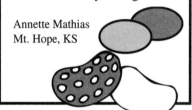

Neatness Incentive

To encourage my students to do their neatest work, I use this simple incentive. I randomly select an assignment to evaluate for neatness. Those students who complete their work neatly earn a special award which I staple to their papers. Awards include a free assignment, extra time on the computer, or a choice of a prize from the treasure chest. Since my students never know which assignment will be evaluated, they are always motivated to do their neatest work.

Cindy Fischer
Bismarck, ND

Traffic Signal Incentive

Control the "traffic" in your classroom with this incentive program which encourages good behavior. Duplicate a copy of a traffic signal as shown for each student. Cut out the circles for each of the three "lights"; then fold in half and glue to form a pocket. To make the three colored "lights," cut a piece of red, yellow, and green construction paper to fit inside each child's pocket. Glue pieces of black construction paper to darken the portions of each color that are not needed (see illustration). Begin each day by displaying each student's "green light." If a student breaks a rule, display his "yellow light." If two rules are broken, display the "red light." Enter the names of those students whose traffic signals display "green lights" at the end of each day in a weekly raffle.

Caroline Zito
Wadsworth, OH

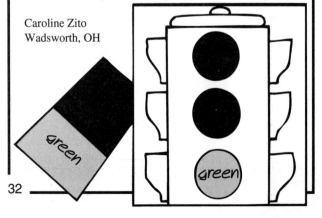

A Positive Note

This behavior modification system is positively successful! Each time another teacher or staff member compliments the class for good behavior or work habits, draw a star near the top of the chalkboard. Continue drawing stars in a line; then celebrate with a popcorn party when the line of stars stretches the entire length of the chalkboard.

Cathy Ignacio
Fort Lauderdale, FL

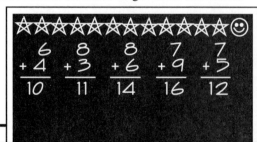

Learning Center Incentive

Motivate students to complete learning center activities with a raffle! Each time a student successfully completes a learning center, reward him with a "ticket" labeled with his name. Have him drop the ticket into a large can or box. At the end of the week, draw a ticket and reward the winning student with a special prize such as a pencil or eraser.

Ann Chiodi
Barnegat, NJ

Free Math Pass

Reward your marvelous mathematicians with a free math assignment. Present those students who earn 100 percent on a predetermined assignment with a pass which entitles them to skip a math homework assignment. When redeeming the pass, have the student staple it to a sheet of paper that indicates the assignment for which the pass is being used. To prevent stockpiling, write an expiration date on each pass. This system helps reduce careless errors and encourages students to recheck their work before turning it in.

Diane Afferton
Morrisville, PA

Homework Raffle

Here's a great way to motviate students to return their homework assignments on time. Each morning, if a youngster turns in his homework assignment on time, have him write his name on a "raffle ticket." Then have each recipient place his ticket in a box or bag. At the end of the day, draw one winner and award him with a small prize such as a pencil, sticker, or pass for a free homework assignment.

Cathy Ignacio
Fort Lauderdale, FL

Pages And Pages

For your next reading contest, keep track of the number of pages read rather than the number of books read. Children list the title, author, and number of pages in the book. This encourages them to read longer books and not just the short, easy ones.

Geraldine Fulton
Sedgewickville, MO

Sticky Transitions

I cut down on wasted time between subjects by occasionally giving a sticker to the first child who has opened to the right page and is quietly waiting. I also mention the names of the next two or three children who are ready.

Nancy Lach
Mandan, ND

Prize Box Cards

Dispensing rewards from the class prize box can be time-consuming and difficult. Make it trouble free by giving out inexpensive stickers for tasks well done. Each child tapes his stickers along the edge of a 4" x 6" card with his name written in the center. When a student collects five stickers, he presents the card at recess and picks a prize from the prize box. Punching a hole in each sticker easily cancels it.

Sharon Snell
Perrysburg, OH

Progress Charts

Progress charts change good grades into gleaming color. Make a paint palette for each student from white construction paper. For a correct spelling test or timed test in math, let each child color in one dab of paint on his palette. At the end of the week, reward students who have a dab of each color on their palettes.

Chris Berens
Bolivar, OH

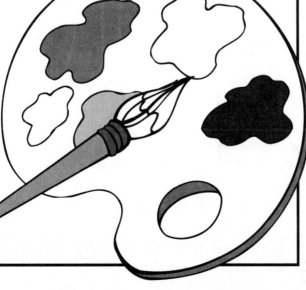

"Caught" Reading!

Encourage students to read in their free time by "catching" them in the act. When a student is "caught" reading, present him with a coupon. Have him write his name on the coupon and place it in a special box or other container. At the end of the week, draw out coupons and award prizes to the lucky winners. The more students read, the better their chances of winning!

Gayle Vledder
Grand Rapids, MI

95 Club

My students go all out for good grades in the 95 Club. I label a class record chart "95 Club" at the top and list the students' names vertically on the left side. Once a week I have each student bring me all of his papers with a 95–100 percent score. I punch a hole by each score and give students one sticker for each punch they have. The students put the stickers by their names on the chart. After completing the chart by his name, each student receives a pencil, eraser, or bookmark as a prize.

Bonnie Jo Kyles
Ennis, MT

Foreign Language Perk

Here's an enjoyable way to practice foreign languages in conjunction with social studies units. Use a simple counting or color-word worksheet from *The Mailbox* and substitute the appropriate foreign words.

Diane Vogel
Chamblee, GA

"100 Wall Display"

To recognize good grades, I always have a seasonal wall display in the school hall. Each time a student makes a "100," he gets to add something to the display. A tree of hearts, a flower garden, and a haunted house are some examples. Everyone in the school can watch our good work grow!

Michelle Martin James
Macon, GA

Reading Is "Ap-peeling"!

I display this clever monkey all year to add appeal to writing book reports. I give a paper banana to every child who writes a book report. At the end of the grading period, the child with the most bananas receives a prize.

Michelle Griffith
Sioux Falls, SD

Prize Bags

Use prize bags as an incentive for students to do their best work. When a student completes an assignment, I give him a ticket with his name on it. The student puts the ticket in his prize bag, which is mounted on a wall. When a student has earned enough tickets, he can trade them in for a prize. For instance, on sticker day students may trade tickets for stickers. This system increases motivation and teaches students to plan and save.

Marsha Goode
Middletown, OH

Seasonal Incentive Chart

Use a trail of seasonal shapes (bunnies, jack-o'-lanterns, turkeys, etc.) to motivate each student to learn vocabulary words. When a student masters a word list, he draws a face on one of the shapes beside his name. When all of the faces in his row are completed, the student may open his "secret door" (a folded-over piece of paper) at the end of the strip. Write the student's prize, such as a sweet treat, stickers, or free time, on the inside of the secret door.

Margo Tilton, Effingham, KS

Adventures Extraordinaire

For our Awesome Adventures Reading Club last summer, we painted a gameboard with tempera paints on the windows. For every five books read, each child moved his paper hot-air balloon to another place on the board: a baseball diamond for 10 books, a waterfall for 15 books, and buried treasure for 20 books. For 40 or more books, their balloons went on a special Adventures Extraordinaire poster. Use this for any contest—the kids love it!

Mary Stanton
Houston, TX

Inchworm

Begin creating an inchworm in your classroom to promote good work and teamwork. Make a large circle from tagboard and decorate it to look like an inchworm's head. Attach to a classroom wall. Then duplicate a smaller circle pattern. Every time a student accomplishes the specified task, he writes his name on a smaller circle and adds it to the inchworm. When the inchworm has extended all the way around the room and back to the starting point, have a popcorn party or pass out stickers.

Beth Hendricks
Auburn, AL

Team Spirit

When students have trouble getting all of their assignments in on time, work on "Team Spirit." Divide the class into teams of three or four students. Draw a class "football field" on the blackboard. Each time every member of the team brings in an assignment, let the team move its football five yards down the field. Reward the team that scores the first touchdown.

Linda Reeves
Grand Junction, CO

Erasing The Chalkboard

Children love to erase the chalkboard. After I've written sentences and the children have read them, I allow them to choose a sentence, read it again, and then erase it.

Gail Felker
Park City, IL

Sparkling Stars

"Sparkling Stars" is a bulletin board theme I use to reinforce a child's good work. When a student has done a good job or shown good behavior all week, give him a precut star with his name on it and have him decorate the edges with glitter. The child puts the star on the bulletin board himself. This display is especially attractive if a dark background is used.

Rebecca Gibson Calton
Auburn, AL

What's Right With Your Paper?

After correcting a student's paper, we tend to ask the child to explain what's wrong with a response. Instead, ask the child, "What's right with your paper?" He'll become aware of all of the things he did correctly, and the errors won't seem so bad.

Cindy Ward
Rustburg, VA

Plastic Eggs

To encourage completion of homework and following class rules, give every student a plastic egg with a number in it each morning. Students keep the eggs at their desks unless they have to return them to the basket on the teacher's desk. A student must return his egg if his homework is not completed or if he breaks a class rule. At the end of the day, the teacher draws a number to select the student who receives a treat.

Debbie Retzlaff

Fishbowl Fun

This poster-board fishbowl comes in handy when rewarding students for learning their addresses and phone numbers, weekly spelling words, or basic math facts. Cut out a large poster-board fishbowl and decorate it. Each time a child accomplishes a particular task, he puts a fish that bears his name in the bowl.

Karen Wallace
The Woodlands, TX

GROUP 1 IS #1!

Incentive For Good Workers

Establish a quiet working environment with nonverbal clues and a colorful banner. Cluster students' desks to create several groups or teams. Recognize hardworking teams by drawing a smiley face or star on the board. At the end of a given period, have each group add up its score. The group with the best score gets to display a colorful pennant in its area. In the event of a tie, one group keeps the pennant in the morning, one in the afternoon.

Les S. Holt III
Waverly, MD

Tracking Awards

Here's how I make certain that all of my students are equally represented for their positive accomplishments on our awards bulletin board. I keep track of the awards I present on the extra pages in the back of my grade book. This system also helps me observe my students more closely for positive achievements.

Mary Anne Haffner
Waynesboro, PA

Give-away BOX

Tamara
Jimmy
Austin
Caroline

Give-away Box

Put the name of each student in a box or some sort of interesting container. Whenever you have extra worksheets, posters you no longer use, or samples of booklets or other things received in the mail, pick a name from the box and give the extras to that student. This is a fair way to distribute these goodies. When the box is empty, start over.

Cynthia Albright
Tyrone, PA

Reading Paper Chain

I read to my students each day. When we finish a book, I write the title and the author of the book on a strip of colored construction paper. I make the strips into a paper chain and hang it on the classroom wall. Every month the chain grows longer. By the end of the year, students are amazed to see how many books we have read. Sometimes we take the chain down and reread the titles to refresh our memories. I encourage students to make their own paper chains for their rooms at home. If they read a chapter a day, they can add links also.

Gail Cross
Piney Falls, TN

Chain Of Names

It's a difficult task to remember who has or hasn't been recognized with a positive reinforcement note or a privilege. Keep track of these things using this paper-chain method. Program a link with each of your students' names. After recognizing one of the students whose name is on the end of the chain, tear off the link.

Sr. Ann Claire Rhoads
Greensboro, NC

Party Plan

Encourage your students to display super behavior outside the classroom. Make and laminate popcorn cutouts. Each time your students leave the classroom, a popcorn cutout is given to the teacher in charge. If the entire class behaves, the cutout is returned with the students and placed in a bowl in the classroom. When the bowl is full, have a popcorn party! For your next party plan, try cookie or ice cream cutouts.

Marlene Schriefer, Halliday, ND

Achievement Chains

To encourage children to learn personal information, make achievement chains. For each achievement, attach a cutout to a length of ribbon. Here's a list of some achievements and recommended cutouts.

Achievement	Cutout
stating full name	boy or girl
stating home phone number	telephone
stating home address	house
identifying colors	paint palette
identifying numbers	card with numbers on it
identifying shapes	triangle

Each child takes his chain home when it's complete.

Jean Busby
Caldwell, AR

The No-Name Game

Encourage students to write their names on their papers with this idea. Every Monday display a piece of construction paper entitled "The No-Name Game." The owners of nameless papers are found and their names are placed on the list. Check marks indicate additional nameless papers. On Friday, any student whose name is not on the list earns a special treat.

Kathy Quinlan
Lithia Springs, GA

Attendance Incentives

This idea will improve the daily attendance of your students. Draw a cone on your chalkboard. Add one scoop of ice cream to the drawing when all children are present for the day. At the end of three weeks, award the class two minutes of free time for each ice cream scoop they have earned. Try adding length to a worm or ladder, birds to a tree, eyes to a monster, eggs to a basket, or spots to a dog.

Rebecca Gibson Calton, Auburn, AL

Saving Stickers

To encourage an active student to stay seated and on task, I present him with several stickers at the beginning of a period. The student gives a sticker back each time he forgets to use his time wisely. At the end of the period, he may keep all of the stickers he has saved.

Sara Kennedy, Bedford, VA

Mailbag

To improve students' homework practices, I labeled an old book bag as the "Mailbag." Each day, a different student receives a letter from me with activities to be completed for homework. The contents may include worksheets on a particular area, an encouraging note, and any other items I feel are necessary. The students are eager to know who will be getting the letter each day, which delights me. The homework is returned in the same envelope and placed in the mailbag for me to check.

Pat Butler
Killen, AL

Warm-Fuzzy Jar

Encourage your students to work quietly and remember their manners with a warm-fuzzy jar. Simply place a cotton ball in a pint canning jar each time a positive behavior is displayed. A full jar of warm fuzzies earns an extra class recess.

Teri Butson
Lancaster, PA

Name Lottery

Try this positive approach for reminding students to write their names on their papers. Provide a decorated shoe box and several strips of writing paper. Each time a child correctly writes his name on an assignment, he earns a lottery ticket (paper strip). He neatly writes his first and last name on the paper strip, folds it, and places it in the box. The next morning after seatwork has been assigned, a drawing is held. The winner exchanges his lottery ticket in place of one assignment. The box is then emptied and a new lottery begins. A nameless paper voids that student's lottery tickets for the day.

Mary Dinneen
Bristol, CT

Quiet Workers' Chart

At the beginning of each week, I attach individual photos of my students to a Quiet Workers' Chart. On Friday afternoon, the students whose photos remain on the poster earn a "no-homework coupon." These coupons have been a great incentive for positive behavior in my classroom.

Sara Kennedy

Surprise Sticker

Each week I select one sticker to be my "surprise sticker" for the week. I tape the sticker on a laminated piece of construction paper so that the front of the sticker is hidden from my students. The children are encouraged to earn stickers for good work throughout the week. On Friday, I have my students take out all of their papers on which stickers have been placed. Then I turn over the surprise sticker. If a student has at least one sticker that matches the surprise sticker, he wins a small prize.

Rebecca Gibson Calton, Auburn, AL

Special Homework

Some students need extra practice or drill exercises to reinforce basic skills. Glue decorative pictures on the outside of a file folder. Write the directions and practice activity inside the folder, or insert a special assignment to take home. Have extraspecial treats ready the next morning for completed assignments.

Claire Batchelor
LaGrange, GA

Self-Esteem Stamps

My rubber stamp collection has grown over the years. Selecting a stamp to use on good work is fun. Passing this honor on to the students has worked wonders for neatness in our class. When we start an assignment, I announce that one student will get to choose the stamp I will award for this set of papers. The lucky student will be a quiet, neat worker. I select the winner after everyone has completed his paper. The papers are beautiful, and the room is quiet.

Mary Dinneen
Bristol, CT

Manners Count

Want your students to practice good manners? Assign one student to mark a card each time he hears a classmate say, "Please," "Thank you," "Excuse me," or any other statements you have decided to reward. Then give one minute of recess for each set of five marks on the card. This reward system really makes students aware of what they say!

Kathy Beard
Keystone Heights, FL

Incentive Puzzle

Promote super behavior and completed work with an incentive puzzle. Place the puzzle at the back of the room where small groups of children may work on it. They'll love the challenge of a large puzzle that takes several days to complete.

Rebecca Gibson Calton

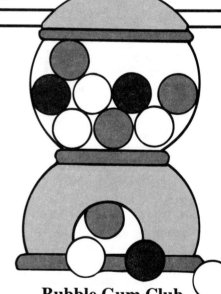

Classroom Motivator

Here's a motivational idea for any grade level! Place pencil toppers on lengths of yarn and display on a bulletin board. Move the toppers to indicate good behavior, books read, points earned, etc. Use them for individual and group progress.

Rebecca Gibson Calton

Bubble Gum Club

For a motivating bulletin board, I make a cut-out bubble gum machine for each child. Each day that a student finishes his work, he puts a circle sticker on his machine. At the end of the week, we count the stickers. Whoever has the most "gum balls" gets a penny to buy a piece of gum from our class gum ball machine.

Jana Jensen
Gillette, WY

Spot The Mistake

Have a "Spot The Mistake Day." Give a small prize to the first child who notices the wrong date on the chalkboard, a bulletin board picture hung upside down, or the wrong spelling of a word somewhere in the room. This helps encourage attention to detail.

Isobel Livingstone, Rahway, NJ

Thank-You Chart

Thank your class for cooperative behavior and build unity among students with a Thank-You Chart. Place a sticker on the chart each time good behavior is displayed by the group. When the class has received 20 thank-yous, reward your students with a special field trip, movie, or popcorn party.

Kenneth T. Helms
Greensboro, NC

Spelling Incentive

Here's an idea that has worked well as a spelling incentive for my students. At the beginning of each month, I label the area above my blackboard with a caption like "Spooky Spellers" for October or " 'Egg-cellent' Spellers" for April. For each perfect spelling paper during the month, I award the student with an appropriate seasonal cutout such as a bat or an egg. The student then colors the cutout, puts his name on it, and displays it on the board under the caption. At the end of the month, the student with the most cutouts receives a special surprise.

Susan Fowler
Portsmouth, OH

Homework Lottery

Motivate students to do their homework by occasionally holding a homework lottery. Simply pick a paper at random and award the owner a small prize.

Isobel Livingstone

"Earn A Compliment" Game

Play this secret game to assure a well-behaved class outside the classroom. Whenever the class behaves in an outstanding manner and receives a compliment from any adult observer, I provide a popcorn party! The only rule is that NO ONE may know of the secret game. My class has "won" parties due to good behavior noticed by parents, other teachers, and even tour guides. The students love to make up new ways to earn a party, and it's great not to have to nag!

Cindy Newell, Durant, OK

Homework Coupon

Having trouble getting homework returned? Give students a "Free Homework Coupon" after completion of an allotted number of assignments. They'll love it!

Barbara Partridge
Rustburg, VA

FREE HOMEWORK COUPON

Assignment: _____
_____
_____
_____
_____

Date Used: _____
Student: _____

Activity Center Reward

I have ordered about 120 preprinted centers from The Education Center. They are grouped according to subject. Each student receives an "inventory sheet" listing all of the centers by name and number. When a student completes a center, he brings his sheet to me for credit. After completing a specified number of centers, the student receives a pop from the pop machine in the teachers' lounge!

Cindy Newell

Good Work Reward

Promote good study habits. Before a big test, give each student a list of points to study. At the bottom, explain that a parent or older sibling may sign the paper to show that the student studied at home. A passing test grade with a signed study sheet earns a special reward. It really works!

Jan Drehmel
Chippewa Falls, WI

Point Bank

Students in my science and health classes are motivated by our "point bank." Students earn points by bringing in things needed for class, by bringing in newspaper or magazine articles about a current topic of study, or by answering the "point question" correctly. The point question is asked at the beginning of a class period. It pertains directly to the previous night's reading assignment and can be answered in one word. Points accumulated in the point bank may be added to a homework grade to improve it.

Norma Stephan
Allegany, NY

Military Badges

My first-grade class is required to learn the Dolch word list. I have broken it down into five levels or ranks, and the children move through the ranks from private to general, earning military badges. The students are highly motivated and proudly show off their badges. This activity is easily adapted to math facts.

Barbara Masiulis
Wolcott, CT

Coloring Incentive

When students are working on a favorite worksheet that requires coloring, be sure to save one that is neatly colored. Also save one that has been completed carelessly. Next year, when your students are working on the same worksheet, pull out the two samples. Have students discuss the differences and what makes one better than the other. Then challenge students to complete their copies so they are even better than the "neat" sample. Reward any student whose paper becomes the "neat" sample for the next year.

Mary Dinneen
Bristol, CT

Mind Challenge

Every week I challenge my students to a brainteaser on "Wise Wednesday." Each student may submit one answer into the brainteaser jar. Correct answers are eligible for our Thursday prize drawing.

Bernadette Carnevale
Buffalo, NY

M&M's Chances

Fill a jar with a predetermined number of M&M's. As a bonus for reading a book or some other achievement, allow the student a chance to guess the number of M&M's by writing his name and guess on a slip of paper. At the end of the time period you've set, such as a nine-week grading period, give each of the ten students who were closest a free book. Award the M&M's to the one who was the closest.

Jan Drehmel

"Hole-y" Rewards

Here's a simple way to provide immediate positive reinforcement. Label a colored index card with each child's name; then decorate it with a seasonal sticker. Have students store their cards in library pockets that have been taped to their desks. Each time a child displays desired behavior or especially good work, reward him by punching a hole in his card. Each time a student's card has been punched five times, reward him with a small prize. After the card has been punched 25 times, reward the student with a larger prize and a new card to fill.

Betty Jane Tiller
Anderson, SC

Attention!

Do your students seem to have cotton in their ears sometimes? Here's a way to perk them up. Like a drill sergeant, I dramatically say, "Attention!" They love it. They straighten right up, then salute. Then I give the necessary directions.

Mary Dinneen
Bristol, CT

Patchwork Quilt Incentive

As an incentive for good work and behavior, piece together a giant patchwork quilt. Cut different colors of construction paper into four-inch squares. Whenever a student displays good behavior or earns a good grade, write his name on a square and allow him to color it. Display completed squares on a wall or bulletin board and watch the quilt grow!

Rebecca Gibson Calton
Auburn, AL

No-Tattle Monitor

When you have to leave the classroom during a lesson period, encourage students to maintain good discipline in your absence. Place a tape recorder in the center of the classroom and turn it on as you leave. Replay the tape when you return. This method discourages tattling while promoting self-discipline.

Joni Isaacson

Raise Your Hand

Use this quick test to determine whose attention you have. Say, "If you're listening, raise your hand." When students start raising their hands, you'll soon have the attention of the inattentive students. If the class is getting noisy say, "If you're sitting quietly, raise your hand." Since talkers will notice hands going up, they'll get quiet to see what's happening.

Joanne Davis
Orlando, FL

Neat Nick

This nifty incentive will turn your students into "neatniks." While your students are out of the room, check their desks for neatness. Place a small stuffed animal or puppet, "Neat Nick," inside an especially neat desk. The student whose desk was selected gets to take "Neat Nick" home with him for the night, along with a special certificate congratulating him on his good "deskkeeping."

Michelle Gnazzo
Farmington, CT

"Bear-y" Good Incentive

Use this incentive bulletin board to motivate your students. Using construction paper, duplicate a teddy bear for each child. Have each child decorate his bear; then display them on a bulletin board. Determine a desired goal, such as reading a specified number of books or turning in homework a certain number of times. When a student is halfway to his goal, attach a small reward to one of his teddy bear's paws. When the entire goal is reached, attach another treat to the teddy's other paw, remove it from the bulletin board, and present it to the student.

Marilyn Borden
Bomoseen, VT

School Zone

Solve the problem of speeding students in the hallways and the classroom by issuing speeding tickets. Payment for each ticket can be determined by the student and teacher. My students have slowed down considerably!

Jill Fitch
Bloomdale, OH

Motivating Kids To Do Their BEST

May I Have Your Attention, Please?

Recapture your students' attention with this unusual signal. Blow into a cola bottle. Because the noise is a unique type of sound, students respond quickly.

Rebecca Gibson Calton
Auburn, AL

Me

(Do actions as described; then bring hands down slowly and place in lap.)

My hands upon my head I place,
On my shoulders, on my face,
On my knees, and at my side,
Then behind me they will hide.
Then I raise them up so high
Till they almost reach the sky.
Then I place them on my knee,
And see how quiet they can be.

It's A Snap!

Here is a unique way to keep students' attention during oral reading. As one student is reading, I snap my fingers. The next student must begin in the exact spot. The trick is to avoid letting students read the same amount or stop at ends of sentences or paragraphs. The students enjoy trying to keep up, and we seem to get through stories quicker with better comprehension.

Sarah McCutcheon

Young Aerobics Class

After taping selected songs from the Top 40 hits, I play a song during class. During this time, we do a series of exercises, such as toe touches, arm rotations, stretches, deep breathing, and walking to the music. The kids look forward to this enjoyable break.

Mary Anne Haffner
Waynesboro, PA

Magic Wand

"Shh!" isn't needed in my room. When group time is approaching, I wave my magic wand and say, "Magic, magic wand, make the noise disappear." The children love the magic wand (a wooden star covered with glitter at the end of a wooden stick), and I love its effect.

Carrie L. Bowyer
Vinton, VA

Problem-solving Students

I involved my class in solving the problem of students leaning back in their chairs. We discussed the dangers of this practice and brainstormed possible solutions. The class then evaluated each solution and chose the best one. We also determined a method of rewarding the entire class for every day no one leaned back in his chair. The students recognized the seriousness of our problem because they were given the opportunity to solve it. We never had a "chair leaner" again!

Pat Schied
Valparaiso, NE

Noise-Level Signal

Remind students to be quiet with this signal. Display a large stoplight cutout. Add a red construction-paper circle to indicate silent time, yellow for whisper time, and green for recess.

Martha Alfrey
Ironton, OH

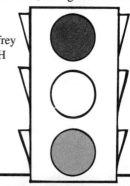

Management Tips

Keeping Pencils Sharp

Are students disturbing the classroom with pencil sharpening? Each morning allow students to come by reading groups to sharpen their pencils. No more than two pencils per student are allowed. Extra sharpened pencils go into a "pencil basket" for students to exchange their pencils for if necessary.

Ruth Wolery
Lexington, KY

Morning Messages

Start your day in an organized way! Each morning write a short greeting to your students and a five-minute task to complete on the chalkboard. The students will look forward to the greeting and the unpredictability of the task, while it allows you time to tend to messages from parents, homework assignments, and so on.

Brr! It's cold outside. Warm up by using the letters in "hot chocolate" to make words. Make as many as you can.

Martha Cranfill
Winston-Salem, NC

Attendance And Lunch-Count Chart

Office and cafeteria workers will appreciate your punctuality with morning attendance and lunch reports when you use this system. For each student, mount a labeled, library pocket on poster board. Provide color-coded cards marked *purchase lunch, purchase milk, packed lunch,* and *eating at home.* As each student enters the room, he chooses a card and places it in his pocket. At a glance, you can see who is absent and what types of lunch purchases students need to make.

Kathy Mobbs

Exercise For Alertness

Morning exercise makes students more alert and ready to work. Begin the day by exercising to the students' favorite songs. Lead the class in some warm-up exercises. Then have students take turns leading the class. Students enjoy creating new exercise steps as well as improvising with old ones. Shy students may develop greater self-confidence as a result.

Pamela Barni
Bloomsburg, PA

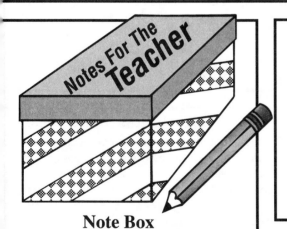

Note Box

A shoe box covered with wrapping paper has helped simplify my mornings. As my students enter the room, they place any notes or papers for me in the decorated shoe box labeled "Notes for Miss Myhowich." After the children are settled and working quietly, I read each note. Questions are clarified by speak-ing to individual students. This note box has been a real lifesaver!

Pamela Myhowich
Selah, WA

Sharpened Pencils

Help students save time by keeping a can of sharpened pencils in the classroom. If a student breaks his point, he puts his broken pencil in the can and takes a sharpened pencil out. Every few days, have a monitor resharpen the can of pencils.

Vita Campanella-Feldstein
Brooklyn, NY

Getting Ready

I have a getting-ready time in my classroom each morning. On a sign by the pencil sharpener, I post a list of things for students to do before class starts. Pencils sharpened? Homework in order? Library books returned? Snack at your desk? Office notes ready?

Sr. Ann Claire Rhoads
Greensboro, NC

☞ Management Tips ☜

No More Lost Tickets

Some schools in our district have begun issuing credits instead of lunch tickets. The cafeteria record keeper receives an attendance roster for each class. As credits are purchased, she puts slash marks in the appropriate number of boxes beside each child's name. The children arrive in the lunchroom in alphabetical order. When a child goes through the line and uses one of his credits, the record keeper changes a slash mark to an X. The record keeper can easily see when to remind students to purchase more credits. If a child brings his lunch, the credit (which is not dated) is retained until lunch is purchased.

Chris Christensen
Las Vegas, NV

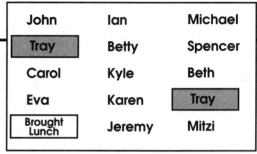

Lunch Count

To make lunch count a simple matter, I use a seating chart and two colors of poster-paper rectangles. The rectangles are labeled Tray or Brought Lunch according to color. As soon as a student arrives, he places the appropriate rectangle over his name. It is easy to count those buying lunch and eliminates roll call as well.

Carolyn Martin
Blanchard, OK

Question Marks

To cut down on interruptions when working with a reading or math group, I give each child a laminated index card with a question mark on it. When a child has a question, he puts the card on the top corner of his desk. Between group activities, I go around and answer each question. Often by the time I get to their questions, they have already figured out the answers!

Jane Dickert
Bath, SC

Spool Hall Passes

Plastic spools from gift-wrap ribbon make great, durable hall passes that students slip over their wrists. They are easy to recognize by school officials and not easily lost.

Debbie Wiggins
Myrtle Beach, SC

Student Attendance

You'll never have to take attendance again with this system! Even kindergartners and first graders can do it while learning name recognition. Make a poster-board chart with a pocket for each child's name. Place the chart near the door. In the morning when children come in, they remove their name cards and place them in the "I'm Here!" basket. Names left on the chart show you at a glance who's not present.

Lissa Swazey
Tucson, AZ

LUNCH COUNT

Hall Passes

Use tongue depressors for handy hall passes. Tape a picture of a nurse, telephone, or library book to the sticks. Write a message on each stick, such as "This student has my permission to use the phone." Put magnetic tape on the backs of the passes, and store them on your filing cabinet.

Connie Connely
Tulsa, OK

Lunch-Count Board

Here's a time-saver when it comes to taking lunch count. Make a lunch-count board from poster board, library pockets, stickers, tongue depressors, and large self-adhesive dots. Glue one pocket for each student onto the poster board, decorate with stickers, and laminate. (You may want to include a few extra for any new students.) Slit pockets open and label with students' names using a permanent marker. Put a green dot on one end of a few tongue depressors. Place a red dot on one end of each remaining tongue depressor, and a blue dot on the other end. Red means hot lunch, blue means sack lunch, and green means going home. As students enter the room, they place tongue depressors in the pockets on the chart to indicate their plans for lunch. Use the board again next year by removing names with hair spray or fingernail polish remover.

Amy Vorderbruegge

Photo Find

Looking for a creative way to divide students into study groups? Find one large magazine photograph for each group you wish to form. Cut each photograph into four, five, or six pieces. Mix up the pieces. As each student enters the room, give him a piece of a photograph. On your signal, students try to reassemble each photo by locating the other pieces. The students whose pieces make up a photograph become a study group.

Sr. Ann Claire Rhoads
Greensboro, NC

Partner Search

Put used Christmas and/or greeting cards to use with this fun management game designed to pair children with partners. You will need one card for every two students in your classroom. Using various patterns, cut the illustrated portions of the cards in half, placing the pieces in a large envelope. When an activity requires partners, pass one card piece to each student. Instruct each student to find the classmate who is holding the other half of his card. When the match is made, the two students return their card to the envelope and become partners for the activity at hand. What a fun and simple solution to a time-consuming task!

Mary Dinneen
Bristol, CT

The Lottery

Assign each pupil a number based on alphabetical rank, and keep a container with numbered Popsicle sticks for drawing lots. The lottery is so handy for an endless number of situations, such as assigning chores, determining the order of presentations, or raffling off extra materials.

Patricia M. Salerno
Manville, RI

Seating Variations

Let your class take charge with this seating arrangement plan. At the beginning of each month, the first child in each row moves his desk to the back of the row as everyone else moves forward one position. In addition, all desks are moved to the right one row. The row on the extreme right moves to the left side of the room. My students really look forward to these monthly variations.

Sandy McKinney
Vienna, WV

Classroom Management By Number

On the first day of school I assign each student a number. We use these numbers in many ways. When I call evens and odds, we quickly have two teams. To regroup after a field trip, we simply count off. The numbers also help to avoid hurt feelings. When I need to choose extra student helpers, I draw student numbers from a can on my desk. My students understand the luck of the draw.

Hannah Means
Cheshire, CT

Surprises For The Day

Sometimes the simplest idea can add fun to a classroom. Place a number (1 to 5, or higher depending on your class size) on each child's desk. That day, use the numbers to direct groups of students in learning tasks. For example: "All *fours* go to the board," "All *fives* line up first," or "All *threes* do the math drill."

Sr. Ann Claire Rhoads

Pick A Stick

Quickly organize center or rotation work with Popsicle sticks. Code each stick with a set of numbers. Control group size by monitoring number repetitions. When ready to use, pass sticks out and assign a number placement to follow. Store sticks in a can.

Sr. Ann Claire Rhoads

☞ Management Tips ☜

Hula-Hoop Corrals

Use a few Hula-Hoops to keep students on task and keep up with small game pieces. Lay Hula-Hoops on the floor with a game inside each. The student or students who wish to play the game sit inside the Hula-Hoop. Playing pieces are less likely to get lost since the playing area for each game is clearly defined.

Sandra Grigsby

Test-taking Tip

Before administering a math or reading test to students, I make a permanent transparency of the test. I use it on the overhead projector to direct children to the area of the test that we are working on. This helps to remove one barrier between good grades and kids.

Mary Lou White
Spartanburg, SC

My Message Is…

To minimize disruptions while you are working with small groups, duplicate "My Message Is…" forms. Students who need immediate help silently hand you the completed form. Often you can write your response without interrupting the flow of the group.

Lydia Chibanes
Paramus, NJ

Color Cards

Check students' understanding of a new skill at a glance. Give students one red, one yellow, and one green 3" x 5" piece of construction paper. Students hold up cards as you explain the lesson. Red means "Stop; I'm lost"; yellow means "Slow down or repeat"; and green means "Go on; I understand." It's an instant evaluation. You may also use these cards to involve the whole class while asking an individual student a question. Green means "I agree with the answer," and red means "I do not agree with the answer."

Rose Rasmussen
Mountain City, TN

Your Own Workspace

Add color and interest to simple activities with personal "workspaces." Glue commercial borders around the edges of construction-paper sheets and laminate. As each student counts with counters, he places his counters on the construction-paper workspace. Workspaces are useful at tables, on the floor, or in learning centers, and may be used in conjunction with any manipulative practice.

Deborah Giamber
Annandale, VA

Memory Jogger

Post a wipe-off board near your desk to cut down on interruptions. When you're busy, a child who needs assistance may write his name on the board with one word to describe the nature of the question. As soon as you're available, you can glance at the board to see who needs your attention.

Sr. Mary Catherine Warehime
Emmitsburg, MD

Computer Name Chart

On computer days, this name/assignment chart cuts down on teacher supervision. Students complete the assignment at the computer, in turn, and cross their names off the list. A timer is set to give each child equal time at the terminal. When the timer goes off, it is the next child's turn.

Mary Dinneen
Bristol, CT

My Message Is…

Name_____

I need help ☐.
• _____
_____
_____

I am finished ☐.
• _____
_____
_____

I need materials ☐.
• _____
_____

Date: _____ Time: _____

Computers
What to do: _____
_____
_____
_____

Ryan Ricky
Susan Taylor
Pam Anderson
Jeff Jones

☞ Management Tips ☜

"Uno, dos, tres, ..."

Foreign Language Counting

Often, to hurry my students in clearing their desks or getting out textbooks, I use the standard system of counting: "one, two, three." To make it interesting, though, I count in French or Spanish. Not only do the children complete the task quickly, but they enjoy counting along with me. Later on, I count in a different language. What a great way to learn bits of other languages while performing routine classroom tasks!

Martha Ann Davis
Greenwood, SC

Line-up Flag

To curb class noise and confusion at line-up time, attach a homemade flag to an old broomstick. When classes line up to come in from outside, the teacher on duty gives the "Olympic Flag" to the quietest class. That class gets to go in first. They also receive a check mark on a hall chart. The class that earns five checks first gets a reward: free video time, free reading time, or stickers. This idea is so successful, you will have trouble deciding which class carries the flag!

Mary Dinneen
Bristol, CT

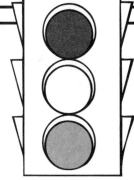

Class Lineup

To avoid confusion, I seat my students in five rows throughout the year. I assign each row a day of the week. On the appropriate day, that row lines up first whenever we leave the classroom. This way, everyone gets to go first sometime during each week.

Cheri Richardson
Columbia, MO

Quiet Room Tip

Keep chattering down to a minimum when you leave the room. Make a bet with your students that they can't stay seated and quiet until you return. If you lose the bet, the class gets extra free time. If the class loses, you take away some of their free time. Bet you'll lose every time!

Rebecca Gibson Calton
Auburn, AL

Traffic Safety

Teach your students that when they're walking in the classroom, halls, and stairways, they are like car drivers. They should always walk on the right, stairways are "no passing zones," and "speeding" is not permitted. Students should also be reminded that "citations" will be given to offenders, while "safe drivers" will receive "commendations."

Mary Anne T. Haffner
Waynesboro, PA

SPEEDING

Lining Up—Creatively!

How do you get students to line up quickly and quietly? Try some creative ways that not only insure order, but are also unique, cooperative learning experiences. Ask students to line up according to their birthday months; in alphabetical order, according to the first letters of their first, middle, or last names; numerically, according to their dates of birth; numerically, according to the sums of the letters in their names; according to length of hair; according to the sums of the digits in their phone numbers; alphabetically, according to the first letters of their moms' or dads' names. Or allow a student to choose the sequence for the day. Not only do kids gain sequencing skills, but they also learn to cooperate with one another.

Cindy Meyering
Marathon, WI

Traffic Light Control

Students learn to monitor their own behavior with this classroom traffic light. Draw a traffic light on the chalkboard. At the beginning of each day, write all of the children's names in the green light. If a student becomes too noisy or too active, give him a warning by writing his name in the yellow light. If the misbehavior continues, write his name in the red light and proceed with appropriate discipline. I have found that seeing a name placed in the yellow warning area is usually enough to remind students to settle down.

Karen Bader
Lake Hopatcong, NJ

☞ Management Tips ☜

Blast Off!

When I'm ready for children to get materials out of their desks, I say, "Eyes up, please." I hold up my open fingers, while the students copy my actions. I list the items that I want them to get; then we all count down from ten to one and say, "Blast off!" "Blast off" is the signal for students to open their desks and get the needed materials. This helps to ensure that students are listening to instructions.

Sr. Mary Catherine Warehime
Emmitsburg, MD

Concentration Caps

Sometimes I have students who need extraspecial help concentrating on an assignment. I solve the problem with broken headphones that can no longer be used. I cut the wires off the headphones and keep them at a center. The class knows that when an individual is wearing a "concentration cap," he is not to be disturbed. The earphones block out annoying noise and really help my students stay on task.

Sr. Ann Claire Rhoads
Greensboro, NC

No More Tattletales

I use Herman the frog to take care of a major classroom irritant—the tattletale. Herman is my pet rock. When children feel they need to report an incident, they write it down and place it under Herman. In the beginning of the year, Herman receives tons of notes. But as the year progresses, he receives only important ones about inner feelings and major conflicts. Herman is a valuable language arts station as well as a solution to my tattletale woes.

Judy Boyle
Oakfield, NY

Multiple Choice

To keep students' attention while preparing them for multiple-choice tests, I give each child four cards of different colors. Multicolored index cards work well. Have children label their cards with the letters *A, B, C,* and *D,* one letter per color. Ask questions orally. Give four answer choices orally, or write them on the overhead projector. On your signal, the students hold up their answer cards. You can see who needs help and give immediate reinforcement. This activity also develops good listening skills.

Brenda McGee
Plano, TX

Window Curtains

Drapes that only cover the lowest windowpane dress up a classroom and help to keep students' attention indoors. Have students decorate the drapes with pin-on or tape-on designs for a class art activity.

Debbie Wiggins
Myrtle Beach, SC

The ? Chair

I've found a simple way to prevent students from gathering around my desk when I'm helping an individual. I have a chair with a large ? on the back of it near my desk. The class knows that if a student is with me and one is waiting in the ? chair, they must wait until the chair is vacant before coming to my desk. I'm able to give quality time to individuals without being constantly interrupted.

Debbie Moreno
League City, TX

Needless Tattling

To put the brakes on tattling and encourage good feelings, I have "Sad" and "Happy" envelopes stapled to the wall. If my students have something to "tattle," they write it on cards and slip them into the "Sad" envelope. Most tattlers won't take the time to write it down, so it'll be forgotten. Positive messages go in the one marked "Happy." At the end of the day, I check "Sad" to see if any matters need to be settled, and I share the "Happy" messages with everyone.

Pamela M. Hartley
Twin Falls, ID

Line Leaders' Chart

Reinforce name recognition with this management aid. List student names in two uneven columns on a poster board chart. Clip a clothespin at the top of each column. Every morning move the clothespins to the next names and announce the new line leaders. When the class lines up, one leader leads the line and the co-leader stands behind him. Leaders switch places on the return trip. Students are line leaders more frequently, and the uneven columns enable them to work with different co-leaders.

Susie Fendley
Montgomery, AL

LINE LEADER

Jon	Dawn
Avis	Amber
Michael	Dwayne
Dena	Linda
Dave	Tony
Marcus	
Samuel	
Sara	

Class Helpers Chart

This is an easy way to assign classroom jobs for the year. Cut two circles of contrasting oaktag, one about 16 inches in diameter, and the other about 24 inches. Divide the smaller circle into wedges for the names of the children in the class. Label the outside circle with job names. (Try to make the number of jobs a factor of the number of children.) Laminate both circles. Assemble them as shown with a brad. Move the wheel one notch to the right each week. Students can see at a glance which jobs are coming up for them.

Pat Garton
Fairbury, NE

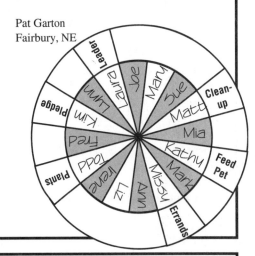

Returning Papers

An easy, effective way to return students' papers is to use baskets designated "pass back." Place papers in the nearest basket and let assigned students do the rest. Reassign new helpers each week or month.

Marilyn Borden
Bomoseen, VT

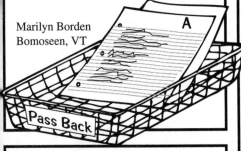

The Big Cheese

Assigning classroom helpers has become a breeze with The Big Cheese! Make a Big Cheese poster and slit the middle as shown. Make and label a mouse for each student. Laminate all pieces. The mouse in the poster is The Big Cheese of the day. He takes attendance, collects papers, cleans blackboards, and changes The Big Cheese at the end of the day. Everyone knows at a glance who is helping out for the day, including me!

Susan Kunda
Naknek, AK

The Big Cheese

Class Librarian

Assign a class librarian to keep books in order and check them out to classmates, incorporating library skills where possible. This helps my students to be more responsible about using my personal books and frees me to do other tasks.

Cindy Newell
Durant, OK

Student Helpers

I allow two of my "quick finishers" each week to help other students with class assignments. This lets me teach without interruption and gives my top students an additional challenge!

Judy Kramer
Houston, TX

Library Card Pockets

Give each student a library card pocket to decorate and label with his name. Prepare cards to indicate jobs to be done in the classroom. Place the cards in pockets to designate helpers. Move the job cards in an "S" configuration as assignments are changed so that everyone gets a turn performing each job. As a reward for exceptional behavior, surprise a student by placing a special card in his pocket. The card entitles him to skip one assignment.

Beverly Hash
Marietta, GA

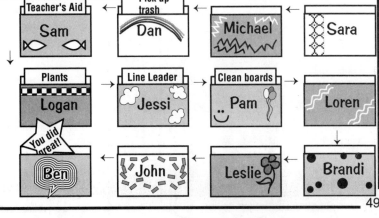

☞ Management Tips ☜

Early Bird Work

Give your "early birds" who fly through assignments a special treat to keep them busy. Create an "early bird" folder from tagboard, and hang it on a door or wall. Fill it with art activities, fun sheets, and writing ideas to complete while others are still at work.

Pamela Myhowich
Selah, WA

Time Filler

Promote creative thinking with this short and simple activity. Each day, write a different topic for list-making on the board. Sample topics might include a list of green things, wet things, happy things, or school things. After five minutes, total the lists. Give a reward to the student with the most items.

Becky Shanklin
Corinth, MS

Speed It Up!

To get my slow beginners off to a speedy start, I use this trick when assigning small-group work. I have students write their names on the board as soon as they've finished the assignment. When we come together and check the work, I award the first one listed who got a "100" with a special sticker. It really picks up the pace!

Mary Dinneen
Bristol, CT

Find The Facts

For those early finishers who say "What now?" here's an activity to brush up on research skills. Glue library card pockets to the front covers of several encyclopedias. On library cards, write questions that can be answered in the volumes, and place them in the pockets. Reward your students with bonus points for the questions they answer correctly.

Linda Piper

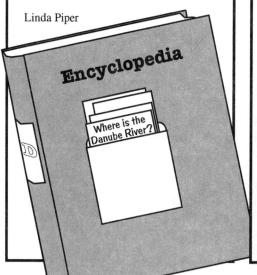

Daily Schedule

I put my daily schedule on the chalkboard by writing the name of each subject on a separate card and attaching magnetic tape to the back. When a subject is completed, the card is taken off the board. My first graders are able to see how the day is progressing and rarely ask, "When do we go home?"

Rhonda Peterson
Baltimore, MD

Spelling

Lunch

Social Studies

Music

Question Jar

My class "question jar" is a great way to fill odd minutes at the end of class or review basic facts before a test. I write increasingly difficult questions to put in the jar as the year progresses. Humorous questions are a nice break from academic ones, on occasion. A student draws a question and answers it. If he is correct, I reward him with a sticker or applause from the rest of the class.

Linda Brewer
Ivanhoe, TX

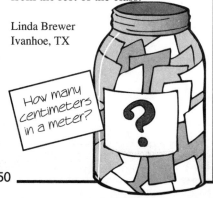

Extra Credit Box

I keep blank ditto masters in a box for students who want to earn extra credit. In their spare time, students may take one and make a worksheet, game, or puzzle for their classmates to complete. I make copies of the best ones for our "student-made" center. This really puts creative minds to work and saves me a lot of time, too.

Sr. Ann Claire Rhoads
Greensboro, NC

Five-Minute Filler

When you find yourself with an unplanned five minutes, put them to good use by brainstorming with "what if" situations. For example, discuss the pros, cons, and interesting aspects of the following:
—What if we lived near the equator?
—What if we had winter vacations from school instead of summer vacations?
—What if we went to school Tuesday through Saturday?
—What if a computer was our teacher?

Mary Anne T. Haffner
Waynesboro, PA

Beat The Clock!

A kitchen timer can help children stay on task. The child decides how many minutes he needs to complete his assignment. The timer is set, and he works to "beat the clock"! There is no time for daydreaming.

Sara Kennedy
Bedford, VA

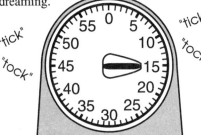

Some Extra Time?

Even though I have centers throughout my classroom, some students finish their work and ask, "What can I do?" I developed a list of activities to remind students of their choices. It is displayed in the front of the room as a constant reminder.

Debbie Wiggins
Myrtle Beach, SC

What do I do?

Some Extra Time?

1. Bulletin Board Activities
2. Journal
3. Math Incentive
4. Folders
5. Basic Skills Packets
6. Writing Tables

Book Of Mazes

To provide an activity for students who finish their work quickly, buy an inexpensive book of mazes and glue the individual puzzles onto construction paper. After laminating the sheets, you'll have a durable and reusable set of mazes that students love to do with wipe-off markers.

Becky Martin
Bergton, VA

Timing The Task

Use a kitchen timer to help motivate students to clean up quickly. Set the timer. If students beat the timer, the class earns a sticker. When students have earned a predetermined number of stickers, award a treat such as extra recess or a popcorn party.

Sue Volk

Computer Time

To simplify scheduling computer time, I circulate a sign-up sheet every Friday. The sheet lists the available computer time slots for the following week. Students choose from the times (English seatwork, morning recess, silent reading time) and are responsible for remembering their choices. I select the disks they are to work on that week. Most students are able to schedule computer time twice a week.

Jan Drehmel
Chippewa Falls, WI

Free-Time Management Form

Monitor your students' use of free time. Duplicate a free-time form for every student to fill out at the end of each day. Have students place completed forms in individual work folders.

Sandra Steen
Corinth, MS

Seth

Name __Seth__
Date __February 5__

Today during my free time I:
X Did some art (staple your work to this sheet).
__ Played a game with _____ Name of game _____
__ Worked a puzzle (staple it to this sheet).
X Worked on an activity in the __math__ center.
__ Other _____

☞ Management Tips ☜

Transition Apron

Be prepared for students who complete assigned tasks by wearing a "transition apron." Make or buy an apron. Sew on several pockets in different colors. Write tasks on index cards and place them in the pockets. After students complete classwork, they may either select an activity from a pocket on the apron or be assigned a card by the teacher.

Betty Ruth Baker
Waco, TX

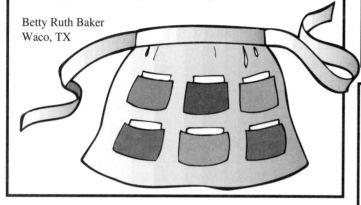

Marker Magic

To encourage students to finish their work on time, I allow them to correct assignments with permanent markers. The chance to use the markers is such a treat that more and more of my students are finishing their work on time.

Mary Dinneen
Bristol, CT

Open A Can Of Worms

Need a time filler for those extra few minutes during the day? Open a can of worms! Cover an oatmeal container with contact paper. On poster board "worms," write tasks and questions that require students to really think. Store the worms in the can. Have a student volunteer pick a worm from the can. Read the task to the class so that everyone understands what to do. Then let the students work independently on completing the task.

Dena Perlenfein
Otis, CO

List all the prime numbers up to 30.

Extra Time

My students' desks are arranged into "tables," with four or five students making up each table. So that students know what to do when their regular work is completed, I have a chart posted with the title "Extra Time." Across the bottom of the chart are library card pockets labeled with the number of groups I have. On colorful poster board strips cut to fit the pockets, I list activities that students can do during free time. I include thinking games, drawing books, reading area, puzzle table, science center, mail center, folder games, and flash cards. Every other day, a helper rotates the strips so that each group has a new activity. One poster board strip that is especially popular is the one with "Join the group of your choice."

Debbie Moreno
League City, TX

Good Use Of Time

To help your students stay on task, make a poster entitled "Good Use Of Time." Include a list of tasks the students need to do daily. Students can refer to the poster rather than interrupt you when they are finished with their regular work.

Good Use Of Time
1. Do all assigned work.
2. Check makeup work chart.
3. Do daily skill.
4. Choose a learning center.
5. Write in your journal.
6. Practice flash cards with partner.
7. Read with partner.

Time On Task With Problem Solving

For a time filler, type up problem-solving questions. (I like to use the large print on the computer.) Cut the questions apart, and glue them on strips of poster board with rubber cement. Color-code the strips according to question categories or difficulty. Put the answers on the backs, and laminate the cards. Because the cards are self-checking, a student can be in charge of this productive way to fill time.

Janet Taylor
Rockport, TX

If you can run a mile in 15 minutes, how ma miles can you run in two hours?

What are three synonyms for the word "pretty"?

Makeup Work

I've found a simple solution to the problem of keeping up with the daily work that absentees miss. I place a clean sheet of notebook paper on the absentee's desk, taping the top and bottom of the sheet to the desk. On the paper, I list each subject covered during the day and page numbers of assigned lessons. If worksheets were handed out, I slide a copy underneath the taped sheet. I also write the student's name on his assignments in red ink; this reminds me that the work was completed for a day the student was absent. If a graded assignment is returned during the day, it is also placed under the taped sheet. This system is very handy and timesaving, especially when a parent drops in at the last minute to pick up a child's work.

Rebecca Abney
Richmond, KY

Coloring Answers Yellow

Before students correct their own papers, have them color all answers with a yellow crayon. Highlighted answers can be spotted quickly and can't be changed.

Joanne Velasquez
Yakima, WA

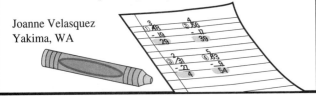

Colorful Corrections

I keep a can of colored pencils handy for my class to use when making corrections in their work. Instead of erasing mistakes, students write their new, corrected answers in color. With this method, parents can see the first answer as well as the corrected one. Also, students can use different colors to correct their work as many times as necessary. I've found this method to be very successful and have received positive feedback from parents. The students like working with the colored pencils, too. It helps eliminate some of the drudgery of "do-overs."

Jeanine Peterson
Bainbridge, IN

Daily Helpers

Keeping track of daily helpers is easy when you let the students do it. Arrange a large cluster of grapes on a bulletin board. Write each student's name on an individual grape. Provide a pushpin for each student. The teacher begins the process of picking daily helpers by putting pushpins in several grapes and assigning jobs to those students. Every morning, each helper from the previous day takes a pushpin from the top of the board, places it on a grape without a pin, and informs that student of the job he has been chosen to do. Continue this method until every student has a pushpin in his grape; then begin again.

Debbie Fischer
Waldron, IN

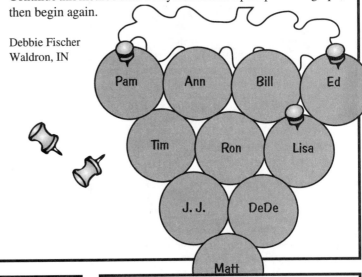

Highlighting Key Words

When reading worksheet directions together, I have my students use crayons to underline and circle key words that will help them remember directions. If there's a Bonus Box at the bottom of a page with additional directions, students circle the entire box. Children often rush and forget to do the "extra" things, especially if something is supposed to be done on the back of a sheet. Highlighting the key words in directions helps considerably!

Mary Dinneen
Bristol, CT

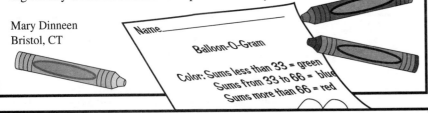

Please Feed The Dog

I have very little trouble getting my students to clean up the classroom. Each trash can has a picture of a dog pasted on the side. I simply say, "Please feed the dog," and our housekeeping is under way.

Francine Reinel
Sarasota, FL

A Helper By Any Other Name...

To save time and to give my students a sense of responsibility, I have developed a unique list of student jobs. My students may choose from a variety of jobs, which they do for a week. Some of the jobs require hard work and patience, while others are fun and always in demand. My jobs include a *butler* (errands), the *zookeeper* (cares for our classroom animals), the *chalker* (cleans the chalkboard at the end of the day), a *line person* (line leader, one per line), a *sanitation worker* (picks up paper at the end of the day), and a *paper manager* (distributes papers to students).

Kathleen Martin
Cincinnati, OH

☞ Management Tips ☜

Lost-And-Found Can

I put books or items left scattered on the floor at the end of each day in a large decorated trash can. To recover the items, students must pay a small penalty. This is a very effective method of teaching responsibility. The trash can helps students learn rapidly to keep up with their things.

Debbie Wiggins
Myrtle Beach, SC

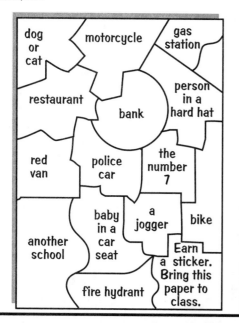

Field Trip Puzzle

Use this idea to keep students busy during a long bus ride. Develop a puzzle similar to the one shown, adapting items for the area through which you will travel. Give each child a copy and a crayon. As each student spots a listed item, he colors that section of the puzzle.

Carole Pippert
Laurel, MD

Post Office Field Trip

A trip to the post office will be more meaningful if your students have something to mail. In advance, purchase a postcard for each child. Have him draw a picture and sign his name in the space for messages. Collect the postcards and address each one to a fellow classmate. Mail them while visiting the post office. Students will be delighted to receive mail from classmates.

Debbie Neumann
Ocean Springs, MS

Hi!

Your friend, Tina

Keesha Teal
3712 West Ave.
Greensboro, NC
27407

RIGHT TO PETITION FOR REDRESS

Field Trip Thank-Yous

Whenever we return from a field trip, I have each student write a thank-you letter to the people who work where we visited. It gives students practice in letter writing, creates goodwill in the community, and gives a real boost to some fascinating and dedicated people.

Sr. Madeleine Gregg
Portsmouth, RI

Field Trip Helper

When parents are assisting you on field trip ventures, consider this identification tip. Attach nametags to the front and back of each child's shirt. This is extremely helpful when a child is walking away from the group and your parent assistant is not familiar with the child.

Francine Reinel
Sarasota, FL

Progress Reports

This report form is a timesaving way to keep parents updated on their child's progress in school. The teacher or the parent can use the "Comments" section to provide additional information. After both parties have signed the form, make a copy for the parent and put the original in the student's file for quick reference.

Arthur Seldney
Sasebo, Japan

Student: _____	Teacher: _____
Date: _____	Grade: _____
Area child does well	Area child needs help
What school will do	What home can do
Comments: _____

Ticket Please!

Cleaning up the floor was a dull chore until I tried this idea. Before my first graders may line up at the end of the day, they must bring me a ticket (a piece of paper from the floor). Some children even bring three or four tickets! If the floor is really messy, I collect tickets several times during the day. The children love collecting tickets, and our classroom looks great!

Rhonda Peterson
Baltimore, MD

Cleanup Patrol

If your classroom has no sink for cleanup time, try this idea. Ask each child to contribute a container of commercial wipes. These containers are easy to use and store. No more running to the bathroom to wash sticky fingers!

Sue Ireland
Waynesboro, PA

Baby Wipes

Keep a container of "baby wipes" in your teacher workroom. Since there may not be a sink nearby, these wipes are great for cleaning purple duplicating ink or copier toner off fingers. They're also useful for other fast wipe-ups and leave hands soft and fresh smelling.

Chris Christensen
Las Vegas, NV

Don't Forget

Notices to be sent home with students are often forgotten. Hang a basket labeled "Don't Forget" beside your classroom exit door. Place homebound handouts in the basket. Even if you forget, it is unlikely that your students will.

Kathy Brown
Florence, SC

Dear Parents,

Don't Forget!

End-Of-The-Day Music

To keep students seated at the end of the day, I play music. As long as everyone is sitting, the music plays on. Students bring in music for me to play during this time, too. Because they enjoy it, I don't have to remind students to stay in their seats.

Catherine Cannon

Cool-down Work

Preplanning some class "cool-down" activities can help you through the last few minutes of the day. Rotate three or four self-graded, self-directing activities such as storybooks with tapes, reinforcement or seasonal worksheets with answer keys on the backs, listening kits, and filmstrips. Tidy up your desk while students cool down.

Cindy Newell
Durant, OK

Don't Forget!

Spelling test tomorrow
Permission forms
Math homework
Science Fair projects
    due on Monday

End-Of-The-Day Reminders

Do you sometimes forget some of the things you should remind students of at the end of the day? Write "Don't Forget" at the top of a sheet of construction paper. Laminate the paper and tape it to the inside of your classroom door. During the day, as you think of things that students will need to be reminded of, jot them on the paper with a wipe-off marker. At the end of each day, refer to the "Don't Forget" reminder before sending the students home.

Mary Beltz
Gillette, WY

☞ Management Tips ☜

Conference Sign-up

Have parents sign up for the fall parent/teacher conferences at the first Open House. This gives parents the opportunity to plan in advance and to let the teacher know if they need an especially early or late appointment. Be sure to send home a reminder right before the conference time.

Diana Curtis
Albuquerque, NM

Sign-up Time!		
Name	Date	Time
Adams	Oct. 9	2:30
Cox	Oct. 10	4:00
Wright	Nov. 6	3:30

Parent Survey

Prior to conference time, send home a survey for each parent to complete and return at the conference. This helps parents examine their child's education and prepare for the conference. (Some sample questions are: What do you feel is your child's best subject? What do you think is your child's weakest subject? How does your child feel about school?) Add questions to the survey that pertain to your class.

Sharleen Berg
Red Wing, MN

Scheduling Conferences

To keep things running smoothly, I put up a sign that says "Knock when it's your conference time." I post a list of parents and times on my door. This helps me keep on schedule by drawing long-winded conferences to a close. Prompt arrivals do not end up waiting because the previous person was late. Having this reminder takes the burden off me.

Paula K. Holdren
Chalfont, PA

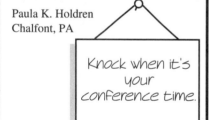

Knock when it's your conference time.

Extra Help

Provide old worksheets and workbooks in boxes labeled according to subjects. Let parents choose from these for their children to use as reinforcement at home. While the parents are waiting to talk with you, they can pick up worksheets on the subjects indicated on their students' work folders.

Mary F. Williams
Miamisburg, OH

Open House Videotape

Our first P.T.O. meeting is always an Open House during which teachers explain their programs. This year, I videotaped my explanation and included segments of our day showing the children working. It was well received at the Open House and stayed quite popular afterward, too. There were many parents unable to attend the Open House, so I let each child have a turn taking the tape home. These parents loved seeing the video, and many who attended P.T.O. enjoyed seeing it again. Along with all of this positive feedback came requests for copies!

Mary Dinneen
Bristol, CT

Miss Paschal's Class

Welcome, Mom And Dad!

I have parents sit at a reading table with me during the conference. Before conferences, I cover the table with yellow butcher paper and let two children at a time come to the table to write and decorate a message for their parents. This table covering has started many conferences on a pleasant note. Parents enjoy searching for their child's message.

Pamela Myhowich
Selah, WA

Sample Table

During parent conferences, set up a table and chairs in the hall outside your classroom door. Display textbooks and workbook samples along with informative letters for parents to view while waiting. Be sure to include a current class newsletter. Post student artwork in the hall to brighten the waiting time.

Cindy Newell
Durant, OK

Mini-Homework Ideas

Sometimes parents want to know how they can help their children at home. I tell them to attach an envelope to their refrigerator. I direct parents to cut worksheets and other assignments into strips or blocks (depending on the format) and place them in the envelope. Then when the child wants or needs extra practice, he can go to the refrigerator!

Sr. Ann Claire Rhoads
Greensboro, NC

Canned Communication

Improve parent communication by ensuring that your notes arrive home in good condition. Have each student label and decorate a Pringles can. Children use their canned creations to carry notes, messages, or forms home to their parents. Parents can, in turn, send their replies back to you in their child's can.

Patricia D. Shulman
Englewood, CO

Letters To Parents

Before conferences, I have my students write letters to their parents telling them what we've been doing in class and what grades to expect. The children are usually quite candid. These letters are a good way to begin conferences and also provide nice handwriting samples.

Deborah Marko
Lancaster, PA

Home Activity Bank

For each unit that I teach, I make up a list of activities to send home that children and parents can do together. I keep the activities in a "home activity bank" file. Each time I begin a unit, I simply go to the file and the list of activities is ready to send home!

Summer Tucker
Knoxville, TN

Contacting Parents

With so many moms and dads working, it's sometimes difficult to call a parent during the school day with concerns about a child. Be sure to keep a class roster at home that has each student's name, his parents' name (last names may be different), and the home telephone number. Often it's more convenient to contact parents at night.

Jane Miles
Pocatello, ID

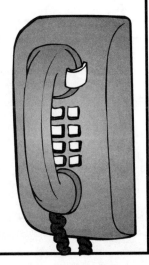

Parents As Partners

Because it's so important to involve parents, I have had great success using this idea to promote reading aloud. I purchased audiocassettes of *The Read Aloud Handbook* by Jim Trelease. Since they have busy schedules or younger children at home, I allow parents to borrow the cassettes and listen to them at their convenience. I plan to look for other quality audio- and videocassettes with information that can help parents maximize their children's school success.

Kathleen Darby
Cumberland, RI

Parents Need Rewards, Too!

To encourage my students' parents to sign and return notes I send home, I hold a "parent raffle." Each time a student returns a permission slip or other note signed by a parent, I put the parent's name in a picnic basket. At the end of a term, I draw a name from the basket. The lucky parent receives a gift certificate from a local restaurant (usually donated by the merchant). Students, and especially parents, really respond to our raffle, and I benefit with notes returned on time!

Amy Kunst
Madison, IN

Getting Organized

Organizing Lesson Plans

Eliminate those last-minute struggles to collect materials for lessons. Label five folders Monday through Friday. While writing lesson plans, highlight the extra supplies needed for each day. Stock each folder with the necessary supplies.

Sharleen Berg
Jefferson, SD

Check Marks

Use a red pencil to check off parts of your lesson plan that are completed. This makes it easier for a substitute to follow your plans.

Mary Dinneen
Bristol, CT

Helpful Checks

Organize your lesson plans by using a check mark whenever classroom worksheets or extra materials are needed. After preparing the materials, circle the check mark in your plan book to indicate that you are ready for the lesson. It's easy, and there are no unwanted surprises in your day.

Kathy Graham
Filer, ID

Modifying Methods

To ensure all learning modes are taught, use the letters *V, A, K,* and *T* to stand for Visual, Auditory, Kinesthetic, or Tactile. Place one letter by each day in your plan book and use that learning style to present lessons. This ensures students have their preferences honored during the week.

Sr. Ann Claire Rhoads
Greensboro, NC

Plan Book Reminders

I use colored dots in my plan book to remind me of things to do. For example, a red dot reminds me to gather art supplies; a green dot tells me to sign up for the computer room. Each color stands for a different item and reminds me to do it now for next week.

Sr. Ann Claire Rhoads

Lesson Plan Reminders

Here's an easy way to stay on top of upcoming events. Jot information down on a stick-on note and place it in your plan book on the appropriate date. You'll be pleasantly reminded of the event when you complete your plans for that week.

Vail Neal
Cleveland, MS

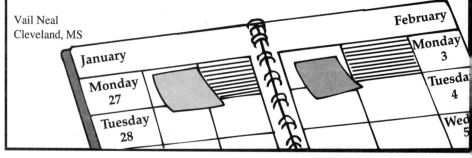

Press-on Pocket Pleasers

The press-on pockets from The Education Center have been a lifesaver for me! Try these ideas:

- Place a press-on pocket inside your grade book to hold grading supplies.
- Store future ideas in a press-on pocket inside your plan book.
- Decorate boxes to hold center activities. Press a pocket on each box to hold the supplies needed for that center.

Cindy Newell
Durant, OK

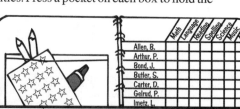

Daily Board Work

Keeping up with daily board work was a hassle until I put each day's assignment on an index card. I file each card by subject: language arts, math, science, seasonal, etc. After I use a card, I turn it backward in the file box so the activity will not be used again until the following school year.

Jenny Kieswetter
Bowling Green, KY

Noting Special Times

I use a Hi-Liter to highlight in my plan book the special times of the school day, including physical education, library, lunch, music, recess, and assembly programs. Then, at a glance, I know when to get ready for these classes and events. Highlighting is especially helpful for substitutes; they're more likely to follow your schedule.

Cindy Fischer
Bismarck, ND

Spillproof Files

When I need a file folder to hold small materials, I save money by using self-locking plastic storage bags. I put in the pieces, zip it closed, turn it sideways, and file it away. To recognize each file, I put a piece of masking tape on the top and label it with a colored marker.

Mary Dinneen
Bristol, CT

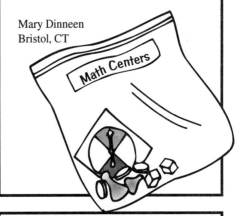

Skipping Around

I skip around in some of the textbooks that I use, often covering chapters out of order. To help me remember which topics and chapters I've taught, I keep a chart taped to the inside front cover of each text. Then when I've completed a particular unit, I check off the chapter and jot down the date. Sometimes it's so easy to forget what you've already taught—this method will help you remember!

Mary Dinneen

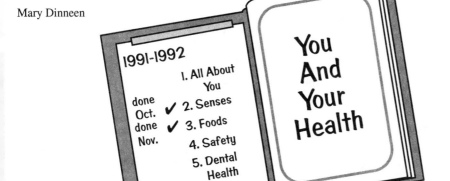

Early Dismissal

Be prepared in case of an early dismissal. Tape a student list inside your plan book, which includes student addresses, phone numbers, and their normal transportation home (walker, bus rider, picked up by an aunt, etc.). Then when there's an early dismissal, you'll have all the necessary information about each child at your fingertips.

Ruby Pesek
Lake Jackson, TX

Achievement Test Skills

I add a special note to an activity or original worksheet I use to teach a skill that's included on a standardized test. This helps remind me to cover this item thoroughly.

Mary Dinneen

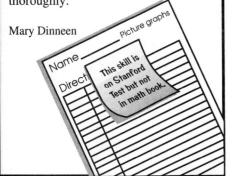

Everything For The Week

This simple idea takes only minutes on Friday afternoon but will save you time and help you avoid last-minute confusion the following week. Label one manila folder for each day of the week. On Friday afternoon, consult your lesson plans for the coming week. Take a few minutes to gather all of the materials needed for each day. Place flash cards, charts, seat work, etc., in the appropriate folder for the day. Your materials folder will also be a tremendous help to a substitute teacher.

Sarah Horton
Fort Payne, AL

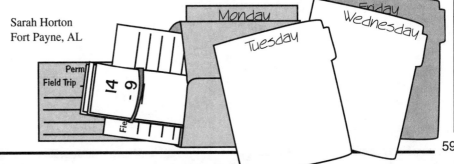

Getting Organized

Game Index

Need a way to organize activities and games? On an index card, list the title, subject, skill, and level of an activity. Provide a description, and file by subject. Use the back to record dates assigned.

Cynthia Huffman
Lawrenceville, GA

Title: "Bowled Over"
Subject: Math
Skill: Multiplication with two-digit numbers
Level: Medium to high
Description: File-folder activity for two players. Each player will spin and multiply the number on the spinner with the number on the bowling pin.

Working Bibliography

In order to efficiently record good literature and/or reference materials, photocopy library cards. All pertinent information is quickly available for future use. Make personal comments or evaluations on the copies of the cards. As new resources are discovered, add them to your bibliography.

Sandra Edgington
West Carrollton, OH

Poetry File

I keep a poetry card file for poetry study and student use. I pull some poems from magazines and cover them with protective plastic. Others I type and laminate for durability. Children choose poems to read or pick out a favorite for handwriting practice.

Nancy Lach
Mandan, ND

Organizing Your Classroom Library

Use colorful sticky dots (available from The Education Center) to organize your classroom library. With your students, decide which category of books each color will represent. For instance, yellow dots can be placed on all mystery books, orange dots on all biographies, blue dots on animal books, red dots on fiction, and green dots on nonfiction. Then get plastic crates in matching colors, and students will know at a glance where a book should be stored. This storage method is also very helpful when students prepare reports. It saves the time of looking through all your books when only a certain category is needed.

Diane Vogel
Macon, GA

Films And Videos

To keep track of the films, videos, and filmstrips that correspond to the various units I teach, I attach a press-on pocket to the inside of each file folder holding my unit materials. I record all the audiovisual materials on an index card and slide it into the pocket. When I pull the file, I have everything ready to prepare for the unit.

Sr. Mary Catherine Warehime
Lynchburg, VA

Tracking Resources

To help you keep up with good books that supplement your teaching units, make copies of the books' covers and file them with your other unit resources. When you're preparing to teach a unit, the copies of the book covers will remind you to check out those books from the library. And since you know what the books look like, they'll be easier to spot!

Mary Dinneen
Bristol, CT

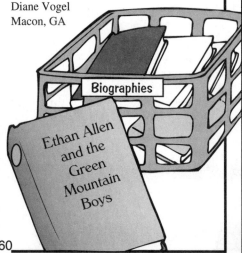

Biographies

Ethan Allen and the Green Mountain Boys

Place Holder

When working with paper and reports to be filed, I use a ruler as a place holder. When a child's folder is pulled, my ruler goes in its place. The finished folder is easily returned to its proper place. When I am working with a set of folders, I place my ruler at the back of the last completed folder. If I am interrupted, I know exactly where to resume working.

Arlene M. Johnston
Bradenton, FL

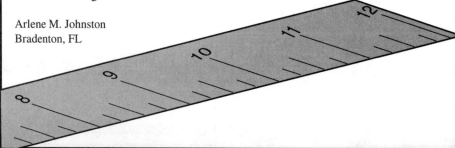

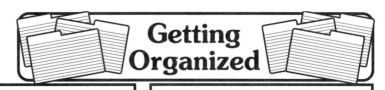

File Helpers

To help organize my files, I place a piece of colored construction paper in the front of my file folders. As I use worksheets, I place the leftover ones in front of the construction paper. I never have to guess which papers have already been used.

Kathy Graham
Filer, ID

File Organization

When your files get bigger and bigger, sometimes it is difficult to remember to which file to return an item. To solve this problem, write a small reminder on the bottom of the item or worksheet. Write the same note and the name of the item on the appropriate page in your teacher's manual. This way, you will always know where to find or store materials.

Mary Dinneen
Bristol, CT

Decofile Organizers

To help file my teaching materials, I purchased several colored Decofile organizers. I color-coded them by subject and used them to hold individual files labeled according to skill. This method eliminates searching through ditto books for a particular worksheet. I can also see at a glance what materials I need to order for next year.

Linda Crissman
Gratis, OH

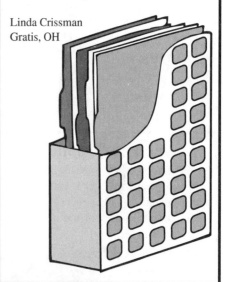

Systematic Subscriber

To avoid digging through my supply of *The Mailbox,* I photocopy the table of contents of each issue. Notes in the margin alert me to how I used the units. I file these copies with old issues in a shoe-storage box that provides one compartment for each issue date. Note: A yearly index is now included in the June/July issue of each edition of *The Mailbox.*

Carole Pippert
Bowie, MD

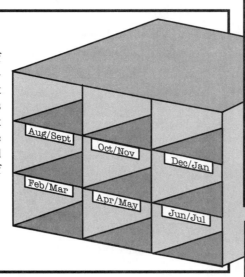

Mailbox File

As soon as I get my new *Mailbox* magazine, I pull out my index cards. I list each unit in the issue on a separate index card with the month and year. Then when I decide to do a unit, I just glance through my alphabetical index file to find which issue to grab.

Pamela Myhowich
Selah, WA

Mailbox Idea Management

Organize small ideas from *The Mailbox* so they'll easily be seen and not get lost among larger papers. Copy and cut apart the ideas you plan to use. Flip through your organizational files to determine which unit of study each idea best complements. Tape each idea to the outside of the appropriate file folder where it will serve as a reminder just when you need it most.

Mary Dinneen

Worksheet Management

Whenever I receive my copies of *The Mailbox* and *Worksheet Magazine,* I photocopy the worksheets and answer keys. I cut out the answer keys and attach each key to the back of its corresponding worksheet with double-stick tape. Now I never have to search for a key or create a new one!

Debbie Moreno
League City, TX

Getting Organized

File It In A Folder

Organize your units of study for easy access year after year. Keep a folder for each unit. Use the folders to store sample worksheets, brochures, art projects, etc. On the outside of the folder, note related activities, bulletin boards, books, and films. Be sure to write the call numbers of books and films. This will save you lots of time in the future.

Sandra Grigsby
Amarillo, TX

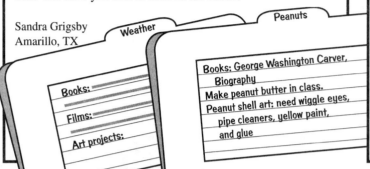

Weather

Peanuts

Books:
Films:
Art projects:

Books: George Washington Carver, Biography
Make peanut butter in class.
Peanut shell art: need wiggle eyes, pipe cleaners, yellow paint, and glue

Monthly File Folders

File folders give quick access to materials from September to June. Label a folder for each month. File dittos, timely art ideas, magazine clippings, and letters to parents. Subdivide the material within the folder by subject area using paper clips. Use the folders year after year, discarding worn-out dittos and adding new ideas.

Lucille Sisti
Yeadon, PA

November
October
September

School Supplies

Be prepared when ordering time rolls around. Keep an index card in your desk drawer, and write down needed items as they come to mind. When it's time to place your order, you'll have your list of reminders.

Mary Dinneen
Bristol, CT

Supplies:
construction paper
chalk
blue tempera paint

Orders

It's Mine

For a quick and easy way to identify personal belongings in your classroom, use sticky dots. Fluorescent dots are visual aids for locating materials or identifying ownership. This is particularly helpful to long-term substitutes or beginning teachers.

Sandra Edgington
West Carrollton, OH

Identify Your Pencils

If you like to keep a supply of pencils at a reading table or interest center, paint the metal near the eraser with nail polish. If a pencil disappears, you or the child who removed it from the center will be able to identify and return it.

Joanna C. Day
Marion, IN

Seasonal Storage

Here's a practical way to store all your seasonal supplies! Label three large cardboard storage boxes *fall, winter,* and *spring.* Put your large bulletin board pieces in the appropriate box with seasonal borders. Also include an accordion folder for each month of the season. Inside each accordion folder, place folders for these topics: bulletin board ideas, arts, crafts, stories, poems, worksheets, calendar pieces, display pictures, and precut letter captions.

Paula Holdren
Chalfont, PA

Monthly Boxes

Get a supply of boxes with lids (boot boxes work well) and label each one with a month of the school year. In each box, place art projects, monthly activities and books, patterns, certificates, birthday prizes and certificates, teaching aids, each week's folders with worksheets, bulletin board letters, and a copy of the month's lesson plans. This system makes it simple to get what you need, when you need it.

Louise Philpot
Sallisaw, OK

Name Tags

Back To School

Art for August

Getting Organized

Post-it™ Notes

The Post-it note has quickly become a "teacher's aide." It's a great way to leave a happy note or reminder on a child's desk without having it blow away. One of the most helpful uses for a Post-it note is as a bookmark for the book I'm reading to my class. The students can also enjoy reading the book without losing my place, and it puts an end to lost bookmarks and bent pages. Best of all, the note can be used for an entire book or more!

Sandy Reid
Durham, NC

Mr. Popper's Penguins

Brian, Don't forget your makeup assignment.

Seth, You did great on your science project.

Susie, Don't forget to take Spike home for the...

Seating Chart

Cut costs and save time with a do-it-your-self seating chart. Using a permanent marker, draw student desks on a 9" x 12" piece of oaktag; then laminate. Write a child's name on each desk with a wipe-off marker. To change the chart, the names wipe off and the desks remain.

Mary Dinneen
Bristol, CT

A Season Of Reading

Organize all the reading books in your classroom by holiday or season. Place them on a spare shelf and put labeled cardboard dividers between each section. Color-code each book so that children can return it easily. When a holiday is approaching, pull that section and place the books in your reading corner for a free reading center. When the holiday is over, return that section and reach for another!

Pamela Myhowich
Selah, WA

Managing Supplementary Materials

When you want to remember an important item that supplements a subject, tape a reminder to the front of that subject's book. Each time you open the book, the reminder will be there and you won't forget whatever it was you wanted to remember.

Mary Dinneen

Convenient Case

Use an old glasses case (preferably one that opens at the top) to hold pens, pencils, or markers. The cases can be left at a center, near the overhead projector, or on your desk for students to use conveniently.

Dr. Rebecca Webster Graves
Burlington, NC

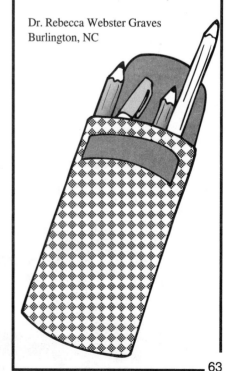

File Folder Storage

File folder centers easily slip into The Education Center's large-sized string-tie envelopes. This makes for excellent storage when separate pieces or cards are used in the centers. Label the envelopes to identify each center, and include a list of pieces.

Geraldine Fulton
Sedgewickville, MO

Big Bear Hug

Notes To Teacher

Keep track of incoming notes by taping a "Notes To Teacher" file folder on your desk. After notes have been read, place them in the folder. If they need to be referred to, you know exactly where they are. At the end of the grading period, clean out the file after recording necessary notations.

Ruby Pesek
Lake Jackson, TX

Notes
To
Teacher

Getting Organized

Letter Rack

I hang a letter rack by my chalkboard for handy storage of flash cards and an extra box of chalk. There are three key hooks at the bottom that I use to hang hall passes. The uses for it are probably endless!

Cathie Weaver
Springfield, GA

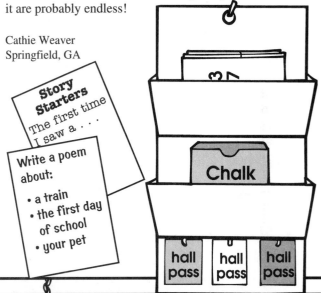

Story Starters
The first time I saw a . . .

Write a poem about:
• a train
• the first day of school
• your pet

Chalk

hall pass   hall pass   hall pass

Poster Storage

To store posters and maps neatly, roll them up and insert them into small orange juice cans that have both ends removed.

Sandra Steen
Corinth, MS

juice

Here's a convenient storage system for large display pieces such as posters, charts, and large bulletin board characters. Clip them to pant or skirt hangers, and store the hangers on a closet rod. When you're in need of a display piece, flip through the hangers to view your selection with a quick glance.

Debbie Burns
Irrigon, OR

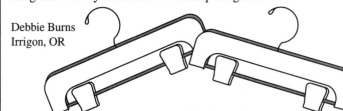

Center Baskets

Hanging metal fruit and vegetable baskets make sturdy center racks. They are excellent for holding those odd-sized games and activities. Spray-paint them to match your classroom colors.

Sr. Ann Claire Rhoads
Greensboro, NC

Pocket Chart

Cards and characters don't slip out of sight with this pocket chart. Divide a large piece of colored poster board into eight sections. Cut eight two-inch-wide strips of clear vinyl, available at most discount stores, and attach them to the poster board with colored tape. The see-through pockets are great for storing flannelboard pieces, too.

Nancy Farlow
St. Joseph, MO

space
plastic strip
space
plastic strip
space
plastic strip
space
plastic strip
space

24 41
-19 36
    -18

Pocket It!

Here's another great use for stick-on pockets. Keep them spaced under the chalk ledge. Fact cards, questions, handwriting exercises, and even story starters can be stored at the blackboard. Keep your art center organized, too, with pockets full of materials.

Sr. Ann Claire Rhoads

Rubbermaid To The Rescue

Need a solution to neat storage of markers, scissors, grading pencils, or other school supplies? Rubbermaid silverware caddies are perfect for the job! Place in a convenient location. Students' desks will not be cluttered by the supply box, and you will not waste time passing out supplies.

M. Jacqueline Kriemann
Riverdale, GA

glue   glue   glue

Handprint Sensation

To dress up my classroom and hide some of the inevitable clutter, I cover the front of my shelves with bed sheets. I have my students make handprints on the sheets using fabric paint. Fabric paint will not wash out of the sheets, so they last year after year.

Sr. Margaret Ann Wooden
Martinsburg, WV

Cutout And Skillboard Storage

Are the corners and edges of your learning center activities becoming ragged? Try this organizational method. Punch a hole at the top of each center. Using S-shaped hooks, hang centers on a sheet of pegboard covered with Con-Tact paper.

Sharleen Berg
Jefferson, SD

Costume Closet

Ease the confusion of dress-up time in your classroom by making a closet just for costumes. Decorate the outside of a large box. Insert a dowel for a hanging rod, and display the costumes on hangers. Children can see at a glance what their costume choices are.

Nancy Dunaway
Forrest City, AR

Hang It Up!

Use hook-type clothespins to organize your bulletin board borders. Just clip strips of border with the clothespin and hang them up in a closet. At a glance, you can see your supply of borders.

Sue Ireland
Waynesboro, PA

Cabinet Stuffers

Place stick-on pockets on the inside of your cabinet doors. Use them to store flash cards, worksheets, and daily reminders. Handy items are right where you want them in a space-saving place!

Sr. Ann Claire Rhoads
Greensboro, NC

Rack Full Of Ideas

Use clip clothespins on a fold-out drying rack to display learning centers in your room. Attach folders, Pocket Pals, learning posters, and other center activities to the drying rack with clothespins. At a glance, students will see the activities from which they may choose.

Kathleen M. Parker
Largo, MD

Versatile Shower Curtain Hooks

Inexpensive shower curtain hooks can serve several purposes in your classroom. Some types can be clipped on chalkboard trays to hold record and book sets or games. Others clip over window bars to hold headphones. Some are great to hold mobiles suspended from rods, beams, or light fixtures. These hooks may even be used as plant hangers for tiny, student-made hanging baskets.

Marge Maginnis
Lakeland, FL

Workbook Checker

To ease the job of checking workbook pages, I use an old pair of pinking shears. When an assignment has been graded and corrected by the student, I "pink" off the edge of the page. Then both the student and I can easily tell which pages have not been corrected. If a student turns in a perfect paper the first time, I use a pink marker to highlight the "pinked" edge.

Diane West
Big Horn, WY

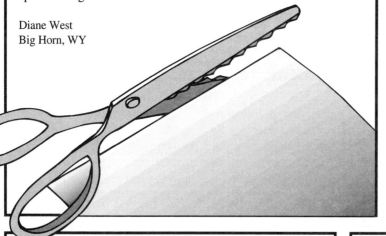

Saved By The Card

Try this to prevent running out of frequently used worksheets. Place a piece of red oaktag in the worksheet pile about 15 sheets from the bottom. Label the oaktag with the words "Help! We need more. Give this to the teacher." When you receive the card, there's still time to run off more worksheets.

Mary Dinneen
Bristol, CT

Did It Go In The Grade Book?

My fourth graders are constantly wanting to know which daily papers are recorded in my grade book. Now they know at a glance. I simply cut the corners off all papers that I record.

Jenny Camarata
Athens, TN

Cutting Corners

Master copies of dittos can get lost in the shuffle on a busy school day. Cut the corners off each original reproducible. It will be easy to spot and save when passing out student copies.

Anne Runyon
Littleton, CO

Rating Correct Responses

To motivate my students, I rate a correct response with a + sign. I remind the student that he can change the + to a * by revising his response. If the child can respond with a higher-level skill or a more creative answer, I change the + to a *. This provides a challenge in even the simplest of lessons.

Jacquelyn Bohen
Wauwatosa, WI

Attention Getter

When photocopying items that need special attention, trim them with pinking shears, and mount them on black paper. Your readers can't miss them!

Linda Piper
Waverly, KS

Don't forget the School Bake Sale on Saturday!

Self-checking Riddle Worksheets

Many worksheets are in riddle format, which means the correct answers provide the answer to a riddle. To change these pages to teacher-checked rather than self-checked, and to provide students with motivation for reviewing checked work, cut the answer blanks off the bottoms of the pages. After checking the answers, return the worksheets with the slips containing the answer blanks. Students will be eager to check and correct their work in order to find the answer to the riddle.

Wendy Sondov
St. Louis, MO

Classwork Organizer

Students do the organizing for you with this quick trick! Label several boxes for subject or skill areas you're covering. Each day, place work assignments beside the corresponding boxes. Clip a number to each box to show which assignment needs to be done first, second, and third. When a student finishes his paper, he places it in the correct box and moves on to the next number. At the end of the day, the papers are already sorted and ready for grading.

Janice M. Thames
Thomson, GA

The Name Patrol

The "Name Patrol" ensures that all papers in my class have names on them. After giving out an assignment, I count to 10 and announce that I am on Name Patrol. I then walk around the classroom looking for names on student papers. Names should already be written on their papers before I reach students' desks. Sometimes I let student helpers "patrol" for me.

Susan Grimm
Brusly, LA

Paper Return

A beanbag can help you save time returning papers. Make or purchase a beanbag character to sit on a carpet square. Whenever there are papers to be returned to students, place them under the beanbag. Inform students that papers placed on the carpet may be handed back by whoever notices them. Name your beanbag character, as he is likely to become a class mascot.

Shirley Kohls
Beaver Dam, WI

"Whooo?"

Rather than try to identify papers without names, decorate a tray or basket with a big owl saying "Whooo?" Place assignments without names in the tray. The children missing papers know to look for them in the "Whooo?" tray.

Bernadette Carnevale
Buffalo, NY

Extra-Mileage Basket

Do you have a basket in which students put their completed assignments? Here's a way of getting a little "extra mileage" out of it. Clip a different picture of an insect, bird, or other animal to the basket each week. Then refer to the basket by its new name. For example, "Please put your finished papers into the *cardinal* basket."

Kathy Galewski
Franklin, WI

IOU Chart

I keep a set of IOU charts on a clipboard for students with incomplete assignments. When a student has not completed an assignment, I write an IOU. Each week I send copies of the IOUs home to the parents. This keeps students and parents up to date on work that has not been finished.

Debbie Retzlaff
Fort Knox, KY

IOU

Name: _Steven Snyder_

Three math sheets

Teacher : _Ms. Dankin_

Paper Management

I have three sets of stackable paper trays to organize all of my paperwork. Each set has an individual tray for each subject. In one set, I place the worksheets that I plan to use; they're easy to find, yet out of the way. In the second set, I put all the papers that need to be graded or that need to be recorded in my grade book. The third tray set is for the students to put their work in as it's completed. This system has really cut down on lost assignments and has helped me to become better organized.

Kim Maxwell
Temple, TX

The Make-up Pad

I keep a pad of assignment sheets on my desk. When a student is absent, I fill out a sheet from the pad as assignments are made during the day. I tape the sheet to the absent student's desk at the end of the day. The next morning, the student has all his assignments at his fingertips. I hold a short conference with him to explain the assignments. Use carbon paper between the sheets if more than one person is absent.

Karen Wigger
Maysville, MO

Daily Assignments

Student _____
Date absent _____
Math _____

Spelling _____

Language _____

Science _____

Social Studies _____

Reading _____

Special message:

Just Hanging Around

Keeping track of make-up handouts is as easy as hanging papers on a clothesline. Stretch a colorful vinyl clothesline with plastic clothespins across a chalkboard, and secure the ends. After passing out papers, immediately write names of absent students on extra sheets and attach them to the clothesline. Students quickly learn this is the first place to look for make-up work. I can also use this to display "no-name papers" so owners can claim them.

Janet Taylor, Rockport, TX

Volunteers!

Take advantage of parents, students, or anyone who is willing to give your students individual help! As you introduce or review a skill, run extra copies of the worksheets you use and keep them in a file. Label folders with skills and file your extra copies in them. Keep a stack of "tutor" forms handy. When you have a student who would benefit from extra help, fill out a form. Provide a special place in the classroom for volunteers to work. When it's time for the volunteer to visit, he can pick up the forms, call the students, and pull worksheets from your files. When the volunteers are not with students, ask them to make centers and manipulatives.

Subject Checkoff Station

To keep track of when students turn in assignments, I put a box for each major subject at a "Checkoff Station." I attach a piece of paper with the class roll, subject, page numbers, and date on each box. Students put completed assignments into the correct box and place a check by their names on the sheet. I then can see, at a glance, who has completed the assigned work at the end of the day.

Gayle A. Brecka
Cumberland, WI

A Week's Worth

Each Monday, my students take home the previous week's papers in a folder. On the front of each folder, I've put a square for each week of the school year. The parent signs the square, indicating he's seen the folder that week. When the child returns his folder signed, I put a sticker in that square. This becomes a sticker collection for the child to keep at the end of the year. Lost and forgotten folders are few now, and the children like seeing their collections grow!

Cherry Evans
Ormond Beach, FL

Make-up Work

Take the headache out of make-up work with this clever idea. Label and laminate a file folder. Mount the folder in a place students frequently visit, such as directly above the pencil sharpener. Appoint a student volunteer to label and place the work for absent students in the file folder. When the absent students return, they check the file folder for their make-up work. This folder is also very handy when parents or friends stop by for work.

Ruby Pesek
Lake Jackson, TX

Post It

Use Post-it™ Notes (available through The Education Center) to keep track of homework assignments for absentees. Jot down the assignment on a note and stick it on the outside of the absent child's book. When the student returns, he immediately knows the work he missed.

Sue Ireland
Waynesboro, PA

Getting Organized

Open Notebook

Our school office keeps a loose-leaf notebook on its counter to list announcements and other information that may not get into the weekly bulletin. Anyone may write a suggestion, memo, or greeting in it. Staff members also cut and paste classroom ideas from various publications for teachers to read and use. It really helps to bridge any communication gaps!

Sandy Docca
Silver Spring, MD

Walking Billboards

Do you know how often those homebound messages to parents aren't delivered? Turn your students into walking billboards by putting "Hello My Name Is" stickers on them for reminders. Stickers can also be used to remind parents/students of overdue books, uncompleted homework, or report cards not returned.

Francine Reinel

String-Tie Envelopes

When I am sending home a special letter or paper, I put it in a colorful string-tie envelope. They are easier for the students to keep track of, and the parents are more likely to look at the contents carefully. The next day, the child returns the envelope with a return message from the parent.

Nancy Dunaway
Forrest City, AR

Paper Sandwich

When toting papers back and forth from school, here is a way to keep them together and wrinkle free. Insert two sturdy pieces of cardboard into a heavy-duty Ziploc freezer bag. Place papers between the cardboard and there you have it. Note reminders can go on the outside of the cardboard and easily be seen.

Mary Dinneen
Bristol, CT

Weekly Work Folders

Every Monday, each of my students makes a folder in which to keep his assignments. He staples an assignment chart to the inside cover of the folder. Each day the student adds new assignments and gets to work. This encourages organization and helps me quickly see what should be there when checking folders. Grades are written on both the papers and the chart. The folder is taken home on Friday for parents to review. Parents sign the chart and keep the papers. On Monday, I collect the charts and reward those who remembered to bring them with stickers. These charts are excellent for record keeping and parent conferences.

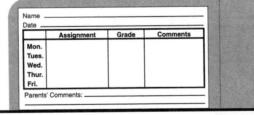

Tube Telecast

Save cardboard tubes from paper towels for carrying longer notes home. Students can also write letters in handwriting class, roll, and insert.

Sr. Ann Claire Rhoads
Greensboro, NC

Identifying Homework

Since students often take home lots of papers, it's difficult for parents to know which ones are homework assignments. To solve this problem, I have my students code homework by coloring red dots in the upper corners of papers that they are to complete. When I check through the work the next day and don't see a red dot on a paper, I remind the child. Usually after a week or so at the beginning of a school year, everyone remembers to include the red dots. Parents have responded favorably to this method and now know which papers should be done as homework.

Vivian Campbell
Piscataway, NJ

Getting Organized

Parent Tags

Here's a clever way to send a note home. Fold a piece of construction paper in half and cut out a price tag shape. Write your note inside; then seal the note with tape or a sticker. Punch a hole in the top, add a rubber band, and slip it on the child's wrist. It's a "big seller" in my classroom.

Rebecca Gibson Calton
Auburn, AL

Tony is very excited that you will be eating lunch with us tomorrow.

Mr. and Mrs. Pope

Special Delivery

Very special artwork deserves to be sent home in a very special way. Save wrapping paper tubes and paper towel tubes. Either roll the artwork and place it inside the tube, or roll it around the tube and secure with tape. Wrap in colored tissue paper and tie the ends with yarn or ribbon to resemble candy. For rainy or snowy day protection, cover the tube and artwork with colored cellophane.

Cathryn Cleaveland
Avondale Estates, GA

Missed Homework

To keep track of missed homework, I write down the assignment on an index card. The student signs the card, and I send it home at report card time. Parents think this is a great idea.

Catherine Cannon
Glen Burnie, MD

Homework Calendar

Here's a quick and easy way to help your students keep track of their homework assignments. Using the calendar feature of The Print Shop Companion disk, my Apple IIe computer, and Imagewriter printer, I create a calendar for each month of the school year. On each calendar, I list days off, special events, and long-range homework assignments. After printing one copy of each calendar, I simply duplicate the number of copies that I need. The kids keep them handy so they can add additional assignments as needed. This seems to help the students get organized, and the fact that the calendars are made by the computer helps catch the students' interest.

Kathy Peterson
Alpha, IL

Pocket Treasures

Save empty plastic breath-mint containers to keep baby teeth and little earrings that have fallen off. Breath-mint containers are small enough to fit in a child's pocket, but large enough not to get lost. Decorate the outsides of these containers with stickers. Children can keep their treasures in a safe place until they get home!

Ellen Allaire
Fredriksted, St. Croix, USVI

Homework Chart

A handy checkoff chart gives students and teacher an up-to-date report on homework assignments. To make, list student names down one side of a piece of poster board and homework assignments across the top. Post the chart in an accessible location. After a homework assignment is turned in, the appropriate box on the chart is checked by the student.

Rose Rasmussen
Mountain City, TN

	Math p.2B	Book Report	Science Project	Vocab. WS	
Cary	✓	✓	✓	✓	
Jimmy		✓	✓	✓	
Trish	✓	✓	✓	✓	
Joe	✓	✓		✓	
Susan		✓	✓		

Assignment Notebook

Save time and teach your students responsibility. Write each day's lessons in a spiral notebook. When absent students return to class, they simply check the notebook to find out what they missed.

Lee Ann Gallagher
Femley, NV

Shelf Markers

I have many of my own books and games that I allow students to use. They were often replaced on the shelves in a mess until I gave each child his own marker—a 3" x 18" strip of oaktag with his name at the top. Now when a student gets an item, he puts his strip in its place so he knows where to return the book or game. I can also see who is using each item.

Betty Ann Morris
Houston, TX

Next Day's Homework

I use a special washable board to write down the next day's homework. If students have extra time during the day, they may begin the assignments.

Rebecca Gibson Calton
Auburn, AL

Coding Filmstrip Cans

Even your students will be able to locate a matching set of filmstrips and cassettes when you label them with color-coded stickers. Use tiny stickers in a variety of colors to organize your film collection.

Connie Connely
Tulsa, OK

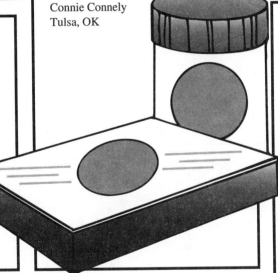

Cardboard Workbook Files

Cardboard magazine files are an excellent place to store student workbooks. I color-code my file boxes and workbooks to correspond with the colors of the tables in my classroom. I place colored adhesive dots on the file boxes and the top edges of the workbooks; then secure each dot with clear mailing tape. Students can easily see which book to pass to which tables and where each workbook should be stored. This saves time and encourages independence.

Christine A. Caruso
Baton Rouge, LA

Giving Clear Directions

After demonstrating how to do something in class, I follow up my visual directions with written directions on the chalkboard. I concentrate on key words, which helps children to organize well and follow directions more smoothly. For example:

Making Flash Cards
1.   Initials on front
2.   Answers on back
3.   Study
4.   Store in desk
5.   Math textbook—page 41

Stir-Stick Helpers

Our librarian uses decorated paint stir sticks so a child can mark a book's space on the shelf while he is glancing through it. Kept in a decorated can, these are placed at convenient places throughout the library for easy use.

Cindy Newell
Durant, OK

Helpful Bookmarks

These easy bookmarks will come in handy when it's time for everyone to find his page for a class lesson. Have students cut the corners off a business envelope, being sure that the straight edges of the bookmarks are at least two inches long. Children will have fun decorating several of these corners to use as bookmarks for each textbook. You can laminate the bookmarks so they will last longer. No more waiting for children to find their places.

Rebecca Gibson Calton
Auburn, AL

Getting Organized

Bagged Photos

When students are asked to bring photos to school to share, I tell them to put their photos in Ziploc bags. The bags are great because classmates can handle and view the pictures without getting fingerprints on them.

Pam Booth
Nashville, TN

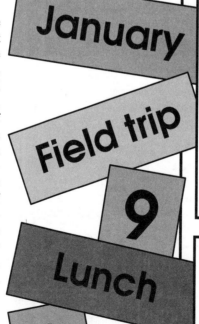

Desktop Organizer

Napkin holders organize my students' desktops and give me a quick indication of unfinished work. Each child in my class has a work folder. At every cluster of desks, a napkin holder holds the folders for that group. When a student completes his morning assignments, he places his folder in a grading basket. Classmates turn in folders of absent students with the work they missed inside.

Dorothy P. Schenk
Sunderland, MD

Using Clipboards

Check out your local discount office supply store for inexpensive clipboards. Clipboards are very handy for small group work when students are not seated at their desks. They're not as bulky as lapboards and are easy to store.

Kenneth T. Helms
Greensboro, NC

Self-made Tests

To help students prepare for a test, I have them make up their own test and supply an answer key. Here's the way the method works: (1) Child A makes out a test and an answer key. (2) Child A gives test to Child B. (3) Child B returns test to Child A. (4) Child A checks answers of Child B. This has proven to be an excellent method of preparing for the real test.

Dr. Rebecca Webster Graves
Burlington, NC

A Schedule With A Flair

For a daily schedule that's flexible and easy to post, I list each content area on a strip of paper. I also make strips for activities such as assembly, lunch, recess, field trip, and physical education. After laminating the strips, I add magnetic tape to the back of each one. The strips are placed on a magnetic chalkboard in the order in which the children will have the subjects. I also have strips to post the date. (Make strips for the months of the year, and for the digits 0–9, including an extra 1 and 2.) As the school year progresses and your schedule becomes more set, assign the posting of the class schedule as a classroom job. It's become very popular with my students, and everyone enjoys seeing what lies ahead for the day.

Deborah Ann Fay
Dover, PA

Table Captains

I keep my classroom organized by appointing a different table captain each week. Table captains are responsible for keeping the tables clean, passing out work, and passing out snacks. This practice helps students develop responsibility and overcome shyness. At the end of each week, I reward table captains for their hard work. I put several different styles of pencils from The Education Center in a paper sack and allow each captain to select one pencil. The students love the recognition and are pleased with the gifts.

Pamela Myhowich
Selah, WA

Personal Mailboxes

I provide a personal "mailbox" for each of my students by attaching press-on pockets to their desks. When papers or notes need to be distributed, I put them in the students' mailboxes. I also have a mailbox attached to my desk. It's a nice catchall for notes and drawings addressed to me.

Diann Poston
Rickman, TN

No More Clutter

To help keep the clutter out of my classroom, I ask each student to bring in a large detergent box in which to store his or her school supplies. I cut a diagonal opening and cover the box with Con-Tact paper. The boxes can be stored upright with students' names prominently written on the sides.

Tami Smith
Canton, GA

Borrowers' Club

Have trouble with students borrowing pencils and paper? Start a Borrowers' Club. Each student puts in 25 sheets of paper and two new pencils to join. When a student runs out, he may borrow up to the amount he paid in. To regain the borrowing privilege, the student must rejoin with more paper and pencils.

LaDonna Hauser
Wilmington, NC

Affordable Desk Organizers

Here's a great and inexpensive way to help children organize their desks. Use a permanent marker to write students' names on quart-sized Ziploc bags. Students place their crayons, pencils, erasers, and other loose items inside their bags. When the bags wear out, I replace them with new bags. Now everyone can organize their desks without needing plastic school boxes!

Jean Busby
Forrest City, AR

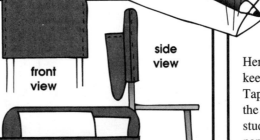

Chairbag

If your students sit at tables with little or no storage space underneath, this idea gets rid of classroom clutter. Make a chairbag for each student. It is made of heavy material (denim works well) and slips over the back of the chair. A large pocket is made on the back side to hold folders and other supplies. A parent volunteer may help with this project.

Sr. Mary Catherine Warehime
Emmitsburg, MD

front view

side view

back view

Keeping Up With Pencils

Here's a way to help students keep up with their pencils. Tape a narrow magnet near the top of a pencil. When the student is not using it, the pencil can cling to the side of his metal desk.

Susan Grimm
Brusly, LA

magnetic tape

Velcro It!

My students were constantly losing their pencils. To help solve the problem, I bought adhesive Velcro circles. I attached one section of a circle to a student's desktop; another section was attached to the student's pencil. When a pencil gets too short to use, the Velcro circle is easily removed and transferred to a new pencil. We not only save pencils, but also the time looking for them!

Delores Alofs
Holland, MI

Notes! Notes! Notes!

What do you do when you're bombarded with notes each morning? Make each student this simple "mailbox." Cut a paper plate in half. Staple the halves to opposite sides of a whole paper plate, creating a pocket on either side. Punch a hole at the top of the plate and attach to a child's chair with yarn. Tell students to put all teacher/office notes in one pocket and that you will put notes for home in the opposite pocket. This system will ensure less hectic mornings!

Sr. Ann Claire Rhoads
Greensboro, NC

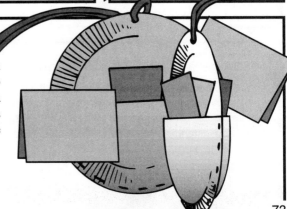

Tax Tip For Teachers

Keep a yellow highlighter pen handy so you can mark in your checkbook any purchases for school materials, books, or your *Mailbox* and *Worksheet Magazine* subscriptions. The highlighted checks are easy to find when calculating business expenses at tax time.

Clarese A. Rehn
Lake Villa, IL

Highlighting Tips

Take a few extra minutes to highlight favorite ideas in your personal issues of *The Mailbox*. Just flip through your issues when you're yearning for new ideas. You'll spot several favorites in a snap!

Theresa Angel
St. Louis, MO

Graph Paper Checklists

Create management checklists quickly by writing your student roster on graph paper. Laminate the checklists for durability. Using a wipe-off marker, check off assignments, permission slips, returned books, etc.

Isobel Livingstone
Rahway, NJ

Field Trip Forms

Joe:	✔	Jeremy:	✔
Niki:	✔	Trish:	✔
Trevor:	✔	Benjamin:	✔
Cathy:	✔	Cassie:	✔

Lesson Plan Lineup

When writing lesson plans from year to year, save time and confusion. On the front of each skill folder, list the order in which you teach the skills in that file. Do it as you finish each unit. Your lesson plans for next year will be a snap!

Mary Dinneen
Bristol, CT

Graph Masters

I tear off the top white sheet of a duplicating master and replace it with a sheet of graph paper. Then I write directly on the graph paper as the purple coating adheres to the back. The grids on the graph paper enable me to write neatly and draw easily. Then I use the graph paper as a master.

Donna Linkous
War, WV

Color-coded Plan Book

In my lesson plan book I use a marker to highlight all extra activities, such as dance, library, and physical education. I use a different color for each subject area. It's great for organization, and I'm less likely to forget something. Substitutes have found my highlighting to be especially helpful.

Susan Deprez
Northridge, CA

Lesson Plan Book

To keep my materials and lesson plans organized together, I use a three-ring binder notebook with dividers for each subject. Behind the day's lesson in each section, I store all of the lesson's worksheets, answer keys, notes, transparencies, etc. Next year I'll have all my materials organized and ready to use!

Kimberly R. Fallin
Rome, GA

Design A Seating Chart

Use the small, self-sticking Post-it™ notes to make your seating chart. Laminate a 9" x 12" piece of oaktag. Label one note for each child in your class. Adhere the notes on the laminated chart to show your seating arrangement. When you change students' seats, it will be quick and easy to redo your seating plan.

Mary Dinneen
Bristol, CT

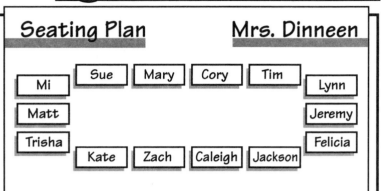

Seating Plan — Mrs. Dinneen

Mi	Sue	Mary	Cory	Tim	Lynn
Matt					Jeremy
Trisha	Kate	Zach	Caleigh	Jackson	Felicia

Handy Word Strips

Sometimes I need word strips or labels for an activity in the classroom. I laminate several pieces of construction paper ahead of time and then I can cut them to size as I need them. The strips last long enough to use again and again.

Beth Gunter
Pocatello, ID

Photo Mount Spray

Tired of gluing and the mess made by rubber cement? Try Photo Mount spray (a 3M product). It's much quicker and great for assembling those small game pieces.

Marthetta Severson
Salem, OR

Sticky-Back Fasteners

To make calendars, helper charts, and games easy to change, attach adhesive Velcro fasteners to the pieces.

Debbie Neumann
Ocean Springs, MS

Tracing Shapes

Make durable patterns using margarine or coffee lids. Trace shapes, numbers, alphabet, or holiday patterns with a permanent marker on plastic lids. Cut out shapes with scissors. These designs are so durable, they will withstand many uses by students. Adapt this idea to make word cards or puzzles for centers, too!

Sr. Ann Claire Rhoads
Greensboro, NC

Timesaving Tracer

Try this technique when you need tracing patterns smaller than 8 1/2" x 11". Make a transparency of your pattern. Tape the transparency to a piece of oaktag. Cut through both the transparency and the oaktag around your pattern. Use the oaktag shape as a durable tracer. You'll eliminate the step of tracing and cutting out your pattern to make the tracer.

Mary Dinneen

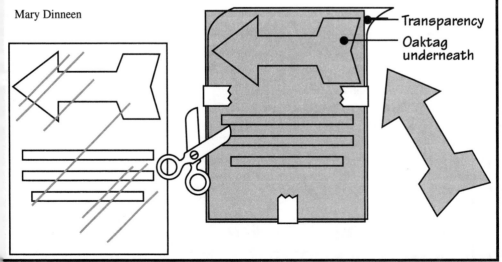

Transparency
Oaktag underneath

Time-Saver

Cut large manila envelopes in half. Staple the bottom halves to the front and back covers of your planning book to make pockets. These pockets can be used to hold faculty meeting minutes, notes from the office, or weekly reminders.

Rosie Troyer
Haviland, KS

Standardized Test Makeups

Giving make-up standardized tests can be a time-consuming interruption in your routine. If a student is absent during testing, record the oral directions as you test your class. When the student returns, seat him at a listening station complete with headphones, pencils, and other supplies. Have him listen to the tape and follow your recorded instructions to complete his test. Share your tape with other teachers on your grade level who had students who were absent during testing.

Mary Dinneen
Bristol, CT

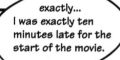

Recorded Plans

Save loads of time by tape-recording lesson plans for your substitute. You will be able to give him or her more information in less time. It works great for me, especially for planned absences.

Rebecca Gibson Calton
Auburn, AL

exactly...
I was exactly ten minutes late for the start of the movie.

Commuting Comments

I have a long trip to and from school every day, so I use this time productively. With a small, hand-held tape recorder, I record things to do, comments for report cards, and general observations about students. I also record any ideas that pop into my head, which I would be sure to forget by the time I arrived at school!

Susan Bell
Florissant, MO

Taped Spelling

Consider this timesaving idea for spelling tests. Instead of reading the list of words, tape-record the test. State the word with an accompanying sentence, allowing a few seconds between each word and sentence. Or choose an articulate student to tape the test for you.

Joni Isaacson
Jefferson, SD

"Extra Box"

Whenever I duplicate worksheets or memos for my students, I run four or five extra copies. I place the worksheets in a special box marked "Extra Box." Whenever a student loses a paper, is absent, or forgets his paper, he simply goes to the Extra Box and finds a copy of the paper he needs. This system has really saved me a lot of time.

Ann Runyon, Littleton, CO

File Markers

File markers make refiling papers quick and easy. Cut several oaktag markers and keep them near your filing cabinet. Each time you remove a file, insert a file marker in its place. Now you can refile with a quick glance instead of wasting time fumbling for the correct place.

Mary Dinneen
Bristol, CT

Straight Stencils

Keep the writing on your stencils in line with this handy tip. Remove the tissue insert from the master; then turn it horizontally and use it as a straight edge. The tissue works even better than a ruler since you can write any letter (even those with descenders) right over top of it. Your stencils will be letter perfect every time.

Chava Shapiro
Monsey, NY

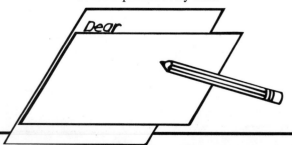

Address Labels

Teacher conventions offer a wonderful opportunity to exchange addresses with other educators and add one's name to company mailing lists. However, writing your name and address repeatedly results in an awfully sore hand! Next convention, bring your address labels to stick on sign-up sheets. They'll save your hands and time!

Wendy Sondov
St. Louis, MO

Little Pocket Camera

Instead of carrying a notebook with me, I now carry my little pocket camera. When I see a cute idea that I can use in the classroom, I simply take a picture of it. This eliminates a lot of note taking that I can't decipher a week later!

Deanna Groke
Misawa Air Base, Japan

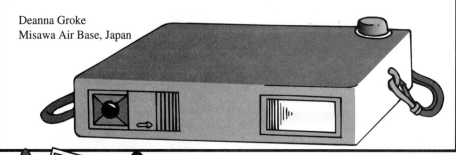

Lesson Plans

Save time writing weekly lesson plans by preparing a plastic cover sheet for your lesson-plan book. In permanent marker, write the daily subjects and other events that occur each week at the same time. Place this cover sheet over your weekly plans with a large paper clip. Include special substitute notes at the bottom.

Sandra B. Grigsby
Amarillo, TX

Handy Track Record

Tape a chart of student names under a transparency and fasten to a corner of your desk. Use an overhead marker to keep track of daily behavior, work habits, etc. A clean wipe, and it's ready for tomorrow.

Cindy Newell
Durant, OK

Instant Posters

Can't draw well or don't have the time to make posters? Make overhead transparencies of pictures you find in *The Mailbox* or other magazines. Let students trace them onto poster board in their spare time or as a reward for good behavior. The students love to help, and it cuts down on teacher preparation time. These transparencies are great to share with other teachers as well.

Sarah J. McCutcheon

Dear Mom And Dad

Writing notes to parents about overdue homework or library books, disciplinary problems, or upcoming events can be very time-consuming. Instead, have students write the necessary notes. Proofread each one and sign it if correct. You may find, as I have, that children respond to parents' questions better when they write the notes.

Rebecca Gibson Calton
Auburn, AL

Quick Notes

Are you spending too much time writing reminders and other notes? By thinking ahead a little, you can save yourself a lot of time. Begin with a copy of your letterhead stationery. Find a clever black-line illustration and attach it to your stationery. List several of your most frequently written messages and duplicate several copies. When you need to send a note, pick up a copy of your personalized stationery and circle the message you want to convey.

Barbara Coon Roberts
Fontana, CA

All-Purpose Frame

Trace the outline of a photo arrangement frame onto a ditto. The pattern makes a worksheet I use several times during the school year. Students use the worksheet to draw favorite characters or scenes from a story, for a family portrait, or to define words from a science or social studies chapter. This format is useful for all subjects and grade levels.

Maureen Pavlik
Allentown, PA

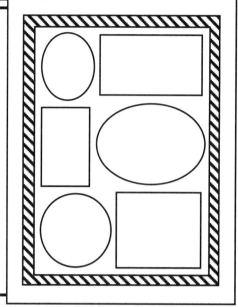

Student Note Labels

To cut comment writing on students' papers, I use preprinted labels ordered from a mail-order company. The manufacturer will print any three-line message inexpensively and promptly.

Diana Curtis
Albuquerque, NM

Correct and return, please.

Thanks for a great job on this paper!

Keep up the improvement!

White-out!

Did you ever make a mistake on a homemade reproducible and not have white-out handy? Just wet the end of a piece of white chalk, and go over the mistake.

Sr. Ann Claire Rhoads
Greensboro, NC

Dotted Lines

The next time you need dotted lines on a master, try using a tracing wheel. For spirit duplicating masters, simply roll the wheel wherever dotted lines are desired. For blackline masters, roll the wheel across a stamp pad before rolling it onto the master. You'll have perfect dotted lines in a snap!

Sr. Ann Claire Rhoads

Laminated Messages

Use your most attractive patterns and designs to send messages. Copy irresistible designs, laminate, and trim. To send a brief note to students, colleagues, or parents, simply write your message on the design with a grease pencil or china marker. Run off as many as you need using a copier. Then rub your message off the laminating film and store the design for later use.

Rebecca Gibson Calton
Auburn, AL

Reusable Shape Cards

To save time making flash cards, I make reusable shape cards from construction paper that has been laminated. For instance, during the Christmas season, I write math problems on Christmas tree shapes. When they finish their regular math assignments, students pair up with buddies to use the cards.

Kathy Graham
Twin Falls, ID

Tracing Tip

When you want to trace something onto a ditto but don't want to write on the original, try this: (1) Remove the tissue paper that is between the sheets of the ditto. (2) Put the original on top of the ditto and the tissue paper on top of the original. (3) Trace away!

Mary Anne T. Haffner
Waynesboro, PA

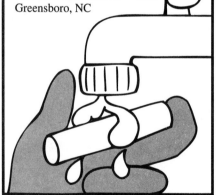

tissue

original

ditto

Grade Book Time-Saver

Instead of writing students' names over and over again on different pages of your grade book, write the names only once and make copies of the list. Attach a Press-on Pocket (available from The Education Center) inside the front cover of your grade book. Store copies of the list inside the pocket. Now whenever you need a new list, simply tape one in place.

Mary Dinneen
Bristol, CT

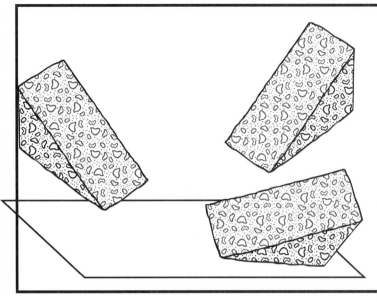

Efficient Erasers

For more precise erasing while using an overhead transparency, use facial or cosmetic sponge wedges. These are found at local department stores. Moistened, they make the ideal eraser for small areas.

Barbara Nivens
LaGrange, GA

Lesson Plan Time-Saver

This handy tip will keep you from having to rewrite your schedule in your lesson-plan book each week. Program the time schedule for your morning and afternoon subjects along with special activities and classes on two blank pages of your plan book. Make copies of the programmed pages and attach them to the pages of your plan book. When you make your weekly lesson plans, your schedule will be easy to see. All you need to do is fill in the daily plans for each subject. Substitutes really appreciate having the schedule included with the plans, too.

Kathryn Smith
Owosso, MI

Knitted Gloves

Collect old gloves and mittens. Place them at worktables. When students need to wipe off grease pencil marks, they slip on a glove or mitten and begin rubbing.

Pamela McKedy
West Germany

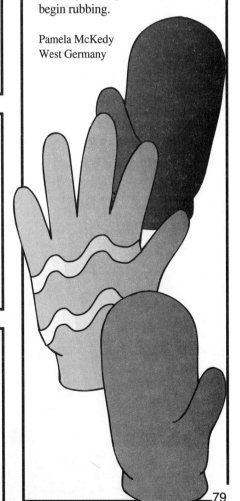

Date Stamp

Whenever a paper you're sending home needs to be returned by a certain date, use a date stamp to indicate the date it should be returned. The official-looking stamp will be easier for parents and students to spot. Students will also enjoy taking turns being the date stamper.

Mary K. Good
Verona, VA

Wipe-off Carpet

Use carpet scraps to erase crayon marks from wipe-off surfaces. They are easy to use and very economical.

Rosie Cowan
Whitewater, KS

No More Scrubbing

Do you need an alternative to scrubbing off grease pencil and wipe-off crayon marks? Dilute a bottle of Glass Plus, spray it on, and the marks can be wiped away like magic.

Debbie McDougal
Greensboro, NC

Dress Yourself

An easy way for a young child to put on his coat is to have him place the coat on the floor, front side up. The child stands at the collar, puts his arms into the sleeves, and flips the coat over his head. He's now wearing his coat, and he did it himself! Try it!

Chava Shapiro
Monsey, NY

Winter Boots

As winter weather sets in, teachers of young children find themselves helping students with their boots. Save time by using long plastic bags that newspapers come in on rainy days. Just slip one over the child's foot, and his boot will slide on easily!

Sr. Ann Claire Rhoads
Greensboro, NC

Play-Doh Mats

Cleaning Play-Doh or clay off desktops can be a tiresome chore. Provide sheets of waxed paper for students to place on their desktops before playing with Play-Doh or clay. Or place vinyl flooring samples on desktops. Flooring samples are long lasting and store conveniently in stacks.

Margaret Paris
Leesville, LA

Knot Picker

Save fingers and time with this simple technique. Loosen a troublesome knot by inserting a nutpick into it. Children will soon learn the procedure and will be using the "knot picker" on their own shoes and jackets.

Betty Lynne Tate
Bristol, VA

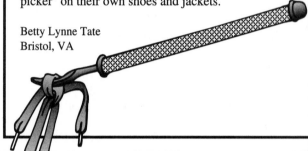

Quick Headbands

To eliminate the time spent measuring heads for headbands, I cut the headband the length of the paper (18") and connect the opening by stapling the same rubber band to each end of the strip. It also stretches to fit adults and is a real time-saver.

Heidi Bode
Sutherland, NE

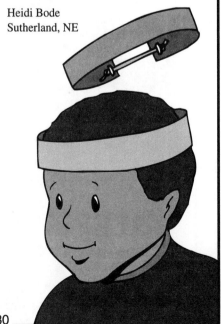

Name Labels

Now children can put their names on their papers before they know how to write them! Print student names on dittos marked off in one-inch lines. Duplicate several copies. Cut the names apart and separate them into individual string-tie envelopes. Glue on labels to the outside of each envelope. Store envelopes in an easily accessible area. Children glue name labels from their envelopes onto their finished papers. Later in the year, duplicate new labels using broken-line letters. Children will trace their names and then glue the labels onto their papers.

Chava Shapiro

Reviving Old Markers

Revive dried-out felt-tip markers by injecting them with water. Using a hypodermic needle, inject a small amount of water into the felt tip of a dried-out marker. This technique can extend the life of the marker up to three times as long.

Marge Westrich
Colby, WI

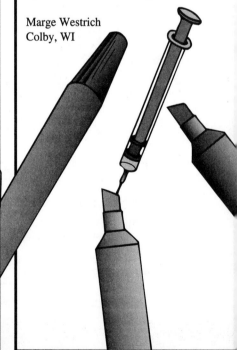

Paper Correcting

This timesaving idea works especially well on papers that can be checked with a quick glance. Set out a stamp pad and a stamp at the front of your desk. Children bring their completed papers to the front of the desk, holding them so you can see them. If you nod your head "yes," they may stamp their own papers. Students making corrections may stamp their papers when they are done. Students receive immediate feedback on their work, and they love stamping their papers, too!

Mary Dinneen
Bristol, CT

Record The Score

Save valuable time used for grading papers. Let the students do this themselves. When a student has finished a paper, have him color the answers with a yellow crayon. The crayon acts as a highlighter and prevents an answer from being changed. All the teacher has left to do is collect the papers and record the score.

Margaret Paris
Leesville, LA

Workbook Time-Saver

This idea will help you save time checking workbooks. Check two workbooks against each other instead of one at a time against the manual. It will really speed up the process!

Marge Westrich
Colby, WI

Time-Saver For Checking Workbooks

Save precious correcting time with this workbook tip. Cut the top outside corner off each corrected page in the workbook. You'll be able to find the workbook page that needs correcting in a snap, and your students will know right where to turn for their next workbook assignment!

Sandra Gonsowski
Euclid, OH

Highlighter

I highlight perfect scores in my grade book so that I know at a glance who has 100 percent. Grades are easier to average at report card time, too.

Cindy Fischer
Bismarck, ND

Correcting By Color

Here's a way to save correcting time and headaches! When a worksheet directs students to "draw lines to connect," have your students draw each line with a different color of crayon. The lines will be much easier to follow when it's time to correct!

Helen Plager
Buffalo, NY

ABC Files

Student helpers can use this filing system! Label a file folder for each letter of the alphabet. Place individual student folders behind the folder displaying the first letter in their last names. Students are able to file test papers or samples of work by first locating the appropriate letter and then the last name they are looking for.

Nancy T. Dunn and Darlene Milholen
Siler City, NC

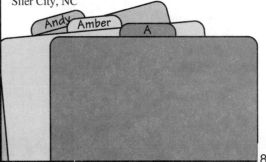

Checking Station

Answer Key

Time-Saving Tip

Speed up the paper-checking process and free up more time for instruction. As you circulate around the classroom spot-checking papers, mark the answers you've checked. Then allow students to finish checking their work by taking it to a checking station. Checking stations should have an answer key and crayons or pens. No pencils are allowed in this area!

Sue Guenther
Waterloo, IA

Turning In Assignments

Save minutes every day by having students establish this habit: always turn in their assignments with the tops of their papers pointing to the front of the room and the front side up. If all students will pass in papers in this manner, the task of checking papers will be easier.

Mary Hemp
Hill City, KS

Answering On The Edge

Do you have difficulty locating student answers, especially for math problems? Have each child number the right edge of his paper and copy the correct answer next to each number. Students can still work the problems on their papers, but you'll be able to find the answers without searching for them.

Joanna C. Day
Lansing, MI

Classroom Management

Numbering your students is a great way to record grades and check for missing work. Assign a student the task of organizing daily sets of papers in numerical order. You can tell at a glance whose papers are still out. List students in your grade book in the same numerical order, and record grades in no time!

Maureen Handler
Richwood, OH

Collecting Assignments

Keep up with who has turned in each assignment by putting a clear press-on pocket wherever papers are turned in. Duplicate a list containing the names of all your students, and put copies of the list in the pocket. The first student to turn in a paper takes a list from the pocket, crosses off his name, and clips the list to his paper. As other students add their papers to the stack, they cross off their names on the list. At a glance you can see whose paper is missing.

Mary Dinneen
Bristol, CT

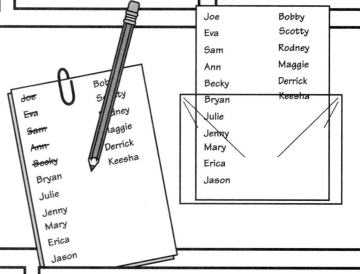

Spelling Grades

The spelling series that I use has four pages for each week's lesson. I go through each lesson and figure the total number of points for each week's work. Then I figure the percentages for each point missed and write these figures on the fourth page of the lesson. Now when I check spelling assignments, I can see at a glance what each child's grade is for the week.

Mary Hemp

Reproducibles In Red

The Mailbox's reproducibles can be made even easier to use by quickly putting the answers directly on the worksheets with a red pen or felt-tipped marker. The answers are then readily available to me and *not* reproduced when copies are made with thermofax and duplicating machines. NOTE: Some copiers will pick up red ink, and some will not.

Sandy Reid
Durham, NC

Keep Those Papers Right-Side Up

Tired of those messy piles of papers? Appoint a child to organize each set of papers as they are handed in. Ask him to count the papers to make sure he has one from everyone. Your helper will save you a lot of time, and he'll feel very important.

Mary Dinneen

Mailbox Organizer

To keep the "goodies" in *The Mailbox* close at hand, I paste the table of contents on the front of the magazine. I also list the reproducibles found in it. That way, I don't miss any of the good ideas, and I save time, too!

Sr. Margaret Ann Wooden
Martinsburg, WV

Correcting Tests

This timesaving method helps eliminate the drudgery of correcting multiple choice tests. After administering oral directions to a small group of students for a specific item on a test, instruct each student to continue darkening the oval for the answer he's selected. Quickly scan the students' answers as they color them in, marking any incorrect ones. Youngsters like the immediate feedback and you utilize wait time in a productive way.

Mary Dinneen
Bristol, CT

Book Club Orders

To help speed up the processing of my monthly book club orders, I ask parents to make their checks out to the book club. This way, all I have to do is tally the orders, fill out the form, and send it in. The canceled checks provide the parents with receipts, and the system saves me time as well.

Mary Anne T. Haffner
Waynesboro, PA

Transparency Checkers

Youngsters can check many of their seat work assignments themselves with these handy transparency checkers. Make a transparency of the desired worksheet; then write the answers with a permanent marker. To use the checker, a student places his paper under the transparency and compares his answers with the ones in red. This method is especially helpful when students need immediate feedback and you're busy with another group.

Mary Dinneen

Weekly Checklist

Use this time-saver to help your students keep track of their weekly assignments and gain independence. Tape a list of the week's assignments to the side of each child's desk. When he completes a task, the student colors in the correct box on his list. By the end of the week, all boxes should be colored in. On Friday, staple all assignments to the checklist and send them home. Give special recognition to the ones who have finished all of the week's work by adding stickers to their checklists.

Cindy Schultz and Nancy Patterson
Deming, NM

Wish List

Keep a wish list of things you would like to have handy in your classroom. When you think of something, jot it down. When ordering time rolls around, your list is already made.

Isobel L. Livingstone
Rahway, NJ

Lesson planning book
Red pens for correcting papers
Highlighter markers (2 colors)
Post-it notes
File folders
Press-on pockets

Classroom Displays

Bulletin Board Storage

To store odd-shaped pieces for bulletin boards, punch a hole in each piece and tie yarn in the hole. You can hang the cutouts on a coat hook or a nail.

Lynn Colquitt
Spartanburg, SC

Bulletin Board Tip

Do you have trouble remembering past bulletin boards? Now I take a photograph of each new bulletin board. I file the photo by skill, month, or subject in my photo file. These photographs also allow student and parent volunteers to reassemble bulletin boards for our classroom!

Cynthia Huffman
Lawrenceville, GA

Storing Bulletin Board Captions

When making a new bulletin board figure, attach a clear adhesive pocket to the back after laminating. Store the bulletin board caption in the pocket. No more missing letters or trying to remember that "catchy title."

Mary Hemp
Hill City, KS

Bulletin Board File

Storing bulletin board pieces from year to year is a breeze with this filing system. Store the cutouts and letters for each of your bulletin boards in a different manila envelope. On the outside of each envelope make a sketch of the bulletin board as it is displayed or, if the idea came from a magazine or book, make a photocopy of the idea and mount it on the outside of the envelope. File the envelopes by subject area or month in a filing cabinet or large box.

Helen M. Hargett
Rome, GA

Memory Sparker

Quickly reassemble a bulletin board next year by taking a photo of the completed board this year. Store it along with the bulletin board letters and pieces. It saves precious time and energy.

Bev Carlson
DePere, WI

Bulletin Board Organizer

I attach a press-on pocket to the back of the largest piece of my bulletin board display. The pocket is used to store the letters and any miscellaneous smaller pieces in the display. With this storage system, I can easily keep all the bulletin board pieces together for future use.

Rebecca Gibson Calton
Auburn, AL

More Bulletin Board Storage

A clear dress bag is a super place to store bulletin boards. You can see what's inside and get to it easily.

Yvonne Hornbuckle
Huntsville, AL

Fabric Backgrounds

Bulletin boards tend to be dull unless covered with colored paper before putting up captions and illustrations. Unfortunately, the paper is often too faded to be reused. As an alternative, try fabric backgrounds. I carry the dimensions of my bulletin boards in my purse and watch for sales in the yard-goods department. I now have several fabric backgrounds in various colors, some plain and some with small prints. The material does not fade and can be folded or rolled on cardboard tubes for storage. A cloth with two- to three-inch stripes can be cut as a border.

Anna Mary Smith
North Loup, NE

A Timesaving Tip

Gift wrap makes a colorful background for a bulletin board, and it doesn't fade. My favorite is a star pattern that lends itself to many themes throughout the year.

Martha Herin
Madison, IN

Bulletin Board Bonus

A one-piece bulletin board is great for storage. Cover your bulletin board with paper. Project your picture and letters directly onto the paper, coloring with oil pastels. Spray with silicon spray or hair spray to prevent smearing. To store, just roll up the paper.

Geraldine Fulton
Sedgewickville, MO

Classroom Calendar

Here's a new twist on a daily calendar for the classroom. Construct a basic calendar and attach a strip of self-sticking Velcro in the center of each square. Make a set of felt cutouts to correspond with each month and number these with a permanent marker. Store pieces in Ziploc bags.

Dorothy P. Schenk
Sunderland, MD

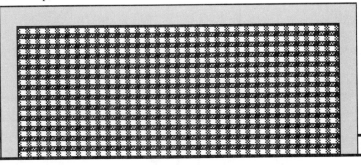

January						
Sun.	Mon.	Tues.	Wed.	Thur.	Fri.	Sat.
■	■	■	1	2	3	4
5	6	7	8	9	■	■
■	■	■	■	■	■	■
■	■	■	■	■	■	■
■	■	■	■	■	■	■

10   22

Make It Special

Vinyl-coated shelf paper makes a bright, attractive background for bulletin boards. Borders can be made by tracing your old ones onto this sturdy paper. Save backgrounds and borders by winding them around paper towel or wrapping paper tubes.

Mary Anne Haffner
Waynesboro, PA

Computer Captions

Create perfect bulletin board captions every time using the Print Shop program and your computer. Type in the desired caption using open-style letters and the "Make Your Own Banner" program. After printing the banner, cut it out and have students color the letters to coordinate with the bulletin board. With the many different letter styles available on this program, you can create many interesting effects.

Don Reiffenberger
Sioux Falls, SD

Pom-Pom Panache

For bulletin boards with a little more panache, try adding some pom-poms. For 3-D captions, glue pom-poms onto the bulletin board to create letters. Rows of pom-poms also make interesting, colorful borders. Pom-pom captions are real attention getters on mini-banners and other displays throughout the school, too.

Sr. Ann Claire Rhoads
Greensboro, NC

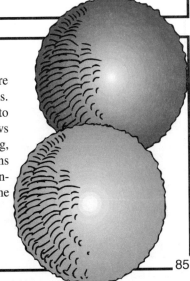

Autumn Leaves Border

Use real leaves as a border for a bulletin board. Iron autumn leaves between two strips of waxed paper and scallop the edges. Place colored tissue paper behind the border to add even more color. To save yourself time, allow students to make the border for you!

Sr. Ann Claire Rhoads
Greensboro, NC

Caption Storage

Here's an easy way to keep bulletin board cutouts and their captions together during storage. Before laminating a cutout, write the caption you use with it on a large envelope; then glue the envelope on the back of the cutout. After laminating the cutout, slit the opening of the envelope with an X-acto knife. Tuck the letters for the caption inside the envelope for convenient storage.

Cindy Fischer
Bismarck, ND

Winter Hint

Make a frosty winter bulletin board caption by writing "WINTER" in glue on dark construction paper. Sprinkle "diamond dust" glitter over it to form icy letters. (This is a clear glitter and can be found at most hobby stores.)

Rebecca Gholston
Plano, TX

Halloween Sky

Miniature silver star stickers on black construction paper make an effective background for a Halloween bulletin board. A witch on her broomstick looks terrific riding across this night sky.

Rebecca Gibson Calton
Auburn, AL

Bulletin Board Magic

White vinyl tablecloths provide durable and economical backgrounds for bulletin boards. They look great with colorful borders, and you won't have to replace the background all year!

Sue Ireland
Waynesboro, PA

Distinguished Backgrounds

Believe it or not, black bulletin board paper makes a beautiful background. Use colorful letters against this, and they really stand out!

Rebecca Gibson Calton

Budget Borders

For economical new borders, fold long strips of bulletin board paper accordion-style. Trace simple coloring-book outlines onto the folded paper, and cut out.

Cindy Newell
Durant, OK

Bulletin Board Letters

Cut letters from wrapping paper to coordinate with bulletin board themes. Laminate to make durable, reusable letters. The comics section of the newspaper works well with cartoon themes.

Cathy Craze
Summersville, WV

Bulletin Board Borders

I cut white paper into six scalloped strips as a bulletin board border for my dinosaur display. The students, working in small groups, decorate the strips with dinosaurs using paints, crayons, or markers. This is adaptable to any area of study.

Carole Pippert
Laurel, MD

Ribbon Borders

Create colorful bulletin board borders with ribbon. Tack a strip of wide (two-inch) ribbon to the edges of your bulletin board. There's no need to cut strips to fit. Since the excess can just be folded under, a long length of ribbon can be used for several different boards. Ribbons are available in a wide variety of patterns and colors and are more durable than most paper borders.

Cindy Fischer
Bismarck, ND

Letter Patterns

To get captions in fancy script, just trace the phrase or title from a magazine, newspaper, greeting card, or calligraphy book onto a clear transparency. Project and trace! Sizes are adjustable according to the distance of the machine from the wall.

Sr. Ann Claire Rhoads
Greensboro, NC

Outlining With Black

If you prefer to outline letters or designs with black marker so they will stand out better, first define the shape inside the line with the colored marker. Outline with the black marker after the coloring is completed so the black doesn't smear into the other color.

Joanna C. Day
Lansing, MI

Letter Lineup

Take the time and trouble out of bulletin board headings! Trace, cut out, and arrange letters on a table. Place a sheet of clear Con-Tact paper over the letters. Turn the sheet over and place another sheet of Con-Tact paper on the back to make the arrangement permanent. When you remove the display, clip the sheet of letters to the other bulletin board pieces. Letters won't get lost, and everything is ready to put up next year!

Rebecca Gibson Calton
Auburn, AL

More Bulletin Board Letters

What do you do with your bulletin board letters once the display has come down? Laminate the letters and place them in a box. On a rainy day, let students play Scrabble or other word games with the letters. Use the cutouts with younger students to practice letter recognition.

Rebecca Gibson Calton

Using Oil Pastels

Coloring in skillboards or large display characters can be a problem when using crayons, which run during heat lamination. Markers are time-consuming and leave "stripes" on large areas. Oil pastels are an exciting alternative. The colors can be smudged or blended to cover a large area quickly and can give a variety of textured looks. The basic technique is simple: outline the area to be colored using the oil pastel and smudge it into the desired area. Use your finger to smudge for a feathered look or a cotton ball for more even coverage. Apply additional colors for contouring or creating new colors. Mistakes or smudges outside the desired area can be erased, and oil pastels will not run in a heat laminator. For best results, use the dull side of the poster board.

Wendy Sondov
St. Louis, MO

Laminating Cutouts

Having problems with cut-out pictures not holding up? Laminate them, but leave a wide edge of laminating film around each one when trimming. This makes the edges strong and keeps small pieces from getting torn off or lost.

Rebecca Gibson Calton
Auburn, AL

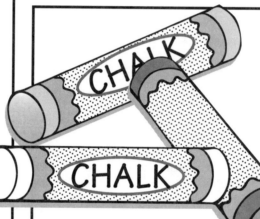

Chalk Characters

Pastel chalk is a wonderful medium to use for bulletin board figures. It spreads easily and gives a soft appearance. To keep the chalk from smearing, use hairspray. It works just like the expensive sprays used for this purpose.

Robert Kinker
Bexley, OH

Wipe Out Ink Smears

I make a lot of posters using white poster board. Many times my hand will accidentally smear the ink from the colored markers. A perfect solution to this problem is a cotton swab dipped in Clorox. I wipe the smear with the swab, and the poster looks as good as new.

Deanna Groke
Misawa Air Base, Japan

Bulletin Board Idea

All thumbs putting up bulletin boards? A wrist pincushion can come in handy when tacking up displays.

Connie Connely
Tulsa, OK

Laminated Scraps

If you are laminating a cut-out shape, mount it on colored construction paper first. After cutting out the shape, save the laminated scraps. These can be used to cut out bulletin board letters that are durable and do not fade as readily.

Suzanne Edmunds
Forest, VA

Air Pockets

How do you get the air pockets out of laminating paper? Just take a pin and punch a hole in the air pocket. The hole is so small it cannot be seen, and your problem is solved!

Rebecca Gibson Calton
Auburn, AL

Tracing Patterns

A technique called the "Bleed Method" is great for tracing patterns for skillboards, colorful cutouts, or large and small bulletin board characters. The time saved is amazing and the results are super.

1. Place tissue paper over the pattern to be copied, and trace with a pencil.
2. Place the tissue paper pattern over poster board to be used for your copy.
3. Using a permanent marker, go over the pencil tracing. The marker will bleed through the tissue paper, transferring the desired pattern to the new poster board.
4. Remove the tissue paper, go over the bleed-through marks with a marker, and color in as desired.

Wendy Sondov
St. Louis, MO

Bulletin Board Under Construction

Sometimes busy teachers are caught with their bulletin boards down by visitors or administrators. Here's a simple solution! Cut a roll of white corrugated paper the length of your bulletin board. Trim the top edge to resemble a picket fence, and decorate as shown. If you are putting up a new board and are unable to finish it, unroll the fence and tack it to the board with a few staples. This not only beats a blank board, but it also creates excitement among your students as they wonder what will go up next. To store, simply roll up the fence and secure with a rubber band.

Jeanne Thomas
Dugspur, VA

3-D Bulletin Boards

Liven up your bulletin boards by displaying three-dimensional artwork. Careful pin placement allows art projects to stand out and look alive. You'll think your birds and butterflies can really fly!

Kathy Mobbs
Farmington Hills, MI

Bulletin Board Technique

Make beautiful bulletin boards with this special technique. Enlarge a picture with an opaque projector, outlining it on cream-colored tagboard with a permanent marker. After coloring the picture with crayons, take a tissue and rub over the crayon to give the picture a smooth effect. These pictures can then be laminated to use from year to year.

Regina Atwood
Pampa, TX

3-D Bubbles

To give bulletin board items a three-dimensional effect, use sheets of packing bubbles and cut-out shapes of graduated sizes. Glue the bubbles between each item's layers with rubber cement, being careful not to puncture the bubbles. This works especially well with clouds, smoke, leaves, waves, and letter shapes. If the finished product will be large, economize by gluing sets of two to three bubbles in small areas around the edges.

Betty Kobes
Kanawha, IA

Long Bulletin Boards

Some rooms have huge bulletin boards that are difficult to decorate and manage. I use commercial bulletin board borders back-to-back to break them into two or three manageable displays. Use the same border throughout for the best effect.

Carole Pippert
Laurel, MD

Fabric Cutouts

Check your fabric store for colorful cutouts, such as Snoopy and Mickey Mouse, to use as bulletin board figures. Trim around the fabric cutout, leaving the seam allowance. Spray the wrong side of the fabric cutout with a spray adhesive, and attach to a piece of tagboard that has also been sprayed with adhesive. Cut away the seam allowance, and your bulletin board figure is ready. Most cutouts have front and back pieces that may be mounted on tagboard and glued together to use as a hanging display. When fabric cutouts become dusty, simply vacuum the dust away!

Vicki L. Dirks
Sutton, NE

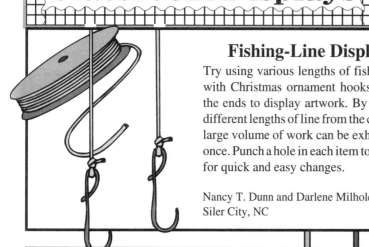

Classroom Displays

Fishing-Line Display

Try using various lengths of fishing line with Christmas ornament hooks tied on the ends to display artwork. By hanging different lengths of line from the ceiling, a large volume of work can be exhibited at once. Punch a hole in each item to be hung for quick and easy changes.

Nancy T. Dunn and Darlene Milholen
Siler City, NC

Wanted: More Room

Here's how I increased the display space in my classroom. I cut several lengths of fishing line; then I tied a paper clip to one end of each length. I tied the other ends to the ceiling lights. Now there's plenty of room to display my students' artwork and papers. Changing displayed papers is also quick and easy!

Regina Atwood
Pampa, TX

Cup Hooks

Here's a fun way to display children's work in your classroom or at home. Attach two cup hooks to the wall about six feet apart. Tie a length of string between the hooks and hang small clothespins on the line to clip completed work. Completed work clipped on the line by students can be easily removed and checked if necessary.

Debbie Giamber
Annandale, VA

Hangin' Around With Good Work

Decorate your room by displaying your students' best work. Hang different colored ribbons of various lengths from your classroom ceiling and staple good work to the ends. Children love to see their work "hanging around."

Kym Smith
Mt. Pleasant, SC

Display Board

Sewing boards purchased from fabric or sewing shops make great display boards. Cover the board with Con-Tact paper or colorful gift wrap; then use it for displaying student papers, classroom projects, or learning centers. The board also makes an attractive backdrop for any work area.

Margaret Paris
Belcher, LA

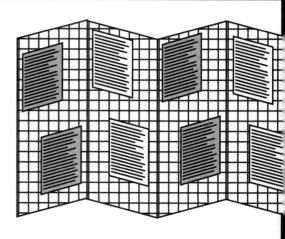

Bulletin Boards To Go

Running out of bulletin board space? Acoustical ceiling tiles convert quickly and easily to small bulletin boards or flannelboards. Cover a tile with fabric, bulletin board paper, or felt. Add a border if desired.

Sarah Joyce
Chicago, IL

Clip Clothespins

Glue magnets or pieces of magnetic strips to colored plastic clothespins. Place these on a metal cabinet for an easy way to display students' work.

Cathy Craze
Summersville, WV

magnet

Laminate The Wall

Do you have a wall area on which nothing will adhere? Cover a small area of the wall with laminating film. Scotch tape or masking tape will then stick to the laminated area, and you will have solved that problem once and for all.

Rebecca Gibson Calton
Auburn, AL

Tack-a-Note Adhesive Stick™

Use the Tack-a-Note Adhesive Stick™ to hang letters or lightweight charts on windows or other smooth surfaces. This product keeps things neat, unlike clear tape, and is available where you buy sticky notepads.

Nancy Phillips
Southern Pines, NC

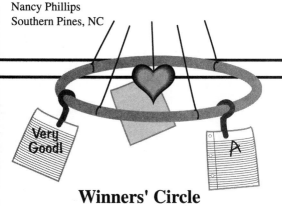

Winners' Circle

Are you looking for a new alternative to a good-work bulletin board? Try this display, which requires a Hula-Hoop; plastic lingerie clothespins with hooks on the ends; yarn; and a seasonal decoration. Use yarn to suspend the Hula-Hoop horizontally from the ceiling. Hang a seasonal decoration in the center. Hook a clothespin on the Hula-Hoop for each student, and clip on good papers. Changing the seasonal decoration will create a new look.

Ruth Thomann
Nobel, IL

Laminated Frames

To keep papers that are displayed in the hall from getting dirty or marked on, I devised an easy, construction-paper frame. Fold one sheet of construction paper in half and cut out the middle. Decorate the frame with stickers and laminate. Don't cut out the lamination in the middle of the frame. Place the frame on top of the paper to be displayed so that the laminated middle protects it. Several students have made their own frames, and other teachers in my school have found the idea quite useful.

Nancy J. Hull
Caldwell, KS

Window Bulletin Boards

Use classroom windows to display art projects. Place two art projects of the same size back-to-back, and tape to the window. The projects may be seen from inside and outside the window.

Mary Dinneen
Bristol, CT

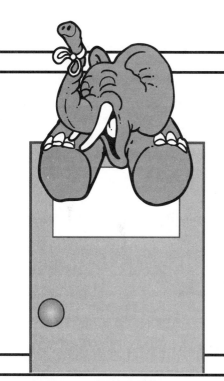

Peek-Overs

The bulletin board Peek-Overs by Creative Teaching Press (sold by The Education Center) look great on a classroom door. My children were so excited when they saw the elephant cutout peeking over our door. I used the Peek-Over as a management device by telling the children that the elephant was looking for quiet workers.

Sr. Margaret Ann Wooden
Martinsburg, WV

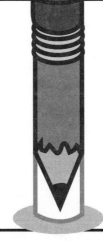

Concrete Poles

Many schools built with open areas have unattractive concrete poles strategically placed in inconvenient areas around the room. To disguise these eyesores, we wrap each pole tightly with paper and use double-sided tape or spray adhesive to put up artwork. These also make great totem poles during Native American studies. You can even decorate the poles to look like giant crayons, paintbrushes, and pencils!

Brenda H. McGee
Plano, TX

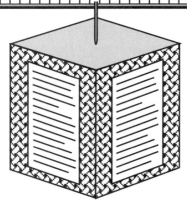

Good Work Display

Think you've used all the available display space in your classroom? Use the ceiling! Decorate several small square boxes with Con-Tact covering. Suspend the boxes from the ceiling using string. Display students' work by thumbtacking it to the sides of the boxes.

Margaret Paris
Belcher, LA

Pocket Charts

Create your own inexpensive pocket charts with this easy technique. Cut a shower curtain liner to the desired size. Then cut several 2 1/2" strips of laminating film the width of the liner. Place the strips atop the liner, leaving 3" to 3 1/2" between them. Use clear tape to tape the bottom of each strip to the liner. Complete the chart by taping all four sides with wide vinyl or duct tape. The durable pockets conveniently hold sentence strips or word cards.

Elke Du Pree
Marietta, GA

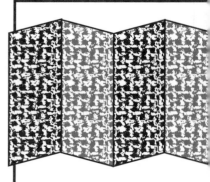

Room Dividers

Fabric cutting boards make durable room dividers. Cover a cutting board with bulletin board paper or burlap. The boards may be decorated if desired and used to create centers or individual study areas.

Nancy Dunaway
Forrest City, AR

Hang It Up!

To make space for mobiles and other hanging projects, install a movable "Mobile Rack." Screw two eye screws into an old broom handle. Add two corresponding eye screws to a wooden beam on the ceiling. Thread heavy-duty fishing line through the screws in the handle and beam. Pull the fishing line down the side of the wall and loop around two additional eye screws attached to the wooden side of the chalkboard. The contraption is then very simple to raise and lower when you need the space.

Sr. Madeleine Gregg
Portsmouth, RI

ceiling beam

broom handle

Pride Line

To display students' good work, stretch fishing line under the chalkboard. Run the line through the center springs of short, colored clothespins to have a handy way to hold up work.

Dorothy Simmons
Memphis, TN

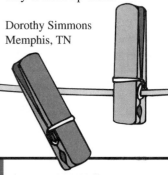

Individual Hanging Displays

Display students' work quickly with these individual hanging displays. Take a picture of each child; then cut it into a three-inch circle. Cut out the center of a small paper plate and mount the picture atop the cutout. Punch a hole near the top of the plate. Cut a 52-inch length of yarn or ribbon, loop it through the hole, and tie the ends together. Slip a paper clip through the knot and attach it to the ceiling. Students' art projects can be attached to the bottom of the hanging cutouts for a personalized display.

Sally Griffin
Ionia, MI

Gooey Charts

When you use masking tape or anything sticky to tack up a chart on the wall, taking it down for storage and reuse can cause a problem. When you remove the tape, the stickiness remains. Use cellophane tape to cover the sticky places on the chart.

Mary Dinneen
Bristol, CT

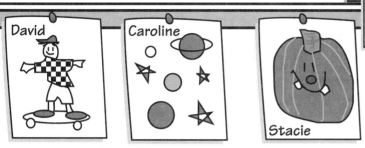

Classroom Displays

Stuffed Bulletin Boards

Create a bulletin board that other teachers will talk about! Cut out a large paper figure such as an Easter bunny or egg, and stuff tissue paper behind it to make it stand out. Staple around the edge as you stuff. The kids will love your giant, 3-D characters.

Rebecca Gibson Calton
Auburn, AL

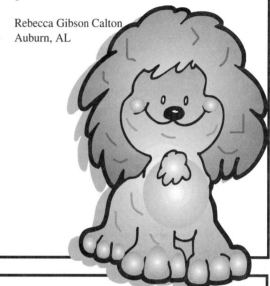

Cinder-Block Wall Display

A few brads and a roll of tape work like magic for displaying children's work on cinder-block walls. Bend one prong of each brad upward to form a hook. Tape the "hooks" on the wall, punch holes in the children's work, and hang!

Peggy C. Vice
New Iberia, LA

Felt Bulletin Boards

Felt and bits of leftover material make great bulletin board decorations. Enlarge a pattern or design, and trace it onto the material instead of paper. Cut out the design, and put it up. There's no coloring or laminating to do. The pieces are easy to store, too. Just fold them up, and put them away!

Rebecca Gibson Calton

Laminated Frames

To display student artwork all year long, make a laminated frame for each child. Cut a one-inch frame from construction paper. Use press-on letters to center the child's name at the bottom, and laminate both sides. If the film is clear, you need not cut out the center.

Melissa Matusevich
Blacksburg, VA

Flowery Bulletin Boards

Make flowers for your bulletin board from coffee filters. Children use crayons or markers to color coffee filters, adding leaves and stems made from construction paper.

Isobel Livingstone
Rahway, NJ

Poster Saver

To protect posters from tearing when you take them down from the wall, cut three-inch strips of masking tape, and tape them flat on the back corners of the posters. Rolled pieces of masking tape can then be put on the flat tape instead of the poster itself.

Sandra Steen
Corinth, MS

Wood Strip Display

A small wood strip nailed across a classroom wall makes displaying classwork a breeze! No more cutting and rolling costly tape that falls off the wall—only thumbtacks are needed. It's easy for students to use, too!

Debbie Wiggins
Myrtle Beach, SC

Classroom Displays

Incentive Bulletin Boards

This activity helps my students stay on task and gives our room an easily decorated bulletin board. Each month I designate one bulletin board that is to be decorated by students who have completed independent reading work. I choose a holiday theme to which students contribute art. Students may only add one art piece at a time, and all of their work must be finished first.

Deborah Fay
Gaithersburg, MD

Waxed-Paper Transparencies

When you don't have a transparency to use, try this! Trace the desired picture onto a piece of waxed paper with a pencil. When you place the paper on the overhead projector, the projected image will show the outline of your picture.

Margaret Paris
Belcher, LA

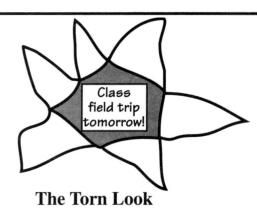

Class field trip tomorrow!

The Torn Look

Try this eye-catching idea to display a special announcement on your bulletin board. Choose and mark your display spot. Tear your background paper away from that point, leaving all the paper attached. Next, staple your announcement inside the torn area. Last, staple back the loose edges of background paper so your announcement is visible. It will not go unnoticed!

Robert Kinker
Bexley, OH

Overhead Lifesavers

Turn penmanship paper, a sheet of clocks without hands, and math drill sheets into transparencies for the overhead projector. The transparencies can be used for class lessons, games, or speed drills. Project the transparencies directly onto the chalkboard for a change of pace. Students can trace letters, mark spots on a map, or race to complete columns of math problems on the board.

Cindy Newell
Durant, OK

Paper Towel Tree

People will do double takes when you display a paper-towel tree. Cut a tree shape from bulletin board paper. Have students glue wadded paper towels to the tree cutout. Allow to dry. Spray-paint the entire tree green. This type of tree looks like the real thing from a distance.

Rebecca Gibson Calton
Auburn, AL

Bulletin Board Idea

Reserve one of the bulletin boards in your classroom for the students to complete. Cover a bulletin board with white paper. Enlarge a picture (large enough to cover the entire bulletin board) on the opaque projector. Have each child color an area of the board. Students will take a great deal of pride in this bulletin board.

Barbara H. Brown
Waverly, VA

3-D Window Displays

Tall classroom windows can sometimes look rather bare, but these 3-D window displays will perk up your classroom from the outside as well as from the inside. Cut two symmetrical seasonal shapes for each child from bulletin board paper. Have each child paint his cutouts. After the cutouts have dried, staple them together, stuffing them with newspaper to create a three-dimensional effect. Suspend the stuffed cutouts from the tops of the windows using yarn or monofilament line. Your display can now be enjoyed by students and passersby.

Pat Allegrucci
Avon Lake, OH

(diagram showing a grid with measurements: 9", 12", 33", 48")

Erasable Chalkboards

The new "dry erasable" white chalkboards are expensive to buy, but you can make a classroom full of them for under $12.00. Buy a 4' x 8' piece of Masonite paneling called Arctic White Royal Tile from your local lumber dealer. (It's used inside shower stalls.) Cut it into 40 (9" x 12") lap boards, or 28 lap boards and a 33" x 48" erasable message center. Be sure to use the "dry erase" markers on your new white boards. No more chalk dust!

Marianne Armstrong
Urbana, IL

Chalkboard Tips

Cover an old or faded chalkboard with white Con-Tact paper. In addition to a neater appearance:
— You'll now have a screen to use with your film or overhead projector.
— Marks from overhead projector pens will wipe off the board easily.
— Charts can be taped to the board without damaging it.
— You can create graphs using colored pens, providing greater contrast and clarity.
— You'll eliminate chalk dust, a problem for computers and allergy sufferers.

Marge Maginnis
Lakeland, FL

Permanent Chalk

Put a cup of water and two tablespoons of sugar in a small jar. Soak one to two sticks of colored chalk overnight. Drain the water off, and keep the chalk in the jar. When you write on the board with this chalk, it won't erase, but it will come off with a wet sponge.

Carole Pippert
Laurel, MD

Fusing Flannel

An inexpensive method for applying flannel to pictures is to use plastic from a dry-cleaning bag. Place a piece of plastic between the flannel and figures. Using a protective covering between the iron and the figure, seal with an iron. The heated plastic fuses the flannel to the picture and eliminates wrinkles and bubbles often caused by glue.

Deanna Groke
Misawa Air Base, Japan

Flannelgraphs

Add to your collection of flannelboard visuals with flocked wallpaper samples available from interior decorating stores. Flocked wallpaper is a durable and inexpensive backing for flannelboard pieces.

Gail Felker

Flannelboard Aids

I've discovered that pink foam fabric softener sheets make great backing for my flannelboard aids. I cut small pieces of the sheets and glue them to the backs of my aids. The sheets help the aids adhere to the flannelboard without slipping.

Pat Bollinger
Leopold, MO

Magnetic Strips For Chalkboards

If you wish you had a magnetic chalkboard, keep reading! Place a magnetic strip along the top of your chalkboard, and purchase a few strong magnets to hold up teaching aids, chart tablets, and more!

June Brantley
Robins Air Force Base, GA

95

Classroom Displays

White Marlite

Try my idea for transportable posters: Buy a sheet of white Marlite (kitchen/bathroom wall covering) and have it cut into eight 2' x 2' squares. Using Dry Erase markers, make temporary posters on these to sit in the chalk tray. These work great for homework assignments, announcements, make-up work, or independent activities. If you need the board space, simply place the posters on the floor below the chalk tray. Posters can be changed by erasing with a dry cloth.

Donna Linkous
War, WV

> Read
> pages
> 57-65.

> Don't forget!
> Test tomorrow
> Bring seeds.

> Today is
> Sophie's
> birthday!

Chalk Talk

Wrap chalk pieces with masking tape to avoid dry fingertips. As your chalk wears down, peel back the tape. This process will also help prevent dropped chalk from breaking.

Ann Sargent
Champaign, IL

Overhead Screen

A sheet of white bulletin board paper makes a good temporary screen for an overhead or filmstrip projector. It works great for small groups or at a center.

J.K. Jacob
Baton Rouge, LA

> Spelling Words
> airplane
> elevator

Using An Overhead

This activity will brighten a rainy day! Select worksheet pages from either *The Mailbox* or *Worksheet Magazine* to use for making overhead transparencies. Project a transparency onto the blackboard and let students take turns working the lesson on the board. My students especially enjoy pages that must be completed with colored chalk. They can't wait until the lights are turned on to see the completed picture!

Karen Wigger
Maysville, MO

Overhead Projector

The bright light from the overhead projector frequently caused me to have headaches. Children found this equipment difficult to write on for the same reason. My solution was to tape a piece of colored transparent paper over the glass to cut down on the light. This worked well, and the colors of transparent paper can be changed for variety.

Sr. Mary Catherine Warehime
Lynchburg, VA

Portable Chalkboard

Do you often find that there's no chalkboard where you need one? Laminate a large piece of oaktag and use wipe-off pens for "chalk." You can then have an instant chalkboard wherever one is needed!

Mary Dinneen
Bristol, CT

Cleaning Laminated Surfaces

I often place grease pencils at laminated centers so that my students can write answers directly on the lamination. But cleaning the marks off is sometimes difficult. I've found that rubbing a regular chalkboard eraser over the marks cleans the surfaces completely, leaving them ready for the next person to use.

Janet Cunningham
Mannington, WV

Reusing and Recycling

Plastic Lids

Plastic lids from bottled water, milk, and juice have many classroom uses. These colorful lids can be used as bingo or game markers or for sorting and patterning practice. To create a matching game, use a permanent marker to program the insides of matching lid pairs with upper- and lowercase letters or numbers and number words. These durable manipulatives are easy to replace if they're lost, and they cost nothing.

Peggy Marcel
Houma, LA

Recycling Tree

This totally recyclable "tree" is a great way to introduce your students to recycling. To create a recycling tree, cut a tree trunk from brown paper grocery sacks. Staple the trunk to a bulletin board. Have students cut or tear leaves from newspaper and attach them to the trunk. For blossoms, have students attach aluminum pop tops, Styrofoam packing peanuts, or small pieces of aluminum foil. This display reminds students of the different types of materials that can be recycled.

Barbara Boldt
Ft. Worth, TX

Basket Bonus

I use round, plastic clothes baskets to store my P.E. equipment. When the baskets can no longer be used for storage, I cut off the tops and use the circular bottoms as giant Frisbees. The children love them!

Elaine Gunterman
New Albany, IN

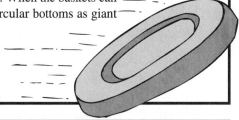

Money Holders

Use 35mm film containers for money holders. They are available from film-processing stores. Label each container with a child's name and teacher's name for easy return if misplaced. Students carry money to and from school in these.

Retha Mancil
Ozark, AL

Durable Book Covers

Add durability to your classroom publications with these clever covers. Cover a matching set of large, plastic margarine or coffee lids with Con-Tact paper and decorate if desired. Mount students' stories on identical construction-paper circles. Tuck the mounted stories between the plastic covers. Punch holes in the tops of the covers and pages; then insert a metal ring through the holes. Stories are protected by these durable covers and can be changed quickly and easily.

Kathleen Smith
Waco, TX

Paint Containers

Plastic 35mm film canisters make terrific individual paint containers. The lids snap on tight to keep the paint from drying out, and they're just the right size for individual student painting projects. The canisters are also durable and can be washed out and used again and again.

Mary Dinneen
Bristol, CT

Game Pieces

The colorful plastic pieces in Flintstones Push-ups make wonderful game pieces. Insert the brightly colored handles into the circular bases to create game markers. Since the flat base won't roll off the gameboard, these markers are easy for even little hands to use.

Susan Keil
Thompson, IA

Reusing and Recycling

Bug House

A gallon milk jug is the perfect home for the bug and butterfly collections of your students. Cut a section out of the side of the jug to make a window. Place colored netting (found in any fabric store) over the window and seal it with masking tape. Add stickers and ribbon to the tape for decoration. Your bug house is now ready for guests and curious bug watchers.

Sr. Ann Claire Rhoads
Greensboro, NC

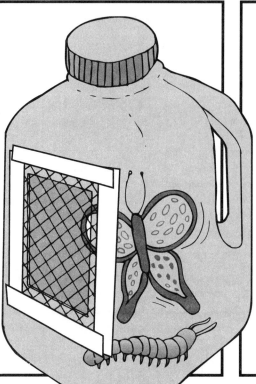

Classroom Ties

Collect wire ties used on garbage and bread bags for lots of classroom uses:

- Attach ties with tape to the back of artwork for hanging.
- Tie extension cords together when not in use.
- Punch holes on the edge of index cards or student booklets, and tie them together.
- Tie tissue-paper flowers together for a class art activity.
- Make a class bread-tie sculpture!

Sr. Ann Claire Rhoads

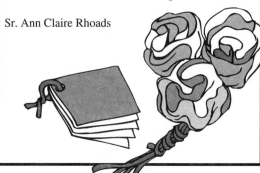

Book Raincoats

If your grocery store has switched to plastic grocery bags, you know how quickly they pile up! Our librarian teaches children that the bags are "book raincoats." Teachers keep them in each classroom, and children are encouraged to use them on rainy and snowy days.

Jane Cuba
Redford, MI

Counter Collection

Start a collection of small, plastic tops from juice and milk jugs. Make them clean and odorless by placing them in a lingerie or stocking bag and washing them in a washing machine. Sort by color into color-coded coffee cans. Students may use them as counters.

Prudence Spaulding
Great Barrington, MA

Reading Bins

To make a reading nook for students, collect the plastic rings from drink cans. Tie them together to make a curtain that hangs from the ceiling. The holes allow light to come through while creating an inviting, private spot.

Rebecca Gibson Calton
Auburn, AL

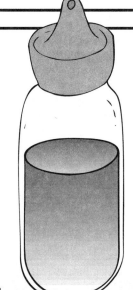

Recycled Perm Bottles

Buying bottles of glue for the classroom can be expensive. Students often ruin the tips by trying to get them unclogged or by pulling the tips off when the glue gets thick. To remedy this problem, I ask the local beauty salons to save their used perm bottles for me. I wash them out and then cut the tip off a little more to allow a fine line of glue to come out. I fill these bottles with glue from one-gallon containers, which are less expensive to buy.

Carolyn Hart
Culloden, WV

Fisher-Price Bottles

Fisher-Price bath products' bottles can be reused in your classroom. For a fun weather-related activity, cut seasonal clothes from cloth or construction paper. Attach a piece of Velcro to the back of each cutout; then attach matching Velcro pieces to the bottle. Youngsters can "dress" the bottles in seasonal attire. Since the bottles come in different sizes with different facial features, they can also be used for sorting or classification activities. The bottles also make great "people" for your block center.

Jennifer Strathdee
Solvay, NY

Reusing and Recycling

Directionality

Children can easily discriminate between their left and right hand with a simple reminder. Make each child his own set of "directional bracelets." When cut apart, the plastic holders on a six-pack of cans make perfect "bracelets" for the children. I mark them with the words "left" and "right" using a permanent marker, and the students wear them during class. When the bracelets are no longer needed, they can be saved for next year's class. If they are discarded, make sure this is done properly, as these rings are dangerous to wildlife.

Vita Campanella-Feldstein
Brooklyn, NY

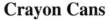

Crayon Cans

We found a good alternative for storing crayons, since crayon boxes tear apart easily. I asked parents to save ready-to-spread icing cans and send them in all year. (This way we have a large enough supply for next year's class, too.) We cover the cans with Con-Tact paper in two colors for morning and afternoon sessions. The children easily manipulate the plastic lids and recognize their names from the labels on their cans.

Judy Wolfe
Tornado, WV

TV-Dinner Trays

TV-dinner trays make great dinner plates at a kindergarten housekeeping center and are easy to stack. Use them to make sorting and classifying activities, too. Place a laminated number in each section of a tray and have the student count the correct number of beans into the sections. Children can also line up trays for sequencing practice.

Sarah Simpson
Orlando, FL

Whoooooo Goes There?

Be wise—improvise. No expensive supplies are needed for these owls—just bottle caps, plastic taken from beverage six-packs, craft glue, and construction paper. Supply scissors and a 6" x 9" piece of construction paper for each student. Demonstrate how to trim off the bottom corners and glue them on the bottom for feet. Have students glue plastic pieces as shown and add bottle-cap eyes. Students may add feather features using black crayon.

Ruth Heinrichs
Larned, KS

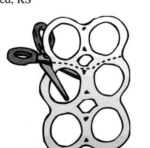

Game Markers

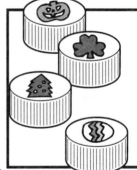

Start a collection of seasonal game markers by saving bottle caps. Just place the appropriate seasonal stickers on top of your bottle caps, and you're ready for the year!

Sr. Ann Claire Rhoads
Greensboro, NC

Pleasing Paint Cups

Empty yogurt cups have many uses in our classroom. They are the perfect size for the paint easel. Cutting a hole in the lid helps with the "drip" problem. These cups are cheap, recyclable, and a terrific time-saver for me. In addition, the children love to contribute these containers to the class.

Karen Botti
West Carrollton, OH

Paint Containers

Start a collection of microwave dishes from frozen dinners. They make great containers to mix paints in, and they are easy to store.

Terri Musser
Lynchburg, VA

Reusing and Recycling

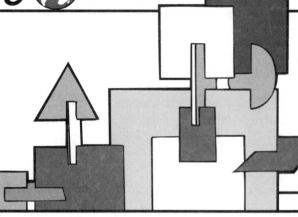

Meat Tray Sculpture

Meat trays are easy for intermediate students to cut. Have students collect trays and cut out shapes. Add a slit in each shape extending from center to the outer edge. (See diagram.) Pieces slide together, forming unique sculptures. Paint with liquid tempera to create interesting effects.

Sr. Ann Claire Rhoads
Greensboro, NC

--- ← **slit**

Styrofoam Printing

Here is an activity to introduce students to the art of printing. Give each student a Styrofoam meat tray on which to draw a picture with a dull pencil. Pour a little tempera paint into an aluminum pan. With a brush or roller, each student covers his picture with paint. Take a piece of construction paper, folded in half, and press it against the painted meat tray. Turn it over for a few seconds. Flip the tray back over and carefully remove the paper. The picture will be printed on it. Repeat the above process to make as many prints as desired. This makes wonderful stationery and invitations.

Laurie Vent
Upper Sandusky, OH

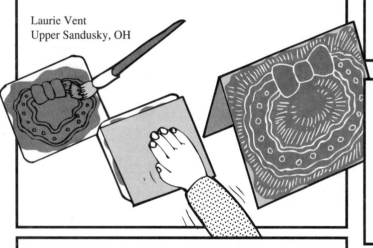

Herbie The Robot

Put your junk to work! Assemble a classroom robot with cardboard boxes, old fuses, plastic lids, colored tape, coiled wire, and anything else you have handy. Bolt the boxes together and spray paint them silver. Attach wire coils to the sides for arms. Add odds and ends for decoration. Rename your six-foot friend every year as a first-day-of-school activity. Program cassette tapes so "Herbie" can give students weekly spelling tests and drill them on basic math facts. Herbie makes learning fun and gives you a break, too!

John T. Finch
Alexandria, KY

Building Blocks

Here's a simple way to make sturdy blocks. Cut the tops off of two half-gallon milk cartons and push one inside the other (bottom side out). Cover with wood-grain or brick Con-Tact paper. For smaller blocks, use pint-size cartons.

Annette Mathias
Partridge, KS

Wallpaper Envelopes

Wallpaper samples make colorful, durable, and free substitutes for manila envelopes. Make a pattern as shown. Trace the pattern on wallpaper and cut out. Glue as indicated. Now you can have a multitude of free storage envelopes in which to store games.

Anne Stickney
Northport, AL

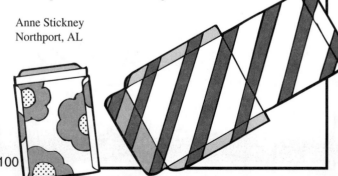

Gameboard Pawns

Remove the plastic squirt tops from empty bottles of dishwashing liquid and reuse them as pawns for your classroom games. The tops are durable and come in a wide variety of colors.

Marge Westrich
Colby, WI

Free Paper

Free paper scraps can be yours for the asking. Sources to check are publishers, printers, and paper companies. These scraps are perfect for art projects, notes, or quizzes.

Reusing and Recycling

Bookstore Boxes

Check your local bookstore for paperback display boxes that are being thrown away. They are great for organizing glue bottles, scissors, paste, and more!

Debbie McDougal
Greensboro, NC

No-dry Dough

Use the new cardboard baby food containers with plastic lids to store small amounts of moist dough.

Joanne Davis
Orlando, FL

Supermarket Posters

Visit your local food store, and ask the manager for any display posters—especially the oversized ones—that are not being used. These are perfect for learning vocabulary, spelling, math, health and nutrition, abbreviations, etc.

Patricia Totaro
Hoboken, NJ

Laundry Soap Boxes

Get organized with soap boxes! Trim large laundry soap boxes to a height of eight inches. Use colorful Con-Tact covering to decorate, and label each box according to skill or subject. Store file folder activities, games, and more in these neat, easy-to-use boxes.

Anne Runyon
Littleton, CO

Desktop Flannelboard Boxes

Make individual flannelboards for desktop skill practice. Cover or decorate a cigar box. Glue a solid piece of felt or flannel to the inside of the lid. Store flannelboard pieces (shapes, numbers, figures, letters) inside each box. These desktop flannelboards are easy to store, and children love using them.

Cindy Newell
Durant, OK

Put A Lid On It

Collect clear, plastic lids as game pieces for your learning centers. Lids work well in centers that require students to give a one-letter, -number, or -word answer. Write the letter, number, or word on each lid with a permanent marker. Rather than writing the answer, the student places the correct lid on each problem. He can view the problem through the lid to check his work. Store lids in a Ziploc bag attached to the center.

Barbara Boldt
Fort Worth, TX

Recycled Covers

Use covers from any children's magazines, especially *The Mailbox* and *Teacher's Helper* (formerly *Worksheet Magazine*), when putting together units. The covers make great gameboards. With help from your students, paste each cover on a manila envelope or folder and use press-on dots for the game trail.

Mary Anne T. Haffner
Waynesboro, PA

Reusing and Recycling

Recycle Your Calendars

Instead of throwing old calendars away, put them to good use by having older students practice Roman numerals in the corresponding spaces. Younger students can simply use the spaces for practicing number writing. The calendars can also be used for multiplication tables. Instruct the students to multiply each calendar number on a page by a certain number and place the answers in the corresponding blocks.

Trudy Naddy
Lake Oswego, OR

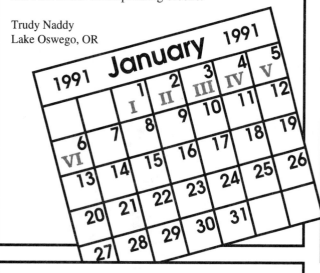

Perfect Paper Towels

Cut a roll of paper towels vertically in half. These two mini-rolls are easy for small hands to handle and can still be put in a dispenser. Students take a towel from left or right.

Debbie Giamber
Falls Church, VA

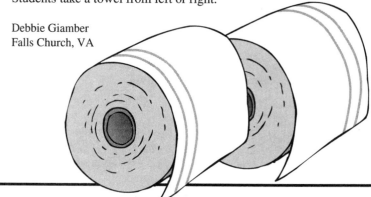

Chalkboard Recycling

Save old chalkboards and recycle them for your classroom. They can be used at a center or as puzzle boards that can be tucked away and brought out at a later time.

Sandra Edgington
Dayton, OH

Paper-Saving Tip

When writing on pads with permanent markers, the ink often runs through to the next sheet, ruining it. To avoid this, tear off the top sheet, turn the pad over, and use the cardboard backing as a pad.

Mary Dinneen
Bristol, CT

Using Old Readers

Put those discarded textbooks to good use. Instead of a paper-and-pencil language assignment, let your students practice important skills by writing in old textbooks. (Explain to students that they should not write in new textbooks.) Write directions on the chalkboard such as "Circle all the nouns in red," or "Put two lines under each verb." Children will enjoy the practice in the textbooks and the colorful pages that will result.

Connie Connely
Tulsa, OK

Wipe-Off Skill Sheets

Invest in a heavy-duty plastic sleeve for each student to reinforce skills and save paper. Insert sheets for math, handwriting, language, or other basic skill practice. Provide wipe-off markers or crayons. When a student has mastered a skill, remove the sheet and insert a new one.

Kathy Beard
Melrose, FL

Wiping Cloths

Don't throw away those old nylons! Save and cut them into pieces for wiping cloths. They are great for cleaning crayon off laminated materials.

Ann Ostrowski
Jefferson, SD

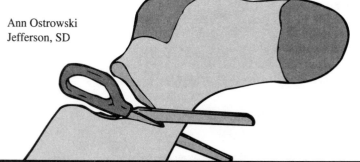

Reusing and Recycling

Popcorn Coffee Filters

I use disposable coffee filters as dishes to hold popcorn for my students. They are less expensive and hold more popcorn than paper cups.

Nancy Lach
Mandan, ND

Old Masters

Don't throw out those old, faded duplicating masters or spend your time copying them. Masters that were originally printed with carbon can be copied using a Thermofax machine. To recycle an old master, white-out any answers on the page, and run it through a Thermofax copier inside a Thermofax master.

Faith R. Ginn
Wardensville, WV

Teacher Trade Day

When it's end-of-the-year cleanup time, designate a place for you and fellow teachers to put any materials to be thrown away. Then all teachers will have a chance to recycle materials by "trading trash."

Rebecca Gibson Calton
Auburn, AL

Freebies For Everyone!

To get rid of items I no longer use in my classroom without throwing them away, I recycle them. Once a year, I let my homeroom students go by rows to choose one item each off my back table. We repeat this until all the items (free samples, outdated workbooks, old books, notebooks, posters, etc.) have been removed. The students are excited by these freebies, and I'm thrilled to get rid of the clutter.

Kathy Peterson
Alpha, IL

Recycled Bookmarks

Make attractive bookmarks from cereal boxes. Clip an illustration or a portion of the text from a cereal or any other similar type box. Punch a hole in the cutout and loop a length of yarn or ribbon through the hole. These colorful bookmarks are a real hit with students.

Eldonna Ashley
Richwood, OH

Playing School

Set aside those extra worksheets, copies of *Weekly Readers,* book club order sheets, and charts and posters from advertising mailers. Put them into packets and distribute to students who want to play school during the summer.

Carole Pippert
Laurel, MD

Lotto Grids

I discovered a way to use the grids that are found around most stickers. After using all of the stickers on a sheet, I peel off the grid and mount it on white construction paper or cardboard. The grids can be programmed with any number of skills such as upper- and lowercase letters, numbers and number words, or math facts. Students can then match corresponding cards to the programmed grids.

Lisa K. Yespen
Geneva, OH

ARTS AND CRAFTS FOR ANYTIME

Soap Flakes Fingerpaint

Out of fingerpaint? Try this recipe for a homemade variety.

- 1 1/2 cups dry laundry starch
- 1 1/2 cups soap flakes
- food coloring or tempera paint
- water
- 1 quart boiling water

Mix starch with enough cold water to make a paste. Add boiling water and stir until clear. Cool and add soap flakes and coloring. Store in a tightly sealed container.

No-cook Modeling Dough

No pots and pans are required for this concoction.

- 2 cups flour
- food coloring or tempera paint
- 1 cup salt
- water
- 2 tablespoons vegetable oil (optional)

Mix the ingredients. Add oil unless you want the dough artwork to harden.

Corn Syrup Paint

Add food coloring to light corn syrup for a beautiful paint with an interesting texture. Mix up a cup of blue, yellow, and red, and put a spoonful of each on a paper plate for each student. Students paint their plates with the colors. Allow five days' drying time. Have each student trace a design onto the bottom of his plate and cut out the design.

Judy Peterson
Delta, UT

Dazzling Tempera Paints

If you want brighter colors, paint that doesn't run when used at the easel, and easy cleanup, use the following recipe:

- 2 cups dry tempera paint
- 1 cup liquid starch
- 1 cup liquid soap (clear or white works best)

Mix the paint and soap; then add starch, and stir. If the mixture becomes too thick, add more liquid soap. Don't add water. Store the paint mixture in one-pound coffee cans with plastic lids.

Delores Camilotto
Fond du Lac, WI

Baking Dough

Your students will enjoy creating dough designs for jewelry, refrigerator magnets, or other decorations. They'll also love the fact that they can measure and mix the dough recipe on their own.

- 4 tablespoons flour
- 1 tablespoon salt
- 2 tablespoons water

Have each student mix and knead the ingredients. Students may create their own dough designs by rolling the dough flat with a rolling pin and using cookie cutters. Bake the dough at 350° for 1 to 1 1/2 hours. Students may then paint and shellac the designs.

Bonnie Pinkerton
Bowling Green, KY

Homemade Play Dough

Homemade play dough works as well as the expensive brand from toy stores.

- 1 cup flour
- 1/2 cup salt
- 2 teaspoons cream of tartar
- 1 cup water
- 1 teaspoon vegetable oil
- food coloring

Mix the dry ingredients. Then add the remaining ingredients, and stir. In a heavy skillet, cook the mixture for two to three minutes, stirring frequently. Knead the dough until it becomes soft and smooth. Stir up several colors and store them in icing tubs.

Nancy Dunaway
Forrest City, AR

Blue
Red
Green

Lacing Cards

Make durable lacing cards from simple coloring-book pictures. Mount the picture on tagboard and laminate. Use a paper drill to outline the picture with holes. For an inexpensive lace, dip the ends of a length of yarn in white glue and let dry.

Delores Pease
Hardin, MT

Color Magic

At the end of a unit on color, bring in a cake with fluffy white frosting. Drop food coloring over the frosting (about five drops of each of the colors—red, blue, and yellow). Swirl through the colors carefully with a small spatula or knife. The colors will mix together to show new colors that are made from the primary colors. Eat and enjoy! (Children may want to try this at home the next time Mom bakes a cake.)

Kathy Thompson
Nevis, MN

Tissue Collage

Here's a new twist to an old favorite. Cut tissue paper into pieces with pinking shears, and lay the pieces on a sheet of white paper. Attach to the paper using liquid floor wax instead of glue. The wax will cause the tissue colors to run, creating a collage with a different look. If desired, draw designs with permanent markers after drying.

Elizabeth Cole
Annapolis, MD

Marble Art

Save this fun project for a wet-weather day. Place a gift box (without the lid), paint, a spoon, and several marbles at an art center. Each student places a piece of art paper (cut to size) in the box. After dropping the marbles in paint, the student spoons them on the paper and tilts the box. The rolling marbles will make a unique and colorful design on the paper. Be sure to provide a bowl of water in which to clean the marbles after each picture. To vary, use golf balls, spools, or acorns.

Rhonda Thurman-Rice
Catoosa, OK

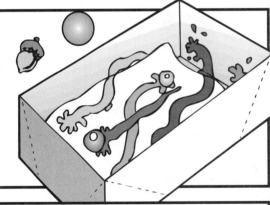

"Scent-sational" Play Dough

Here's a recipe for a brightly colored play dough that smells terrific.

2 packages unsweetened Kool-Aid	1 teaspoon alum
2 1/2 cups flour	3 teaspoons oil
1/2 cup salt	1–2 cups water

Mix the dry ingredients together. Add the oil. Gradually add just enough water to give the dough the desired consistency.

Michelle Sears
Malone, NY

Paper Chains

Here's a way to make paper chains without sticky fingers. Fold three-inch-wide strips of construction paper lengthwise. Make horizontal cuts from the fold to 1/4" from the edge, and from the edge to 1/4" from the fold, alternating the cuts. Unfold, press flat, and gently pull ends apart to create a chain.

Bonnie Pinkerton, Bowling Green, KY

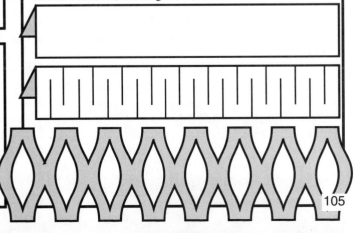

Opaque Projections

The next time your youngsters need to draw a large map or picture, try using the opaque projector to project the picture onto a large piece of bulletin board paper or poster board. Youngsters will be sure to take a little extra time with their drawing when given the opportunity to use this "high-tech" equipment.

Rebecca Gibson Calton
Auburn, AL

ARTS AND CRAFTS FOR ANYTIME

Balloon Creations

You won't blow a minute getting this project prepared! All you need is a variety of colored balloons and various art supplies (colored construction and tissue paper, yarn, glitter, markers, etc.). Students inflate and decorate balloons to resemble animals, using the balloons as the animals' bodies or heads.

Jan Drehmel
Chippewa Falls, WI

Paint On The Windows

For a different and exciting art activity, have your students paint on the windows! Add liquid dish soap to tempera paint and have students paint. I've used this technique for painting Halloween fence posts, Christmas scenes, and Valentine's Day hearts. Just use water for easy cleanup.

Cindy Maxwell
Houston, TX

Paint Extender

Use this mixture rather than water to conserve on powdered tempera paint. Bring two quarts of water to a boil. Mix 1/2 cup cornstarch with 1 cup cold water. Pour cornstarch mixture slowly into boiling water. Cook, stirring constantly, until thickened. Stir in 1/2 cup powdered detergent. Cool and pour into clean jars. When you're ready to paint, add powdered paint to the mixture.

Denise Covert
Long Beach, CA

Box Creatures

This simple art activity using boxes and paint encourages limitless student creativity. Make box creatures in advance by taping together three or four different-sized cardboard boxes for each creature. Divide the class into small groups, giving each group a creature and a variety of colored paints. Then stand back and let smiles and creativity take over. When used as an outdoor activity, cleanup time is minimal.

Judy Bone
Belgrade, MT

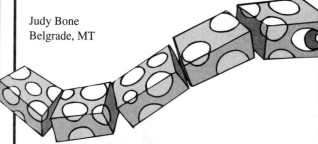

Window Paintings

What do you get when you mix a window painting and sunlight? A spectacular display! Mix 1/2 cup liquid starch into 1 cup brown tempera paint. Paint a large tree trunk and branches on a classroom window. Children create tissue paper leaves and flower buds to complete the spring scene. Make these seasonal changes and keep your window decorated the entire school year: For fall, iron crayon shavings between waxed paper and cut into leaf shapes. For winter, add snowflakes cut from white paper.

Cindy Newell
Durant, OK

Wild And Woolly Worms

Form woolly worms out of ordinary, wrinkled tissue paper. Each student draws and cuts out a worm shape from 8 1/2" x 12" tagboard. Provide students with one-inch squares of different-colored tissue paper. Students wrap one square of tissue on the eraser end of a pencil. A dab of glue is added to the top of the tissue as shown. Holding onto the tissue and pencil, students glue the tissue onto the caterpillar shape. Finally, the children draw, cut out, and glue eyes for the worm. This same technique can be used for other creative art projects for holidays and special events.

Laurie Vent, Upper Sandusky, OH

Fine Designs

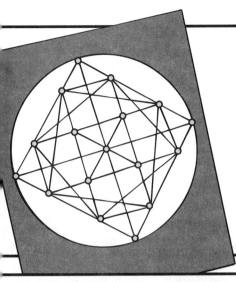

Expect a crowd of admirers when this art project is put on display. Each student needs a dot pattern (as shown), one 9" x 12" piece of colored construction paper, 17 brad fasteners, various colors of thread, scissors, glue, and markers. Cut out the pattern and glue it to the center of the construction paper. Insert a fastener at each dot on the pattern. Beginning at any fastener, wrap a single strand of thread around it; then move to another fastener. Gently pull the thread between the fasteners so it is tight but not stretched. Continue in this manner until the design is complete. To change colors, clip the thread after a wrap. Begin the new thread at any fastener. Add a border to the pattern edge with markers. Students will be thoroughly impressed with the fine designs they've made.

Naomi Reyes
Wilmington, CA

Photo Paintings

Parents will love these photo reproductions. Ask students to bring photographs to school of their homes, bedrooms, family cars, pets, or other familiar objects. Students paint pictures from the photographs and surprise their parents or relatives with their creative interpretations. These are super keepsakes and often end up framed and displayed. Provide photographs of your school or school grounds for those students who are unable to bring in photographs.

Dr. Rebecca Webster Graves
Burlington, NC

Rubber Cement And Watercolors

Have each child make a design by dripping rubber cement on a piece of white typing paper. (Do not use white art paper, as it is too porous.) Let the rubber cement dry. This takes about 15 minutes. Then have children watercolor over the entire paper using several colors in a rainbow effect. The next day, show students how to carefully rub their fingers over the paper to pull off the rubber cement. They'll discover a design of white lines and shapes over their rainbows.

Judy Peterson
Delta, UT

Chalk Shadows

Interesting chalk creations are lurking in the shadows! Cut a simple pattern from tagboard (heart, flower, kite, plane, balloon) and lay it on a 9" x 12" piece of white construction paper. Stroke colored chalk over the pattern while holding it in place. Move the pattern and repeat this process several times. Be sure to overlap the pattern and use an assortment of colored chalks. Spray completed picture with hairspray to prevent smearing. Completed projects create a mystifying display!

Robert Kinker
Bexley, OH

Sand Jewelry

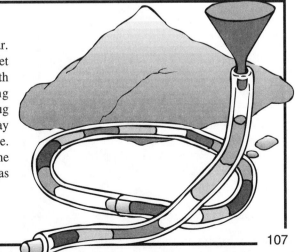

Follow these directions for beautiful sand jewelry. Put some clean sand into a jar. Add several drops of food coloring and shake. Spread the sand on a cookie sheet to dry. Prepare several different colors of sand in this way, or rub sand with colored chalk for varied colors. Cut a length of flexible, clear plastic tubing (1/4" or 5/16" in diameter) to fit around each student's arm or over his head. Plug one end of each plastic tube by pushing a small piece of wooden dowel halfway into the tube. Using a paper funnel, pour the colored sand in layers into the tube. When the tube is nearly full, push the open end onto the dowel plug to join the ends. Your class will have as much fun wearing these necklaces and armbands as they had making them.

Cathie Weaver
Springfield, GA

Sandpaper Printing

Enjoy an easy project that's perfect for fall. Have each student use bright crayons to draw a picture on coarse sandpaper; then place the sandpaper upside down on lightweight paper. Press with an electric iron set on medium until the crayon shows through the back of the paper. Because of the sandpaper's texture, the new picture will look as if it has been painted with hundreds of dots.

Judy Peterson
Delta, UT

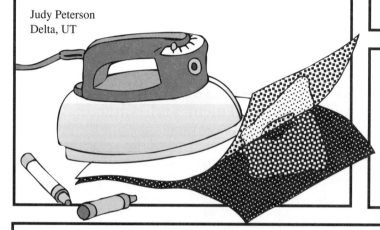

Geometric Art

I have my students cut geometric shapes from different colors of construction paper in their spare time. We save the shapes and use them for various holiday art projects. Students make pictures using the different shapes and glue. They use their crayons only for finishing touches. We save this activity for special holidays, but you can use it any time of year.

Renee Sebestyen
Durango, CO

Graph Paper Art

Graph paper and cross-stitch designs make colorful art projects. Duplicate cross-stitch patterns for students. Give each student a sheet of graph paper and a pattern. The student makes *X*'s in the graph paper squares using the colors indicated. Mount finished work on construction paper for a colorful display.

Esther Thompson
Hendricks, MN

Bits Of Americana

For a fun group art project, create an American flag with bits of red, white, and blue. Tell students to look for blue-jean denim and ketchup-red pictures in glossy magazines. Have students cut or tear the colored paper into little bits about the size of their thumb. Provide a piece of white bulletin board paper (5' x 7') on which the field of blue and the red-and-white stripes have been outlined. Allow students to glue their bits of colored paper on the flag outline, overlapping the pieces. Let students add 50 white cut-out stars to the field of denim blue. Everyone will be proud of her contribution to this star-spangled display!

Ruby Pesek, Lake Jackson, TX

Bubble Painting

For a variation of "Paint With Bubbles" as seen in *I Can Make A Rainbow* by Marjorie Frank, add tempera paint to bottled bubbles. Divide the class into four groups. Each group goes to a parent volunteer who blows either green, blue, pink, or yellow bubbles. The children try to catch the bubbles on poster board. When the bubbles break, they leave circular splotches of color. After everyone catches some bubbles, a whistle is blown to move the groups to another color. Be sure the children wear their paint shirts for this activity!

Joan Steele
St. Louis, MO

Paper Frames

Use paper frames that photographs come in to display students' artwork. At the beginning of the year, ask students to bring unwanted frames from home.

Dr. Rebecca Webster Graves
Burlington, NC

See-through Drawings

Decorate your classroom windows with colorful crayon drawings. On white typing paper, have students draw holiday scenes. Using an iron preheated to a low temperature, press each drawing between two sheets of waxed paper. Have students trim the waxed-paper edges and tape the projects to classroom windows or other glass surfaces.

Betty Brooks
Buhl, ID

Clay Storage

Need an easy way to store modeling clay? Have students roll unused clay in small balls and place in an egg carton. The cartons are both easy to store and pass out for the next art period.

Sr. Ann Claire Rhoads
Greensboro, NC

Meat Tray Paint Pad

Styrofoam meat trays hold paint pads that help eliminate spills and excess paint. Line a meat tray with several layers of paper towels. Pour paint over the towels, and let it soak in. Press an object onto the paint-soaked paper towels; then print it on paper. The trays can also be washed out and used for additional printing projects.

Janet Paczak
Brandon, MS

Q-tip Finger Savers

An easy technique for blending oil pastels or "Cray-pas" is to use Q-tips. This gives the soft, shaded effect to posters and bulletin board displays without the sore fingers and smears that you get when you rub pastels with fingertips or tissues. They are especially good for blending colors in small areas. Use a new Q-tip for each color.

Kathy Floyd
Findley, OH

Art Project Supply Tubs

Organize classroom art projects by providing each student with a "supply tub" to hold all the supplies needed for a project. Margarine tubs or shoe boxes make excellent supply tubs. If a student doesn't finish the project in the allotted time, he can put the supplies back in his tub for completion later on.

Bonnie jo Kyles
Ennis, MT

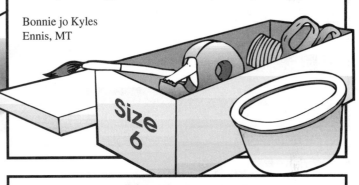

Size 6

Color By Word

This coloring activity is a fun change of pace. Have each child write a color word in each space of a coloring-book picture. Then have him pass his labeled picture to a classmate who colors it as indicated. When the pictures are complete, present them to their original owners. Youngsters really enjoy this cooperative art project.

Sr. Margaret Ann Wooden
Martinsburg, WV

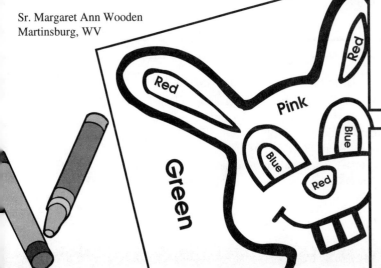

Wind-down Time

In our class, art is the last subject on Friday afternoon. To take advantage of this "wind-down" time after a busy week, I encourage the children to speak up. This way, we have a discussion time while we work, and everyone gets a chance to talk about work we've done, weekend plans, friends, and so on. The children enjoy the open atmosphere and being able to share with each other.

Patricia Celenza
Lodi, NJ

Paint Cartons

Use egg cartons to hold small amounts of tempera paint, one color per section. At the end of the painting session, close each carton, and place in a plastic bag. Paint will stay moist and can be used again.

Bonnie Dennis
Fairfax, VA

ARTS AND CRAFTS FOR ANYTIME

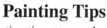

Pipe-Cleaner Needle

Trying to thread large-eyed needles or prepare lengths of yarn with hard glue ends (like shoelaces) for a lacing project proved to be too much for this teacher! Necessity spawned the invention of the pipe-cleaner needle. Students themselves can make it, repair it if yarn should slip, and clean up when the project is complete. We'll lace up everything in sight now!

Judy Faherty
Hopewell, NJ

Painting Tips

Try these painting tips at your classroom easels. Tie a pencil to each easel so you can easily write the names and captions on the children's artwork. Also keep a sponge clamped to a clothespin at each easel. The children will enjoy experimenting with these new "brushes."

Debbie Giamber
Annandale, VA

Scrap Box

Provide a brightly decorated box for children to place construction-paper scraps in. After an art project, appoint a classroom helper to take the scrap box around to his classmates. Pieces of paper that could be used again are placed in the box. During free time, students can visit the scrap box and select scraps to create their own art projects.

Pamela Myhowich
Selah, WA

Paint-Easel Ease

Simplify the use of paint easels in your classroom. Instead of bottles or cans, use half-pint milk cartons to hold paints. They fit well in the easel tray and are tall enough to hold large brushes without tipping. Open the tops of the cartons completely. As the paint dries around the edges, add more paint. The dry paint actually strengthens the carton. You'll only need to change the cartons a few times during the school year.

Beth Jones
Niagara Falls, Ontario
Canada

Apron Assistant

Could you use an extra pair of hands? Try organizing the pockets of an apron with basic supplies (stapler, glue stick, tape, paper clips), and hang it in your closet. When more hands are needed, call on a classroom helper to be the "apron assistant." He may wear the apron and assist you with various jobs.

Sr. Ann Claire Rhoads
Greensboro, NC

Garbage-Bag Aprons

These painting aprons are easy to make, easy to use, and easy to replace! Cut a hole in the bottom of a large plastic garbage bag for a neck opening. Then cut an armhole on each side of the bag. Each student slips an apron over his head. Aprons can be stored and used again.

Rebecca Gibson Calton
Auburn, AL

Disposable Paintbrushes

These inexpensive paintbrushes work great in little hands and cut cleanup time in half! Cut used, pink fabric-softener sheets into fourths. Then fold a section into fourths and wrap it over the end of a drinking straw. Tape in place and it is ready to use. These paintbrushes are great for painting leaves, flowers, pussy willows, and lots more!

Ann Fausnight
Canton, OH

Easy Glitter

Children of all ages love to work with glitter. By adding glitter to a bottle of clear nail polish and letting children apply it to their projects, excess waste is eliminated and the drying time is cut in half. The finished items really shine, and the glitter will not rub off. Parents can provide clear nail polish.

Deanna Groke
Misawa Air Base, Japan

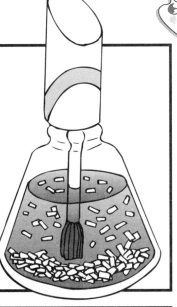

Coating For Making Fossils

When making fossils in plaster of paris, spray the objects with PAM, a nonstick vegetable oil spray. It's cleaner and less expensive than using petroleum jelly. After the object is removed from the plaster, any leftover PAM will evaporate quickly.

Kay Good
Punxsutawney, PA

Papier-Mâché Partner

Since working with papier-mâché can be messy and difficult for primary students, I have asked older children to help. With an older child to guide and direct each group, I can better supervise all groups. Also, to cut down on the mess, I place plastic containers of water at each table for cleaning hands.

Sr. Mary Catherine Warehime
Emmitsburg, MD

Hole Reinforcement

When using a brass fastener on an activity, place a reinforcement on the back around the hole before laminating. This will help prevent the hole from becoming too large.

Joanna C. Day
Lansing, MI

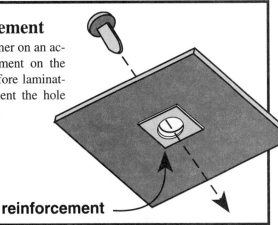

reinforcement

Lock It—Don't Lose It

Give each student a locking plastic bag at the beginning of the year. Put a piece of masking tape with the student's name on each plastic bag. Students use these bags to store unfinished art projects or puzzles.

Mary Anne T. Haffner
Waynesboro, PA

Art Center Assistant

This multipocket shoe bag stores supplies for independent or small-group use. Hang the bag in an art center. Fill the pockets with pens, pencils, crayons, paper clips, scissors, and tape.

Sr. Ann Claire Rhoads
Greensboro, NC

Triangles | Brushes | Popsicle Sticks

Pencils | Markers | Yarn

Scissors | Cards | Thread

Sticky Fingers

For those art projects that leave hundreds of tiny paper scraps on your classroom floor, try this masking tape trick. Wrap masking tape, sticky side out, around your students' hands. Watch their enthusiasm as your room is quickly litter free!

Sara McCormick Davis
Putnam City, OK

ARTS AND CRAFTS FOR ANYTIME

Teaching Secondary Colors

Here's a neat way to demonstrate how primary colors combine to create secondary colors. Put two drops each of two primary colors of paint into a Ziploc bag and close. Have children mix the two colors with their fingers, and watch the magic. Children are sure to remember the concept, and you won't have a big mess to clean up.

Debbie Giamber
Annandale, VA

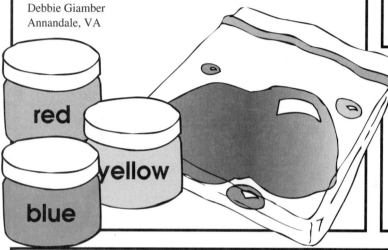

Art Tablecloth

Next time you're ready to tackle an especially messy art project, cover your table with a vinyl tablecloth. The tablecloth stays in place due to its flannel backing, and unlike newspapers, it can be used again and again. Cleanup is a cinch, too. Simply wipe the tablecloth clean with a damp sponge or toss it in the washing machine.

Michelle Sears
Malone, NY

Artwork Driers

Here's a simple solution for drying artwork when space is limited. Clip paintings or gluey artwork onto skirt hangers and hang them out of the way to dry. Valuable table and floor spaces can now be used while your artwork dries conveniently out of the way.

Barbara Hosek
Valencia, CA

Shape Sponges

Making your own shape sponges is easy and economical. Wet a sponge; then place several heavy books on top of it to flatten it. After the sponge is dry, draw the desired shapes on it. Cut out the shapes and use them for various sponge painting projects.

Rebecca Gibson Calton
Auburn, AL

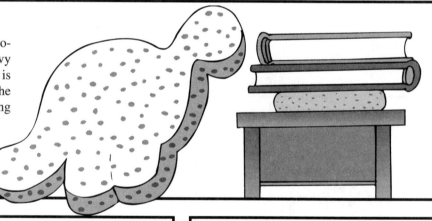

Glue Clue

Do your students have trouble opening their glue bottles? Try teaching them this plumbers' tip: "Righty, tighty. Lefty, loosey." Now your students can easily remember which way to turn the top to open and close their glue bottles.

Mary Anne T. Haffner
Waynesboro, PA

The Perfect Paint Shirt

Toss out those paint shirts that are too baggy and full of buttons! Try men's golf-style shirts instead. Your students can wear them backwards. The neck opening allows the children to pull them on easily, and there is no need for fuss with the buttons. The sleeve length is perfect, and they wash up great. This is a super timesaver for a busy kindergarten teacher.

Beth Jones
Niagara Falls, Ontario
Canada

Beat The Clock

After your art lesson is complete, a quick round of "Beat The Clock" really speeds up cleanup time. Challenge students to attempt to beat the clock and clean up the room before 60 seconds have passed. Students love this fun twist to cleaning up, and you'll have a sparkling clean room in no time flat!

Vickie Simpson
Big Rapids, MI

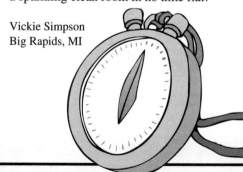

Seasonal and Holiday Ideas

Tree Branch

My students and I have a lot of fun with a large, bare tree branch standing in a bucket of sand in our classroom. We use it in the following ways:

September: Leaves labeled with student names are hung on the branches to welcome students.

October: Students fill out and hang a "batty book review" for each book they read.

November: Students draw and hang pictures of things they are thankful for.

December: Students write wishes for the world on cut-out stars and hang them.

January: Students hang original snowflakes.

February: Students write one homonym on each side of a cut-out pear (*pear* and *pair*) and hang them.

March: Students make cherry blossoms by shaking popcorn in dry tempera paint and stringing it in small bunches to hang on the tree.

April: Students make raindrops for the tree. On one side of the raindrop is a vocabulary word and on the other side is its meaning.

May: Honor-roll students glue their pictures in the centers of paper flowers and hang them on the tree—our blooming scholars!

Michelle Martin James
Macon, GA

Learning The Months

Here's a fun way to help your students learn the months of the year. Divide a large bulletin board into 12 sections, and label each section with the name of a month. Let your children complete the bulletin board display by assigning each section to one or two students, and having them add appropriate decorations.

Connie Moeller

Shape Calendar

Use your monthly calendar to help young students recognize colors and shapes. Cut out the four shapes (circle, triangle, square, rectangle) from construction paper in the eight basic colors. Number the shapes from 1 to 31, and pin to a blank calendar. When observing the calendar each day, your children can also review the colors and shapes. This calendar is attractive and requires little change from month to month—just change the number of days and the name of each new month.

Patty McGuckin
Apache Junction, AZ

Monthly Symbols For Classroom Doors

Make copies of a different symbol each month, laminate them, write each student's name on one, and mount them on your door. Encourage good behavior by rewarding those students whose names have not had to be removed from the door before the end of the month. Some suggestions for monthly symbols are as follows:

August—circus characters: "Mrs. _____'s great performers!"

September—footballs: "Throwing good grades your way."

October—jack-o'-lanterns: "You light up my life."

November—acorns: "We're nuts about _____ grade."

December—Christmas trees: "Oh, Christmas tree,…"

January—mittens: "Warming up to school."

February—valentines: "Be mine."

March—lambs: "Gentle lambs."

April—kites: "Hanging in there!"

May—baseballs: "Homestretch!"

Beverly Moore
Auburn, AL

Personalized Calendar

Instead of purchasing calendar symbols, my students "personalize" our calendar each month. I give each student half of a 3" x 5" index card to decorate according to the month's theme. After numbering their pictures, I pin them to our blank calendar. Students feel good about contributing to our classroom calendar every month.

Ruby Pesek
Lake Jackson, TX

Seasonal Tic-Tac-Toe

Using colored transparencies, cut out two different sets of seasonal or holiday shapes. Add features with markers. Prepare a tic-tac-toe grid by taping masking tape to a clear transparency. Project the grid onto the screen, divide your class into two teams, and let the fun begin!

Sr. Ann Claire Rhoads
Greensboro, NC

Wrapping Paper

Students can make wrapping paper any time of the year by changing the motif. Supply each student with a square sheet of newsprint and have each fold it in half (four times) to make 16 squares. Direct students to create two designs and alternate the designs in the squares. This makes a perfect wrapping for child-made treasures.

Jeanette Lendl
New Alexandria, PA

Holiday Party Tablecloth

Youngsters will enjoy preparing a special tablecloth for your next holiday party. Cut a length of bulletin board paper (long enough for your students to sit around comfortably) and place it on the floor. Have each child color an appropriate table setting and a seasonal table decoration on the paper. Serve your party refreshments atop this kid-created tablecloth as you reinforce good table manners. For quick cleanup when the party's over, place all of the trash in the center of the tablecloth, roll it up, and discard.

Michele A. Gnazzo
Bristol, CT

Fall Mobiles

Take students on a fall nature walk to collect leaves, seeds, seedpods, bark, and dried flowers to make classroom mobiles. Ask them to clean and save plastic pop bottles. Show students how to mount each natural object between two pieces of cold laminating film or clear Con-Tact paper. Then have them cut around each object, leaving an edge of film. Use an X-acto knife to cut off the top of a two-liter, plastic pop bottle for the base of each mobile. Punch holes in it and in each object using a paper punch. Tie yarn through the holes to hang the various objects. Hang mobiles in the classroom where students can examine them.

Judy Peterson
Delta, UT

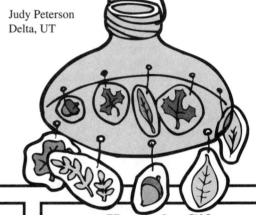

Trip Tasks

On holidays or vacations you can spark new interest in language arts assignments. Have students research and summarize information about a state or city they will be visiting. Provide encyclopedias and other resource books. Assign other individuals to write sentences, descriptive paragraphs, or stories about trips they may be taking in the future.

Dr. Rebecca Webster Graves
Burlington, NC

Monthly Word Lists

Use monthly word lists to perk up your daily review of basic skills. Every month, cut out a supply of appropriate seasonal shapes. Each day, have your students program two or three cutouts with seasonal words. Display the cutouts on the chalkboard or on a bulletin board. Use the words to practice alphabetical order, identify vowel sounds, or reinforce other basic skills.

Susan M. Valenti
Emmitsburg, MD

Shiny Leaves

There's no better time than autumn to turn out a colorful, leafy bulletin board. Collect leaves when they first fall off the trees. Place them in a damp paper towel to keep them fresh. Melt old beeswax candles in a saucepan or coffee can. Dip the leaves in the wax, and brush off the excess with a soft brush. Let them dry. The leaves should keep their color and stay fresh for a long time.

Sr. Margaret Ann Wooden
Emmitsburg, MD

Keepsake Gift

These keepsake booklets make fine gifts for grandparents. Make booklets using lined paper and construction-paper covers. Help students make a list of things they've learned to do in school. (Example: I can write my name. I can count to 100. I can write a sentence.) Have each student write one thing that he can do on a page in his booklet. Then have him demonstrate the task on that page. Have students color or paint the booklet covers before giving them as gifts on Grandparents' Day.

Betty Brooks
Buhl, ID

Mr. & Mrs. Scarecrow

Have student teams design scarecrows. The best source of clothes is Mom's and Dad's old shoes, hats, panty hose, and neckties. Use a pumpkin for each scarecrow's head. If possible, don't allow either team to see what the other is doing until the scarecrows are finished.

Rebecca Gibson Calton
Auburn, AL

Fall Colors Song

Sing this catchy tune when the leaves start changing colors in the fall.

When The Leaves Come Floating Down
(*sung to the tune of "When The Saints Go Marching In"*)

Oh, when the leaves come floating down,
Oh, when the leaves come floating down,
They'll be red and orange and yellow
When the leaves come floating down.

Kimberle Suzan Byrd, Wyoming, MI

Better Breakfast Month

October is Better Breakfast Month. Celebrate by making breakfast with another class. One room may provide the toast, while another brings in hard-boiled eggs. Another may bring in juice. The children learn about nutrition through cooperation.

Lona Hanner and Sharon Hayden
Cape Girardeau, MO

Halloween Treat Bags

For a special treat to give students on Halloween, glue wiggle eyes to a large black pom-pom (available at fabric stores). Glue the pom-pom to a small orange (or brown) paper bag. Use a permanent marker to add eight furry spider legs and a Halloween message such as "Tricky Treats," "Boo Bites," or "Spooky Snacks." Fill the bag with stickers, candy, pencils, or erasers.

Sandra Steen
Corinth, MS

Haystacks

Here is a neat treat for autumn:

2 packages peanut butter chips
1 large package chow mein noodles
1 small can cocktail peanuts

Melt chips in a heavy pan over low heat. Do not stir. Remove from heat and add noodles and peanuts. Stir with a wooden spoon until coated. Drop by teaspoons onto waxed paper and refrigerate to cool. (Butterscotch and chocolate chips can be substituted, but the lighter colors are more attractive.)

Debbie Neumann
Ocean Springs, MS

Halloween Countdown

Tie facial tissues around marshmallows to make 31 spooks. Use a permanent marker to make eyes. Hang the spooks from a tree branch. Have different students remove a spook for each day during October.

Marla Stevens
Pasadena, CA

Fireman Fun

This game is sure to make quite a splash with your students during National Fire Prevention Week. Using colored chalk, draw two blazing campfires on the chalkboard. Divide students into two teams. Alternating between the two teams, ask a child to answer a question or solve a math problem. If he is correct, he helps "put out" his team's fire by squirting it three times with a squirt gun. The first team to successfully "put out" its fire by washing it away is the winner.

Sue Hancock, Seaford, DE

Halloween Recipes

Here are some easy party treats that children can help you make:

Hot Witch's Brew: A cup of simmering apple cider topped with a scoop of orange sherbet creates a popular potion.

Skeleton Bones: Use a pear half and raisins to create a skeleton head. Add crossbones by stuffing celery with cream cheese. It will rattle your bones!

Jack-o'-lantern Sandwiches: Make a shape sandwich with a pumpkin cookie cutter. Add candy corn and raisins for a spooky face.

Ghost Bingo

Play Ghost Bingo at your party using candy corn markers! Duplicate game cards as shown for students. Have each child fill in his bingo card with Halloween vocabulary words at random. Play as you would play bingo, except when someone covers five words in a row, he says, "Boo!"

Tiptoe Through The Pumpkins

Everyone gets to participate in this fast-paced, stepping-stone relay race. Divide the class into relay teams. Hand the first player on each team two orange paper plates. The player lays the two "pumpkins" down in front of him and steps from one to the other, stepping-stone style, to reach a predetermined point. (While standing on one pumpkin, the player picks up the pumpkin behind him and lays it down in front of him.) The player returns to the line and hands the two plates to the next player. Play continues until all members of one team have been to the pumpkin patch and back.

Linda Vicich
Oglesby, IL

Rice Pumpkins

Bring on plenty of smiles with this fun activity. Each child needs 1/8 cup of rice in a Ziploc bag. He adds six drops of yellow and two drops of red food coloring to the rice, seals the bag, and shakes. Then he spreads out the rice on a paper towel to dry. Each child punches one hole in a small plastic margarine lid and threads it with green yarn. Next he cuts a jack-o'-lantern face and stem from construction paper. After spreading glue inside the margarine lid, he sprinkles it with dry orange rice and pats it down. Remind the children to turn their margarine lids over and let the loose rice fall on their paper towels before gluing their jack-o'-lantern faces and stems in place. You may hang or wear these clever pumpkins.

Sr. Ann Claire Rhoads
Greensboro, NC

Halloween Paragraphs

After Halloween, have students write descriptions of their costumes. The students should swap papers. Ask each student to use the description to illustrate the costume of his partner. This is a good way for students to find out if their descriptions were complete.

LaDonna Hauser, Wilmington, NC

Halloween Songwriters

Turn students into songwriters. Begin by brainstorming words pertaining to Halloween and writing them on a chart. Students use these words as "idea helpers" to write their own group song. The next step is to decide on a tune to fit the words. Students can make up their own tune or borrow a tune. The teacher transcribes the words into music and gives each student a copy. Students sing and tape the song.

Sherrill Fujimura, Monterey, IN

Jack-o'-Lantern Relay Race

For a quick Halloween party game, try this relay race. Divide the class into two teams. Draw two pumpkin outlines on the chalkboard. Each team lines up facing the chalkboard. At a signal, the first member of each team races to the board and draws one feature on the team pumpkin. The first team to complete the jack-o'-lantern wins. Use colored chalk for fun.

Cheryl Seachord, Fairbury, NE

Halloween Makeup

Try this homemade makeup to create spooky disguises for your Halloween party. This recipe makes enough for one child's face.

   2 teaspoons white shortening   5 teaspoons cornstarch
   1 teaspoon white flour   food coloring
   liquid glycerine (obtained from a drugstore)

With a rubber spatula, blend shortening, cornstarch, and flour to form a smooth paste. Add three to four drops of glycerine for creamy consistency. Add food coloring. Students use Q-tips and fingers to apply makeup to each other. Be sure to bring in several hand mirrors. Choose the scariest, funniest, and most original faces. This Halloween "greasepaint" can be easily removed with shortening, cold cream, or baby oil.

Elisha Williamson, Elk City, OK

Pumpkin Science

After you clean out your Halloween pumpkin, and before you carve its face, do this experiment. Place a lit candle in the pumpkin, and have students hypothesize what will happen. The candle will go out almost immediately when the oxygen inside the pumpkin is used up. Next cut out the mouth and see if the candle stays lit. Finally carve the eyes and nose, replace the top, and watch the jack-o'-lantern glow in the dark.

Judy Peterson
Delta, UT

Coat-Hanger Characters

Transform coat hangers into floating jack-o'-lanterns and galloping ghosts! To make each character, bend a coat hanger into the desired shape. Apply a coating of white glue around the hanger; then place the hanger, with the hook extending, between two sheets of tissue paper. Pat the layers together. After the glue dries thoroughly, trim any excess paper. Add construction paper features and green tissue stems. Hang these spooky characters from your ceiling.

Lynn E. Teague, Charlotte, NC

Halloween Party

Try this nutritious Halloween snack. Cut bread into pumpkin shapes using a cookie cutter. Spread peanut butter on the "pumpkins" and let students decorate them with raisins. You may even want to have a contest for the funniest or scariest jack-o'-lantern face before they disappear!

Pam Wedel
Montevideo, MN

Marble Painting

Roll into action with this marbleized spider's web! It's sure to be a favorite. Set up several paint stations. Supply each station with a spoon, a gift box lid or bottom (at least 9" x 12"), and one marble in a cup of white paint. Give each child a 9" x 12" piece of black construction paper. Taking turns, each child visits a paint station. First he puts his construction paper in the gift box. Next he spoons the marble onto his paper and rolls it around. When his web is finished, he returns the marble to the paint cup. Children can make spooky spiders for their webs by painting Styrofoam ball halves and attaching pipe cleaner legs. BEWARE!

Sharon Conley
Keansburg, NJ

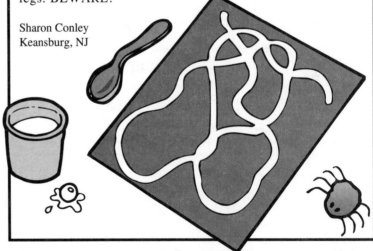

Halloween Costumes

I make a bulletin board with masks that I have purchased at after-Halloween sales. During our parade and party, students are invited to use these masks. I also keep an eye open at rummage sales and flea markets for unusual costumes from foreign countries, such as Japanese kimonos, Mexican sombreros, and peasant-style clothing. Trash bags also lend themselves to a variety of costumes.

Kathryn Marcuson
Elwood, IN

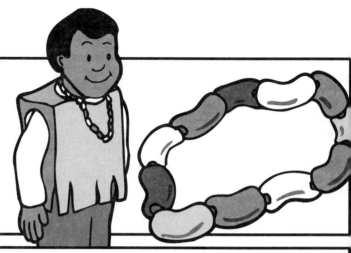

Native American Costumes

Costumes can add a historical touch to your Thanksgiving festivities. Emphasize that Native Americans today wear modern clothing but may dress in traditional costumes for ceremonies and special occasions. Ask parents to send in large, brown grocery bags to make vests. Cut openings for arms and neck as shown. Help children cut fringe along the bottom of vests. Children may use crayons or tempera paints to decorate their vests. For "wampum" necklaces, have students string large macaroni pasta on yarn. Children can paint the necklaces, if desired.

"Scent-sational" Ghosts

Fabric softener sheets, tissues, yarn lengths, and markers are all that's needed to create a batch of sweet-smelling ghosts. Roll tissues into balls and cover with fabric softener sheets. Wrap yarn lengths around necks, and tie. Use markers to add spooky faces to your ghostly creations!

Dr. Rebecca Webster Graves
Burlington, NC

Pilgrim Garb

Children can make their own white paper collars and Pilgrim hats. Have each child fold and cut a 12" x 18" piece of white construction paper as shown to make a collar. For the Pilgrim girl's hat, fold an 8" x 11" piece of white construction paper as shown. Staple the corners together. Turn the paper over and fold up the bottom edge. Attach two pieces of yarn to tie under each girl's chin. For the Pilgrim boy's hat, enlarge a pattern similar to the one shown to fit an 8" x 11" piece of black construction paper. Provide black and gold paper squares for boys to glue onto their hats. Have them cut out the hat patterns and attach paper headbands. Staple the headbands to fit each boy.

collar

Wampum Necklaces

During our unit on Native Americans, my class makes "wampum" necklaces by stringing Fruit Loops cereal onto strands of yarn. Tape one end of the yarn to keep it from unraveling during the process.

Nancy Dunaway, Forrest City, AR

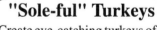

Cheesecloth Ghosts

These ghosts take a little time, but the effort is well spent. Each child needs one yard of cheesecloth or gauze, a 12-inch bottle, a 2 1/2-inch or 3-inch Styrofoam ball, and an inexpensive coat hanger. Bend the coat hanger as shown and clip off the curved tip. Tape the hanger to the bottle with masking tape. Stick the Styrofoam ball on the hanger tip; then secure the hanger to the bottle with more tape. Now you're ready to make your ghost. Place the bottle on a cookie sheet. Dip the cheesecloth in a solution of equal portions of glue and water. Drape the soaked cheesecloth over the bottle, spreading and shaping the hem outward. Let the ghost dry thoroughly overnight. When you remove the bottle, you'll have a freestanding ghost. Glue on black felt eyes for the perfect finishing touch.

Chris Christensen
Las Vegas, NV

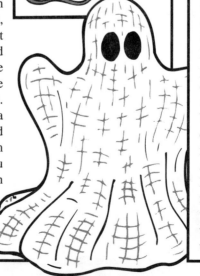

"Sole-ful" Turkeys

Create eye-catching turkeys of a different feather! Divide students into groups of five or six. For each group, enlarge a turkey pattern onto tagboard. Students color their turkeys with markers and mount them on a bulletin board or wall. To make feathers, have each child scuff his feet across the floor, then step on a piece of paper. Students outline their dusty footprints with markers and color the designs with crayons. The footprints are then cut out and added to each turkey.

Christmas Card

Create a special gift for each of your students. Have photographs taken featuring you with each of your students. Design a Christmas card, and paste the photo inside. This gift is appropriate for other holidays and birthdays as well.

Retha Mancil
Ozark, AL

Merry Christmas

Christmas Tree

Decorate your classroom Christmas tree with holiday pencils and bookmarks. Students take the decorations home when they leave for the holidays.

Pat Powell
South Haven, KS

Plaster Picture Frames

My children love this picture frame project using plastic candy molds and plaster of paris. I use a heart-shaped mold with a hollow space in the middle where the picture goes. I mix the plaster with pink paste food color. After I pour the molds, I set a plastic ring at the top of each one to use as a hanger. Remove the plaster from the molds after it hardens. The children color the raised designs and seal the frames with a light coat of enamel spray. Each child then cuts out and glues a small picture to the back of each frame. The finished frames are very inexpensive and make great gifts!

Virginia A. Larsen
Round Lake, IL

Christmas Gift

Trying to think of an inexpensive gift for your students? Buy some Christmas balls. Write each child's name on a ball with glue, then sprinkle glitter on the glue. These ornaments, though simple to make and inexpensive, are appealing to students.

Sr. Margaret Ann Wooden
Martinsburg, WV

Laminated Place Mats

Students' paintings or drawings make nifty place mats to be given as gifts, or just to brighten a holiday table. Collect students' artwork and laminate it, or cover with clear adhesive covering. Your students will be proud to set the dinner table using their special place mats.

Jan Hall
Brighton, TN

Gift Tags

Scraps of holiday gift wrap make terrific gift tags. Loosely cut around a character or design featured on the gift wrap. Laminate the cutout for durability; then add the recipient's and the giver's names to the tag using a permanent marker. These colorful tags add a personal touch to your students' handmade gifts.

Rebecca Gibson Calton
Auburn, AL

Personalized Christmas Ornaments

Decorate your classroom tree with these easy-to-make Christmas ornaments. Write each student's name on a satin ball with Puffy Paint (available at most fabric or craft stores). Students will be delighted with the results and will look forward to taking their ornaments home at the start of the holiday vacation!

Tara Kicklighter
De Land, FL

Stocking Coupon Book

It's time to decide what you're going to give your students for Christmas this year! Consider giving your students coupon books. From construction paper, make stocking-shaped covers and coupons. Program coupons with special privileges. (Example: Pick the job of your choice from the job board. Join your teacher for lunch. Skip one homework assignment.) Students are responsible for keeping track of the coupons. One extra benefit of this Christmas gift is that you'll get to know your students better as they make decisions about when and how to use their coupons.

Gail Kostka
Palatine, IL

From Your Teacher

For Christmas, I surprise my first graders with bags full of treats and surprises. I decorate small, white shopping bags (available from The Education Center) with large cutouts from holiday gift wrap. Fill the bags with fruit, nuts, novelty erasers, seasonal pencils, and Christmas Fun Books. The shopping bags are easy for youngsters to carry and are great for transporting party leftovers.

Gail Cross, Bluff City, TN

Holiday Cards

These greeting cards are both eye-catching and simple to make! Fold any size construction-paper sheets in half. Stick on white loose-leaf reinforcements in a simple holiday shape. Add any additional cutouts—candles for a menorah, a star for a Christmas tree. Students write their own holiday greetings inside.

Joan Holesko
North Tonawanda, NY

Frosted Windowpanes

I put black electrical tape in a gridlike fashion on my classroom windows to create inner windowpanes. In the winter, the class cuts out and mounts snowflakes on the panes. We spray artificial snow along one side of each pane to give it a frosted look. At Christmastime, we hang a paper wreath in the middle. Just add some curtains to give the window a "homey" look.

Wendy B. Morris, Monticello, MN

Present-Wrapping Contest

Announce a present-wrapping contest to encourage creativity; then use the "presents" to decorate bulletin boards and doors. Give each child art supplies and an envelope. Have students decorate the envelopes to look like gift-wrapped packages. Remind students to include nametags.

Rebecca Gibson Calton
Auburn, AL

Gifts For Parents

Have students frame their most prized artwork to give to their parents at Christmas. You'll need a greeting card box, an artwork sample, craft glue, and rickrack or ribbon for each student. Have each student cut his artwork to fit in the bottom of the box, and glue in place. Use an X-acto knife to cut an opening in the cover of each box. Have students paint the box covers if necessary for an attractive frame, and glue on rickrack or ribbon. These frames also make a great display for students' school pictures with a few lines of poetry.

Sr. Ann Claire Rhoads
Greensboro, NC

For Those Who Crochet

Here's a special Christmas gift that you can make for your students—crocheted bookworms! Using brightly colored yarn, follow the crocheting instructions below. Display completed bookworms on your classroom tree. Draw numbers at your Christmas party and let students choose bookworms from the tree in numerical order. Or surprise students with these wiggly friends as they leave for vacation.

Crocheting instructions: Chain 65: 4 double chain in the first 14; then slip stitch through the remaining single chain. Sew on wiggle eyes. Make a tail and a mustache by pulling through several pieces of yarn and knotting it.

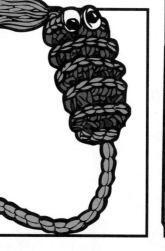

Janet Taylor, Rockport, TX

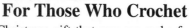

Holiday Relay

Divide the class into two or more teams. Give each student a drinking straw. Make several construction-paper Christmas trees or dreidels. To play, the first child on each team sucks up his team's cutout with his straw and puts it on the next student's desk. If the cutout falls on the floor, the player must pick it up with the straw, not with his hands. The first team to finish is the winner.

Reindeer Twig Puppets

These "rustic" reindeer puppets with real twig antlers are a great holiday art project. Trace patterns onto brown construction paper, and cut out the reindeer. Add facial features with crayons or construction-paper scraps. Attach "twig" antlers and tongue depressors or Popsicle sticks. For additional fun, role-play "Rudolph" by attaching a red pom-pom to one student's puppet.

Judy Peterson, Delta, UT

A Great Christmas Gift

My special gift to students is 20 sheets of personalized stationery, a pencil, and an eraser placed in a Ziploc plastic bag. The children love having personalized stationery, and parents appreciate the educational value of the gift. To make the stationery, prepare an original showing only writing lines and two picture frames. Make one copy for every two children in your class. Glue school pictures inside the frames, and add catchy titles to complete student originals. Make copies and cut in half. Be sure to make yourself some stationery for writing Christmas thank-yous.

Cindy Newell, Durant, OK

Snowflake Tree

Let your students create a stunning winter display. Give each child a 6" x 6" piece of white paper. Students fold their papers several times and cut around the edges to make snowflakes. Cover a bulletin board or door with bright holiday paper; then post the snowflakes in the shape of a tree.

Barbara Sumpter
Florence, KY

Questions For Santa

Enlist the help of an older class to help you add the final touch to this writing assignment. Begin by having your class write questions to Santa. (How old are you? How do reindeer fly?) Have the older class write answers back to your students during their writing time.

Teri Butson
Lancaster, PA

Egg Carton Christmas Tree

This Christmas decoration is easy to make and is an eye pleaser as well. To begin, trace and cut out a tree pattern from poster board. Next, staple Styrofoam egg carton cups in rows across the tree cutout. Glue thin, tinsel garlands between each row and around the outside of the tree. It's done and ready to be displayed!

Standing Christmas Tree

Make an attractive display with a forest of Christmas trees. Fold a 3" x 4" piece of green construction paper lengthwise. Cut out a half tree on the fold. Use this tree as a pattern to cut out three more half trees. Open the trees on the fold and stack them together. Use a sewing machine to stitch the trees together on the fold line.

Dr. Rebecca Webster Graves
Burlington, NC

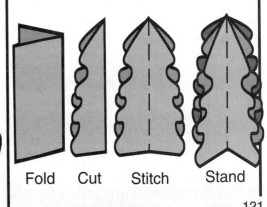

Fold   Cut   Stitch   Stand

Vacation Countdown

Welcome Christmas vacation with a classroom countdown of daily holiday activities. Display a large, cut-out Christmas tree in your room. Provide students with ornaments to decorate by duplicating ornament shapes onto construction paper or providing patterns to trace. Program ornament backs with different holiday activities such as "Sing a Christmas carol," or "Bake Christmas cookies." Next, number the ornament fronts so you can prepare for each activity in advance. Your students can look forward to a surprise activity each day until vacation arrives.

Diane Taylor
Bethlehem, PA

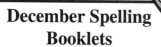

Seasonal Book Jackets

Think ahead so you won't be scrambling in January to find those Christmas books you borrowed from the library. Make book jackets from seasonal gift-wrapping paper and put them on each Christmas book. When the holiday passes, books are easily identified for quick return.

Sr. Ann Claire Rhoads
Greensboro, NC

Christmas Stocking

I hang a stocking in the front of the classroom to help control overly excited students at Christmastime. When a student completes a task on time, I write his or her name on a ticket and put it in the stocking. During our classroom Christmas party, I draw several names from the stocking. These students receive special gifts.

Trudy Naddy
Gladstone, OR

December Spelling Booklets

Stocking-shaped spelling booklets will add a holiday flair to December's weekly spelling tests. For each student, cut out two red construction-paper stocking shapes and a matching test paper for each December spelling test. Staple together at the top. Have students label their booklets and decorate with cotton and glitter. Send booklets home at the end of the month.

Susan L. Pearson
Charlotte, NC

Holiday Surprise

This holiday gift for the custodian will be greatly appreciated! When the custodian is busy in another area of the school, students quickly and quietly clean your hallway, using brooms borrowed from other teachers. When the custodian returns, watch his face light up!

Rebecca Gibson Calton
Auburn, AL

Glitter Grabber

Make your supply of glitter last through the holiday season with this glitter tip! While using glitter, have students work on cookie sheets with sides. We have one cookie sheet for each color of glitter. The mess is greatly reduced and our glitter lasts a lot longer!

Jane Cuba
Southfield, MI

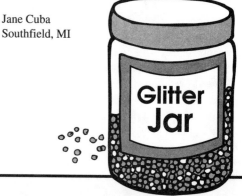

Glitter Jar

Christmas Caroling

Ask your principal for permission to go caroling in the building just before the Christmas holiday. Your students will be eager to practice Christmas carols in preparation for their performances. Their peers will enjoy the festive mood set by traditional holiday songs.

Rebecca Gibson Calton

Rudolph Sandwiches

This nutritious holiday snack will bring shouts of glee! For an added treat, let your students help in the preparation. You will need two slices of wheat bread, peanut butter, jelly, six pretzel sticks, two raisins, and one red gumdrop for each child. Cut bread slices as shown, and fill with peanut butter and jelly. Add pretzel antlers, raisin eyes, and a gumdrop nose. Could they be too cute to eat?

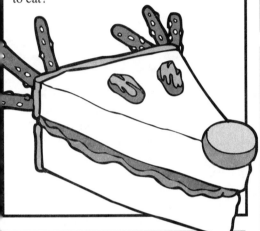

Filling Piñatas

If you're planning to make a piñata for the holidays, make sure that each of your students gets his fair share of the treats! Before the party, have a parent or aide fill plastic sandwich bags with equal amounts of goodies, one bag per student. Tie each bag with ribbon and place inside the piñata. When the piñata breaks, each student grabs one bag. This cuts back on the scrambling and assures that everyone gets a fair share.

Pamela Myhowich
Selah, WA

Christmas Drums

These tiny drums can decorate an entire Christmas tree. Each child needs half of a toilet paper tube, felt to wrap around the cardboard tube, sequins, scissors, glue, yarn, straight pins, one Q-tip, and white construction paper. Have students cut two circles from white paper that are slightly larger than the diameter of the toilet paper tube. Each student glues the circles to the top and bottom of his cardboard tube. Then he wraps the tube in felt and glues the seam. Students decorate with pins, yarn, and sequins. Each child cuts his Q-tip in half and pastes the cotton ends to the top of his drum. Use a needle to run nylon thread through the top and side of the drum for a hanger.

Sr. Margaret Ann Wooden, Martinsburg, WV

Menorah Magic

Try this simple menorah that can stand. Fold a paper plate in half and use as the base. Cut straws in half to use as the candles, and provide small pieces of orange tissue paper for the flames. Students can count out the eight candles and glue them to the folded portion of the plate. Glue one long straw in the center for the shammash. Count off each of the eight days of Hanukkah by placing the tissue paper on the end of the straw to symbolize the lighting of each candle.

Christmas Candle Snack

Your students will enjoy preparing a simple nutritious snack that looks like a Christmas candle. You will need a pineapple ring, half of a peeled banana, a cherry, a paper plate, and a fork for each student. Instruct students to place a pineapple ring on their plates, insert the half banana in the center of the ring, and top it with a cherry held in place by a toothpick. Let your students admire their creations for a moment before munching.

BessAnne McKnight
Memphis, TN

A Party Piñata

This piñata is easy to make. You will need two large, brown paper bags. Cut the bottom out of one bag. Cut away the top half of the other bag. Punch one hole for each student along the bottom edge of the second bag. Tape one length of yarn inside each hole, pulling yarn to the outside. Slide the second bag inside the first one and tape into place. Place one Ziploc bag of treats inside the piñata for each student. Staple the bag closed at the top and decorate. Hang the piñata securely from the ceiling. At party time, each child holds a yarn length. At your command, all the children pull their pieces of yarn at the same time, and the goody bags will come tumbling out!

Sharon Haley

Step 1
Step 2
Step 3
Step 4
Step 5

outside   inside

Catching Snowflakes

How do you keep snowflakes from melting once they're caught? By catching the snowflakes on ice cubes! Next time it snows, send your students outside with ice cubes. They will be fascinated by the beauty of the individual snowflakes. You can even take the snowflakes inside for a short while before any melting will occur.

Alissa Dinneen
Bristol, CT

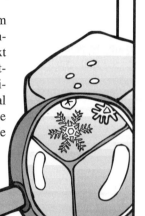

Snowflake Art

Arouse your students' curiosity with the prediction of afternoon snow flurries! To begin, each student cuts nine snowflakes from tissue paper in a variety of sizes and colors (pastels and blues work nicely). Students then arrange their tissue cutouts on 11" x 17" pieces of white construction paper, and glue in place. With paintbrushes and water, the students gently brush outward from snowflake centers to their points. This process helps adhere the snowflake points and gives the project a blended look. Mount dry projects on 12" x 18" pieces of colored construction paper. Bundle up! The snow flurries have arrived!

Clarese A. Ornstein
Lake Villa, IL

Snow Log Recipe

This is a yummy way to celebrate a cold, snowy day at school! As well as being fun and nutritious, this can be used as a center activity if picture direction cards are used. To create one snow log, each child will need:
   1 banana, cut lengthwise
   1 tablespoon of peanut butter
   shredded coconut
The banana halves are spread with peanut butter and then pressed together, sandwich-style. The "sandwich" is then rolled in the coconut. The kids love making and eating these treats.

Mary B. Hines
Kingston, TN

Winter Wall Hanging

A winter wall hanging is a great follow-up activity for studies of the four seasons. Cut an old white sheet into 12" x 16" rectangles. Stretch a rectangle on each child's desk over a piece of drawing paper. Secure with masking tape. Using markers, have each student draw a seasonal picture. Then stitch the rectangles together into a wall hanging. Add a three-inch border of inexpensive fabric. A wall hanging is the perfect cover-up for an unsightly wall.

Prudence Spaulding
Great Barrington, MA

Flowers In The Snow

New deep snow! Everyone in boots? Stamp down the snow somewhere where people can see your handiwork. Then squeeze liquid paint to create a row of simple flowers. Add a big sun!

Sandra Docca
Silver Spring, MD

Let It Snow!

Can't wait for a big snowstorm to hit your area? Create a blizzard in your classroom with the help of your students. Begin by having students cut lots of snowflakes from white paper. After everyone has left for the day, tape the snowflakes all over the room. Save a few small snowflakes to be given as rewards the following day. Post signs outside your classroom telling about the snowstorm. Take this opportunity to give a creative writing assignment about an incredible blizzard.

Rebecca Gibson Calton
Auburn, AL

The Answer Of The Year

This math challenge will help your students get accustomed to the new year. Students try to make as many word problems as they can with an answer of 19_ _.

Janice Scott
Rockport, TX

Bird Feeder

Welcome early birds to this natural bird feeder. Have students save grapefruit shells. After grapefruit halves dry, use a paper punch to make two holes opposite each other near the rim. Tie string in the holes, fill with birdseed, and hang in a tree branch.

Martha Cranfill
Hickory, NC

Abe Mobiles

Honor the birthday of Abraham Lincoln by making an eye-catching mobile of the president himself! Have each student fold a 12" x 18" piece of black construction paper in half, lengthwise, and cut as shown. Students design face parts from the paper scraps, and hang using thread.

Barbara Mace
Topeka, KS

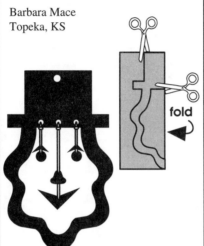

fold

A Sentence A Day

Younger students can learn about Martin Luther King while they practice handwriting. Cut out several construction-paper balloons. Write a simple sentence about Dr. King on each balloon. Post a balloon on the board each morning for handwriting practice. After discussing the sentence, let students practice writing it, adding an illustration on their papers when they finish. Let students compile their papers at the end of the week into a booklet to take home for reading practice with a parent.

Sample sentences:
Dr. King wanted to help all people.
Dr. King helped to make fair laws.
Dr. King believed in peace.
Dr. King gave speeches to many people.

Dr. Martin Luther King, Jr., was an important American.

Dr. Martin Luther King, Jr., believed in peace.

Dr. Martin Luther King, Jr., wanted to help all people.

Edible Bird Feeders

Youngsters will enjoy making these totally edible bird feeders as much as the birds will enjoy eating them. Using cookie cutters, cut shapes from semifrozen bread dough. Punch a hole in the top of each cutout with a plastic straw. Spread the cutouts with peanut butter, and sprinkle them with birdseed. Bake at 300° for about ten minutes or until the dough hardens. After the treats cool, thread a piece of yarn or ribbon through the hole and have youngsters tie them to the branches of a tree.

Kimberle Suzan Byrd, Wyoming, MI

Shiny Pennies

For Lincoln's birthday, surprise students with a shiny penny taped to each desk. Discuss the significance of the words and pictures on the penny. Have them do a "rubbing" of the penny with a crayon or pencil. This could introduce the class to art rubbings.

Kathryn Marcuson, Elwood, IN

Peaceful Solutions

Help your students to begin looking for peaceful solutions to problems they may face with friends or family. Write problem situations on large tagboard cards. After explaining Dr. King's ideas about peaceful protest, post one card on the board. Read it to the students; then ask them to think about a peaceful way to solve the problem. Give them several minutes to think silently before they respond. List solutions on the board and discuss the advantages and disadvantages of each. (To stress that there may be more than one good solution to the problem, avoid voting for the "best" solution.) Continue with the rest of the cards.

Ladder To Equality

Present a visual timeline of Dr. King's life with a wall or door display. Post two long tagboard strips on the wall to make a ladder. Write important events in Dr. King's life on cut-out rungs. Each day, add a rung to the ladder. When the ladder is complete, have students choose an event to illustrate on a paper plate. Tack the ladder and the plates to a "Celebrate Martin Luther King Day" bulletin board for a 3-D display.

7. Was killed in 1968

6. Received the 1964 Nobel Peace Prize

5. Gave important speech in Washington, DC, called "I Have A Dream"

4. Led a bus boycott in Montgomery, AL

Have A Heart

Reward the good things your students do with tiny hearts. Cut out several two-inch construction-paper hearts. Punch a hole in each one. Give each student a ribbon long enough to make a necklace. Tie ends together. Whenever you observe a student doing something positive, jot it down on a heart and have the child add it to his necklace. On the last day of the month, the child may wear his necklace home. Both students and parents will be proud of the positive comments.

Pamela McKedy
West Germany

Colorful Valentine Cards

Provide students with magazines, department store ads, and nursery catalogs to create and decorate their own valentines. To get them started, you may suggest using a clothing ad with the saying "You SUIT me just fine! Be mine!" or an ad for a watch to illustrate "It's TIME to be my valentine!" Use the nursery catalogs to create romantic cards with floral collages.

Clarese A. Ornstein, Lake Villa, IL

Valentine Train

Climb aboard the valentine train! To make boxcars, each child cuts away one long side of a half-gallon milk carton. He then adds wheels, valentine hearts and doilies, and his name. Boxes are arranged to form a train. The train is pulled by an engine (the teacher's car) made from two half-gallon milk cartons and a round dusting powder box . Students then sort their valentines into the proper cars for easy distribution later!

Annette Mathias
Partridge, KS

Valentine Ruffles

Start a new trend with ruffled valentines! Students gather toilet paper strips and glue to their valentines. They are certain to be heart-warmers!

Nancy T. Dunn and Darlene Milholen
Siler City, NC

Candy Kisses

Circulation should increase in the library on Valentine's Day when you announce that each student checking out a book will receive a kiss from the librarian. As the first few students come to get a book, give each a chocolate candy kiss. Then stand back and watch how fast news travels. Be sure you have a large supply of candy kisses for this day.

Cathy Bonnell, Phoenix, AZ

Valentine Award

Even young students can make attractive valentine award corsages using just construction paper and glue. Each child will need nine 5" x 3/4" strips of construction paper. To make, glue one end of each strip to the back of a small cut-out heart. After drying, fold each strip in, towards the center, and glue to the back to make a loop. Attach small hearts to the ends of several more strips and glue to the back for streamers. Students use markers or glitter to decorate the hearts. Use the corsages as student awards or parent valentines.

Debbie Wiggins
Myrtle Beach, SC

A Valentine For The Principal

A few weeks before Valentine's Day, as a daily reward for good behavior, allow students to decorate a big heart for their principal. Each student should get a chance to add his or her personal touch. Paper lace can be added to finish the heart. To complete the surprise, actually mail the valentine instead of delivering it. Your principal will love it!

Rebecca Gibson Calton
Auburn, AL

Pipe-Cleaner Hearts

Give your students an inexpensive and unusual valentine treat. Purchase one red pipe cleaner for each of your students. Shape one end of each pipe cleaner into a heart shape. Wrap the other end around a pencil.

Debbie Wiggins
Myrtle Beach, SC

Heart Cups

Candy hearts help encourage concentration during the valentine season. Hang a valentine cup for each student from a bulletin board. Select special pages throughout the day to be "heart" pages, and have students draw hearts around their page numbers. At the end of the day students place a candy heart in their cups for each heart paper they have completed perfectly. The heart cups are a favor for the Valentine's Day party.

Vicki Rosine, Lebo, KS

Conversation Hearts

A few days before Valentine's Day, I give each of my students six to eight candy conversation hearts. Using the words on his hearts, each student writes a story. Then they may eat their candies. On Valentine's Day, everyone reads his story to the class.

Esther Thompson, Hendricks, MN

Valentine Bingo

Here's a game your students make themselves! Using a pencil and a ruler, each child draws a bingo card (five squares across and five down). Present a theme for the game (synonyms of *love* or popular Valentine's Day words). On the chalkboard, list 40 or more words that the children suggest. Students complete their cards by writing a different word in each square. To play, students cover words that are called out. Five words across, down, or diagonally wins! Students may also fill cards with math answers and cover an answer when a matching problem is called.

Diana Curtis
Albuquerque, NM

Alphabetizing Valentines

Before the children give out their valentines, I have them practice arranging their cards in alphabetical order. I then post an alphabetized class list on the board. Students check the cards, then sit in the listed order. Passing out the cards is then quick and easy.

Carole Donoghue
Bristol, CT

Valentine Party Hats

Potato-print party hats are as much fun to make as to wear. Have children watch as you make a potato printer. Cut a potato in half. Press a heart-shaped cookie cutter into the potato. Cut around the cookie-cutter line, leaving a raised heart. Provide students with three-inch-wide bands of white construction paper. Put a thin layer of red tempera paint on a paper plate. Demonstrate how to stamp the potato in the paint and then onto the headbands. Let children stamp hearts on their bands. When dry, write students' names and staple headbands to fit.

Valentine Cake

You can make a special Valentine's Day cake by using one square and one round cake pan. Prepare a cake mix as directed and bake in the two shaped pans. When cool, cut the round layer, as shown, and assemble with the square layer to make a heart shape. Frost with white icing and trim with candy red-hots.

Michelle Martin James
Macon, GA

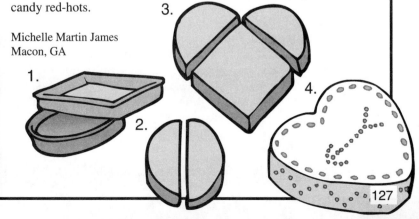

Fresh Spring Hyacinths

Your classroom will bloom with these spring flowers. Each child needs a toilet paper tube, glue, 1 1/2" squares of purple and pink tissue paper, a pencil, floral tape, and a plastic straw. Staple one end of the tube and cut it to a rounded shape. Have children cover the tube with the tissue by folding each square, one at a time, over the end of a pencil. Dab each piece lightly in glue and attach to the tube. Wind floral tape around a plastic straw and attach as a stem. Add construction-paper leaves. "Plant" these pretty flowers in paper cups or post on a bulletin board.

Martha Cranfill
Winston Salem, NC

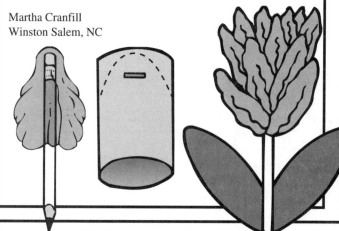

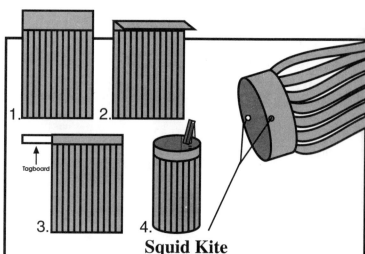

Squid Kite

Soar into spring with colorful squid kites. Each student needs a 24" x 36" piece of paper. Draw a line six inches from the top edge of the paper. Measure strips to the desired width and cut to the line. Fold the top edge down to the six-inch line. Insert a 2 1/2" x 18" strip of tagboard into the folded section of paper for stability. Staple in place. Staple the tagboard strip to form a circle, overlapping the edges. Punch holes on opposite sides of the circle and attach a string handle. Take these kites out on a breezy day, or hang them in your classroom for an attractive display.

Debra Burns

Rainbow Mobiles

Bring a bit of spring into your room with colorful rainbow mobiles. For each rainbow, cut a small paper plate in half. Cut an arch in the bottom of the plate to make a rainbow. Have children roll small squares of tissue paper in balls and glue in arches to the plates. Glue cotton to each end of the rainbow to make clouds. Punch a hole in the top of the rainbow, add yarn, and hang it from the classroom ceiling.

Cynthia Munn, Pamplico, SC

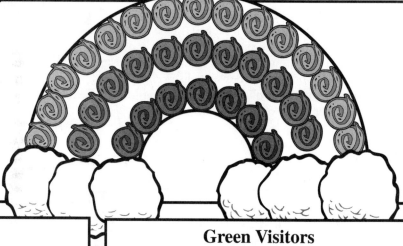

Spring Sprouts

Students can grow their own sprouts for healthy snacks. Each child puts a teaspoon of sprout seeds in a peanut butter jar. Cover the top of each jar with cheesecloth and seal it with a rubber band. Have each student dip his jar in a pail of warm water, shake the jar for two to three minutes, and then drain the water out. Do this every day in the morning and afternoon. Your class can also keep a "by the seeds" journal for a humorous record of the sprouts' rapid growth. When the sprouts are grown, have students bring salad bar items to school for a special Salad Day: pita bread, cheese slices, salad dressing, and chopped vegetables. Students put sprouts and other salad goodies into the pita bread for healthy, do-it-yourself snacks.

Carole Pippert and Sandra Docca
Silver Spring, MD

Green Visitors

Four days before St. Patrick's Day, I kindle my students' interest in the holiday. First, I overturn several desks and chairs and sprinkle green glitter on the floor before students arrive. They are surprised to see this mess and a discussion begins. I suggest that leprechauns could have visited our classroom. The discussion turns into a writing activity when students want to leave notes for their "visitors." Each day, the classroom looks different and students leave notes. On St. Patrick's Day, the room is left orderly with a "pot of gold" (gold-covered chocolate coins) and a note from the "visitors."

Pamela Myhowich
Selah, WA

Easter Baskets

A local grocery store may supply you with plastic containers used for tomatoes or strawberries, or students may collect them for these colorful, easy-to-make baskets. Have students cut out strips in two colors of construction paper and weave the strips in and out of each hole until the row is covered. Cut long strips of oaktag for the handles and have students decorate them. Staple a handle to each basket. Students may cut and curl strips of green paper for grass, or use artificial grass.

Donna Hall
Jennings, MO

Dipped Carnations

Here's an old idea with a new twist. Unfold a facial tissue and tear in half lengthwise. Repeat this step and stack all four sections. Tear off smooth edges for a rippled effect. Pleat and secure with a green pipe cleaner. Gently separate the folds. Then, dip the flower edges in a solution containing equal parts of water and food coloring. Bend the pipe cleaner to form a hook, and hang upside down to dry.

Cindy Newell
Durant, OK

Party-Favor Bunnies

Convert L'eggs panty hose containers into bunnies for cute party favors. To make them stand on end, melt the bottom of each L'egg container with a foil-covered warm iron. Glue on construction-paper features. Fill with cellophane grass and treats.

Bunny Tracks

Surprise your students during the Easter season with a room full of bunny tracks! While children are out of the room, dip two cotton balls into powder or flour. Use the cotton to make "tracks" leading into the classroom, on each desk, and all around the room. Place jelly beans in each child's desk. When children return, they'll love the surprise!

Geri Dugo, Bristol, CT

Bunny Cake

The Easter bunny would be proud of this debonair and delectable cake. Prepare a two-layer yellow cake mix as directed on the package. After cooling the cake, cut it as shown and place it on a cake plate. Frost with either white or chocolate icing. Use thin black licorice for whiskers, black jelly beans for eyes, a red gumdrop for the nose, and thin red licorice for the mouth. Decorate the bow tie with jelly beans.

Matzo Covers

Jewish students will enjoy making these colorful cloths to cover matzos at the Seder during Passover. Provide wallpaper samples with a large circle drawn on each. Students cut out and fringe each circle. Students will be proud to make a contribution to the Seder.

Ruth Brinn
Boca Raton, FL
Author of *Let's Celebrate!*, *More Let's Celebrate!*, and *Let's Have A Party!*

Easter Baskets

Have students bring empty coffee cans from home to help make these unusual Easter baskets. To make each basket, thoroughly wet a paper plate and place over a can, securing with a rubber band. When dry, remove the plate from the can, and attach a yarn or oaktag handle. Decorate with colorful tissue paper, twisted to look like flowers.

Janice Hanson
Rochester, NY

Butterfly Art

Bring the beauty of butterflies to your room. Fold a sheet of 9" x 12" construction paper in half for each child, and draw a butterfly outline as shown. Leaving the paper folded, instruct students to cut on the line. Using crayons, markers, or stickers, have students decorate the wings of their butterflies. Have students paint tissue tubes black or wrap the tubes with black construction paper. Assist in taping bent pipe cleaners to the inside of each tube for antennae. Staple or glue wings to tubes. Display butterflies with large flower cutouts.

Beth Jones
Niagara Falls, Ontario
Canada

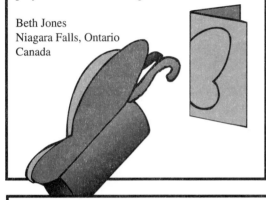

Covered Flowerpots

Choose one of these flowerpot projects as a Mother's Day gift or for a spring planting project. Individual clay pots are needed, but green thumbs are not required! **Simulated Cork:** (Materials—masking tape, any type of brown shoe polish) Cover the pot completely with two-inch strips of masking tape. Polish the pot surface with shoe polish and allow to dry. The result is cork-like! **Rug Yarn:** (Materials—glue, paintbrush, rug yarn) Brush glue over the first inch of the pot, starting from the bottom edge. Wrap the rug yarn around the bottom edge of the pot. Continue wrapping upward, keeping the yarn wraps very close together. Brush on additional glue as needed and continue wrapping until the entire pot is covered. Use contrasting colors of rug yarn to glue additional shapes or designs on top of the yarn surface if desired. **Calico:** (Materials—glue, paintbrush, fabric scraps) Use pinking shears to cut fabric scraps into two- and three-inch squares. Brush squares with glue and apply to pot. Overlap squares for added texture. Cover the entire pot. Protect completed pots with a coat of spray-on clear shellac or polyurethane.

Laurie Vent
Upper Sandusky, OH

Mother's Day Magnet

Cut spool in half.

These refrigerator magnets are lovely Mother's Day gifts. You will need wooden thread spools (from craft stores), small dried flowers, glue, yarn or ribbon, and magnetic tape. Have the spools cut in half as shown. Students glue flowers in the grooves on the back of the spools and tie with yarn or ribbon. Attach a magnet strip to the back of each spool.

Sister Carolee Vanness, Cato, WI

Bouquets For Mothers

Student-made flower bouquets are a lovely thank-you for room mothers or Mother's Day gifts. You'll find that it's time-consuming for students to make these flowers, but the results are gifts your students will be proud to give. Cut leaf shapes through several thicknesses of green crepe paper. Cut a three-inch strip from folded red, pink, or lavender crepe paper, and fringe. After unfolding the strip, gather unfringed side and secure with floral wire. Wrap the wire with floral tape. Wrap your way down the "stem," inserting leaf cutouts at intervals. Spray finished flowers with perfume, and tie several together with a matching ribbon.

Mary Dinneen, Bristol, CT

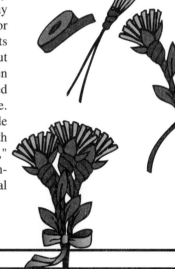

Mom's Special Day

Treat moms on Mother's Day with a special writing project. Have each child write the letters in the word "mother" down the side of his paper. Beginning with each letter, the student writes a phrase that describes something special his mom does for him every day. Roll each finished paper up and tie with a pretty ribbon before sending home. You may wish to complete a similar project before school is out to celebrate Father's Day.

Robert Kinker
Bexley, OH

M=akes my lunch.
O=atmeal fixer.
T=akes time to listen.
H=ugs me.
E=ven loves me when I'm bad.
R=eally is my best friend.

Tea For "Tea-rrific" Moms

Youngsters will enjoy surprising moms on Mother's Day. To make greeting cards, fold a sheet of construction paper in half for each of your students. Then have each student trace or write *You are my...*on the outside and *cup of tea* on the inside. Write *Happy Mother's Day! Love, (child's name)* on the inside of the card. Cut a construction-paper or wallpaper teacup for each child. Have students fold and glue the sides, but not the tops where you will insert tea bags. Then assist students in gluing the tea cups to their cards.

Diana Curtis, Albuquerque, NM

cup of tea.

You are my...

Happy Mother's Day! Love, Jody

Wild Tie Contest

Around Father's Day, provide the students with precut ties or patterns to trace and cut. Instruct each child to decorate it. See who can come up with the wildest tie! Finally, the children can add strings and wear them.

Rebecca Gibson Calton
Auburn, AL

Dad's Pad

To make a notepad for dad, have each student decorate a clothespin using markers. Assist students as they glue their clothespins and tie-shaped cutouts on poster boards as shown. Have each student personalize her dad's gift by gluing a picture of herself on the tie. Using a hole puncher, help students punch two holes and add a yarn hanger. Clip small sheets of paper in place with the clothespin.

Judy Peterson, Delta, UT

Flag Day

Talk about symbols in the American flag. Have a contest to design a flag for your school or classroom. Give each child a chance to explain his flag and choice of symbols. Hang the flags in the cafeteria for a colorful display.

Kathy Beard, Keystone Heights, FL

Father's Day Mobile

Here's a Father's Day gift that sports-minded dads will love. Have students trace and cut a bat from brown construction paper. Then have them trace and cut out four baseballs from white construction paper. Students use black crayons to draw seams on balls. Have each student punch a hole in each ball and six holes in the bat (as shown). Using yarn, have students tie the balls to the bats and make hangers. Using black crayons, students may write Father's Day greetings on their mobiles or list jobs they'll do for their dads on the ball cutouts.

Naomi Reyes, Wilmington, CA

Caps And Gowns

Graduation is a special time for students, parents, friends, and relatives. To make a mortarboard, cut a ten-inch poster board square for each student. Measure a two-inch-wide strip of poster board to fit around each student's head and staple it. Assemble pieces with glue as shown. To make a tassel, wrap yarn around your hand several times. Gather and tie one end as shown. Cut through the loops at the other end. Tie the tassel to a length of yarn. Secure the tassel to the mortarboard by twisting the other end of the yarn around a paper fastener and securing it in the center of the mortarboard.

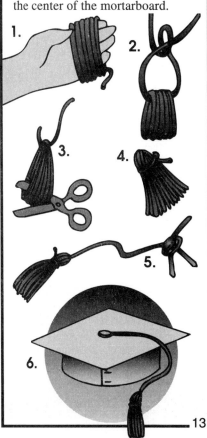

Memorial Day

In preparation for Memorial Day and a trip my sixth graders were planning to Washington, D.C., we discussed the various memorials we would see. Our discussion centered around the Vietnam War Memorial. We talked about the number of men and women who lost their lives in that war and decided to make our own memorial. I gave each student a sheet of 1/4-inch graph paper. The student put ten Xs on each of 20 lines for a total of 200 Xs. We kept a record of the number of Xs completed until we had 50,000-plus. The students stapled together and taped the sheets on a large wall, identifying the memorial with a computer-made sign. To instill some meaning into this activity, we remembered that each X represented a human being, and we discussed all of the people who may be affected by the death of one. The concept of 50,000-plus meant nothing to my students until we made our own memorial. This type of activity works well whenever you are trying to relate large numbers to your students.

Sherry Ostroff
Lancaster, PA

Spotlight on Centers

Learning Centers On The Line

Learning centers don't have to take up a lot of space in a classroom. Nor do they require a lot of daily organization by the teacher. Attach wire or string under a chalkboard or table. Store each of your centers in a Ziploc bag and attach it to the wire with clothespins. When you organize your centers in this manner, students will find that they are easy to store and easy to put away.

Theresa Bruhl
Folsom, LA

Don't Cry Over Lost Parts

To secure small game parts, store them in a locking plastic bag. Then punch holes in the bag and attach it to a file folder, game pocket, or gameboard with a brad.

Sandy Edgington
West Carrollton, OH

Learning's My Bag!

You'll wonder how you ever got along without this bulletin board center! Use pushpins to hang shopping bag centers from The Education Center from a bulletin board. A student chooses a bag and returns it when he is done.

Joanne Davis
Orlando, FL

Chinese Carryout

Those Chinese food carryout containers are great for storing counters, checkers, chalk, crayons, and game pieces. Chinese restaurants will sell them at a small cost. If several people are interested, you can buy 100 containers from a restaurant supplier very cheaply. Decorate and label; then store by hanging on a mug rack mounted on the end of a bookshelf.

Sandra Docca
Silver Spring, MD

Disk Storage

Don't worry about "slipped disks" at your computer center. The Education Center's press-on pockets are perfect for keeping computer diskettes safe and easily accessible when not in use. Press the pockets on a flat surface at eye level. Use a permanent marker to label each pocket with the subject, or insert index cards with titles and a list of student users. Larger press-on pockets can be used to hold program folders.

Sr. Ann Claire Rhoads
Greensboro, NC

Learning Activities Center

I use worksheets from *The Mailbox* to make a learning activity center. First I make several copies of each worksheet. Then I add color to one worksheet, glue it to a manila envelope, and laminate both sides. The extra copies of the worksheets are put inside the envelopes. I bought colorful, inexpensive plastic baskets to store the envelopes. Each day I assign students a color for "basket work" to be completed independently.

Nancy J. Hull
South Haven, KS

Color-coded Cards

When making game cards for folder games, make the cards the same color as the folder. When cards become separated from the games, the color will enable you to locate the correct folder more easily.

Joanna C. Day, Lansing, MI

Organizing Centers

Each day I have an activity period called "Center Time." On a pegboard, I hang games or centers for pairs of students to do during Center Time. In another area, I attach library book pockets labeled with center numbers. Students' names are written on construction-paper crayons. After laminating the crayons, I place two in each pocket to show center assignments. The name crayons are rotated daily to provide center variation.

Sharon Hayden
Perryville, MO

Milk Crate Listening Center

To save preparation time and table space, I store my listening center in a milk crate. The jack is placed in the bottom, and headphones are hung on the edges with cords inside the crate. The crate is easy to move and to store.

Janet Boyd
Chandler, OK

Center Management

Assign each center in your classroom a color. Within each center, provide a designated number of colored, laminated strips of paper. The students make their choices for center time each day by choosing one strip. These are then filed in a personalized library card pocket according to the day of the week. Students must choose a different color for each day of the week. Although this idea originated in our school's kindergarten, it is appropriate for other grade levels.

Sara C. Kennedy, Bedford, VA

Clothespins To The Rescue

Center activities can sometimes be confusing for young children. To organize the activities better in my centers, I use wooden clothespins. Each clothespin is numbered to match a corresponding activity in a center. Then the clothespins are attached to the activities. They're easily clipped right onto worksheets, games, folders, baskets, and bulletin boards.

Vicki Fann
Smyrna, TN

Center Clips

Spot-check center work at a glance using personalized clothespins. Give a clothespin to each child with his name on it. Store the pins on a hanger near your center corner. When a student finishes a center activity, he clips his pin to it. You can easily see which activities each child has completed.

Lori Schmidt
Lima, OH

Learning Centers File

I developed a simple filing system to help me keep track of all the learning centers I use in my classroom. Each time I make a center, I also make an index card to go with it. On the card, I write the title of the center, the skill, and an answer key. An (*) on a card reminds me that the center is a large one and is stored in my closet. All other centers are stored alphabetically in a file cabinet drawer. When it's time to change centers, I simply look through my card file and choose the skills that I want. Then it's a snap to locate the centers!

Beth Price

Learning Center Chart

I made a learning center chart so that my students know which center to go to each day. I wrote the children's names on library card pockets and attached them to a board. To identify the appropriate center, I made lollipops out of Popsicle sticks and construction paper. The color of the paper indicates which group the student is working in that day, and the number on the lollipop identifies the center to be used. I rotate the lollipops until each student has been to all of the centers.

Regina Atwood
Pampa, TX

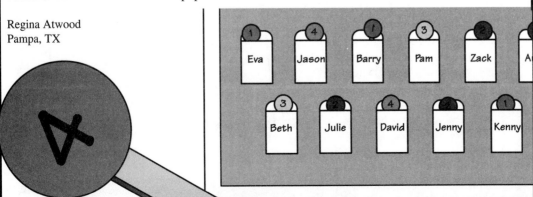

Learning Center Management

This management system is in the hands of the children, and it works wonderfully! Colored clothespins are placed at the top of a center display to indicate the number of activities in the center. When a child selects an activity, he takes the clothespin that matches the dot on that activity. (When the clothespins are gone, all the activities have been checked out of the center.) After completing an activity, the child returns it and the clothespin to the center. Next he finds his name on the "center chart" and colors in the space for the activity he completed. At a glance you can see which activities each child has completed.

Michelle Melson

Center Chart			
Pam	●	●	●
Beth	●	●	
Jason	●		●
Eva			●

Center Choice Board

Operate your classroom centers efficiently and effectively with a center choice board. Cut out, label, and laminate a construction-paper circle for each center. Attach small Velcro squares to each center circle to indicate how many students may attend that center at one time. Display circles. Each student needs a marker backed with adhesive Velcro. When a student visits a center, he places his marker on the appropriate circle at the center choice board. If all the Velcro squares are full, he chooses a different center.

Mary A. Carl
Auburn, AL

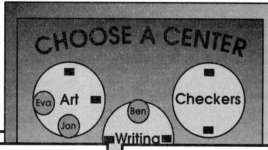

CHOOSE A CENTER

Eva Art Ben Checkers Jon Writing

Coding With Colored Dots

Use assorted colored dots to code file folder activities, games, Pocket Pals, and learning centers. Using the code, children can see at a glance the maximum number of students who may use the activity at one time.
Code:
red dot—1 student
green dot—2 students
orange dot—3 students

Cathie Weaver, Springfield, GA

Fair Chance

To keep students from monopolizing favorite centers, folder games, or skillboards, I tape a class list to each activity. Students cross their names off the lists as they complete the activities. When all names are crossed off a list, a new activity is introduced, or the list is replaced and children may complete the activity again.

Kathy Quinlan
Lithia Springs, GA

Play Area Management

Mark the play areas in the room with different colors and provide a certain number of colored clothespins for each. As each child goes to an area, have him attach a matching clothespin to his clothes. This makes it very easy to regulate the number of children in each area.

Sandy Davis, Lincoln, AR

Center Identification

A center chart with picture clues has really helped my students recognize their daily centers. I cut out and glued one picture to represent each center on a piece of poster board. Then I wrote student names on individual clothespins. Each day I attach two clothespins to each center on the chart. The center partners visit the center pictured. The chart is handy for me to check student placement or to give reminders about cleanup. By changing student partners on a regular basis, I also encourage new friendships.

Janet B. Vaughan, North Augusta, SC

Learning Center Organization

Here's a nifty way to organize your classroom for learning centers. Each week display five learning centers. Label the centers A, B, C, D, and E. Make a classroom center chart as shown. To program the chart, write a different center letter beside each group of students for every day of the week. At the end of the week, students will have visited all five centers!

Pam Miller
Graysville, IN

	Mon.	Tues.	Wed.	Thur.	Fri.
Glen Pam Eva	A	B	C	D	E
Julie Liz Jenny	B	C	D	E	A
Barry Susan Becky	C	D	E	A	B
Beth David Bruce	D	E	A	B	C
Mary Jack Alex	E	A	B	C	D

Cooperative Learning Centers

After years of evaluating center work during my free time or at home, I have finally found an easier way! At every center in my classroom, I place a list of students, which has two blank boxes after each name. The first child to use the center puts a √ in the first box by his name. No one else can use that center until I have checked the first student's work. If the work is correct, a star is added in the second box by the student's name. Then I no longer have any checking to do! Any other student who works in the center must find a "starred" person to check his work. Then that person, upon receiving a star, becomes an additional checker for the others who follow. Not only does this reinforce the work for those doing the checking, but more responsibility is placed on the students for their learning. After all names on a list have received stars, it's time for a new center!

Vivian Campbell
Piscataway, NJ

Jo	√	☆
Mark	√	
Sam	√	
Maggie	√	☆
Beth	√	

Learning Center Pens

My centers were always a mess because students marked on them with china markers and other pens. I started saving old overhead pens that weren't very "pointy" or were going dry. Now I let students use these pens to mark on centers. Students love to use the pens, and the centers can be easily cleaned off with a wet cloth. I store the pens in a coffee can covered with Con-Tact paper. No more messy centers!

Marilyn Borden, Bomoseen, VT

Table Center

I use a round classroom table as a game center. I tape laminated shapes on the table, transforming it into a gameboard. On one of the shapes I write Start, and on another one I write The End. At intervals are shapes with Move Ahead One Space and Sorry, Move Back One Space. Students place their markers on Start. Each player takes a turn drawing a word card. If he correctly identifies the word, he may move the number of spaces indicated on the card. The first player to reach The End is the winner. This gameboard can also be used to reinforce other types of skills and can incorporate a holiday theme or any theme of study. The table gameboard provides a unique change from commercially made cardboard games.

JoAnn Harmelink
Perry, IA

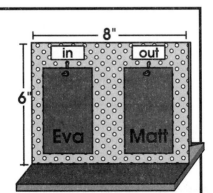

Removing Crayon Buildup

Laminated materials can become dull from crayon buildup. To give them a new sparkle, spray a petroleum-based prewash laundry product onto each one. Spray an extra amount on stubborn stains. After a few minutes, wipe it off. Materials look like new!

Charlene Granger
Olean, NY

Evergreen Center

Leave your artificial Christmas tree in your classroom after the holidays for a three-dimensional center area. Each month, program seasonal shapes with appropriate skills and hang shapes on the tree. Use snowballs in January, hearts in February, shamrocks in March, umbrellas in April, and flowers in May. Near the tree, post directions for the activity and an answer key, if appropriate. Students will complete the activity on their own paper.

Barbara Coon Roberts
La Mesa, CA

Pegboard Pleaser

Taking turns for center work is no problem using this convenient name and idea. Place an 8" x 6" pegboard into a grooved rectangular wood base. Attach two hooks to the pegboard labeled "In" and "Out." Hang all student name cards on the In hook. When a child completes the center, he moves his card to the Out hook and taps the next person.

Spotlight on Centers

The Reading Pool

I use a small children's wading pool as part of my reading center. I inflate the pool and allow children to sit inside it to read their stories. Pool rules are: (1) No more than three students in the pool at one time. (2) You must read in the pool. First-grade students love to read in the pool.

Francine Reinel
Sarasota, FL

Mirror, Mirror On The Wall

Create a personality center with a mirror, tempera paints, and paintbrushes. Students make self-portraits by painting over their reflections right on the mirror. Your daytime personalities will delight in the results!

Sr. Ann Claire Rhoads
Greensboro, NC

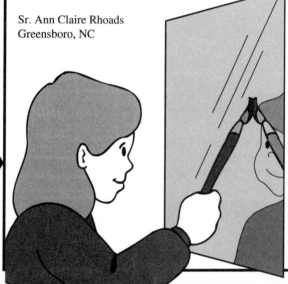

Pill Bottles And Pennies

Make a counting center using clear pill bottles and pennies. Number bottles 0–10 by writing on their sides with a permanent marker. The child will count pennies to place in the bottles. By arranging the bottles in order 0–10, he can see the progression of the numbers. To make the activity self-checking, use a marker to draw the correct number of dots on the inside of each bottle cap. Be sure to write the numeral on the outside of each bottle cap.

Nancy Dunaway, Forrest City, AR

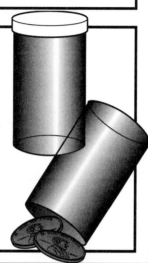

Directions, Directions

To improve reading, writing, and creative-thinking skills, cut off directions from used, duplicated worksheets. Place them in a bowl. Have children match each direction to the appropriate worksheet or guess what the directions for the sheet might be. Compare their answers with the originals. Students enjoy choosing a direction and making up a worksheet to go with it, too. Brainstorm other activities to use with the direction strips for an additional challenge.

Sr. Ann Claire Rhoads

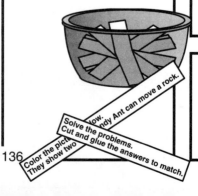

Programming Centers For Reuse

Make file folders or centers reusable by laminating them and then using wipe-off markers to write directions. Remember to also laminate all pieces of an activity for reuse.

Sue Guenther
Waterloo, IA

Magnetic Album Centers

Many department stores have regular sales of magnetic photo albums. These inexpensive albums are perfect for creating minicenters:

- Use the children's pages of newspapers to make album pages. Simply place a section under an acetate sheet and provide an overhead pen for writing.
- Make album pages of appropriate puzzles and problems that you find in magazines.
- Make album pages with math practice.
- Make a vocabulary album with context clues practice. Write sentences using vocabulary words, but leave blanks for the words. The student must supply the missing words.

Marilyn Borden, Bomoseen, VT

Center Time-Saver

If you have a lot of pieces to color for a center or activity, spray paint them instead of using crayons or markers. It's an easy way to prepare centers quickly.

Sharon Mitchell-Pierce, Bedford, VA

Wheels Made The Difference!

I never would have guessed that adding wheels to the bottom of our block storage cart would renew my students' interest in block play! But it certainly did. Now the children can easily move the cart around to disperse or pick up the blocks. It has really made a difference!

Chava Shapiro
Monsey, NY

Spinners

Do you have an empty margarine tub with lid, a brad, and a large safety pin? If the answer is "yes," you can make a homemade spinner. Using markers, divide the lid into several sections and number them if desired. Insert the brad through the loop in the safety pin and then through the plastic lid. Store game pieces in the tub and snap the lid in place.

Barbara Masiulis
Naugatuck, CT

Rubber Cement Trick

Instead of using Velcro or magnetic tape on matching activities, put a drop of rubber cement on the back of each piece and let dry. You can press the piece to the activity and it will stick, but it will also be easy to remove. Rub the rubber cement off and replace after a month's use.

Nancy Farlow
St. Joseph, MO

Student-created Centers

My kindergarten students love making their own centers! Some of their ideas include matching apple cutouts to numbered trees, and matching ghosts with lowercase letters to ghosts with uppercase letters. The student who created a center checks the other students' work and gives out stickers. Students take the centers home and share them with their families.

Sandra Falsioni
Lackawanna, NY

Shape Spinners

Make seasonal games more fun by making shape spinners. Cut out hearts, bunnies, jack-o'-lanterns, Christmas trees, and ghosts, and put numerals in a circle. Laminate and add the spinners!

Sr. Ann Claire Rhoads
Greensboro, NC

Edible Game Markers

Treat your students to edible game markers. Some good choices are "conversational" hearts in February, jelly beans during the Easter season, candy corn for Halloween, and Sweet Tarts for any time of year.

Lona Hanner
Cape Girardeau, MO

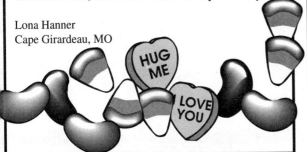

Student Centers

When making learning centers, file folders, or posters, save the coloring part for your students. They delight in seeing their work used and take better care of things they've helped to create.

Nancy Lach
Mandan, ND

Quiet Spinners

This inexpensive, easy-to-make spinner can be used instead of dice at an activity table. Simply draw a hexagon pattern onto sturdy poster board, mark a dot in its center, and cut out. Write numerals 1–6 as shown. Use a pen point to poke through the center hole. Place a pencil stub or a short piece of a wooden dowel in the center hole. Kids really enjoy using this spinner, and it's very quiet!

Jane Cuba
Redford, MI

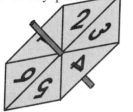

Mini-Math

Prepare a week's worth of math fact practice in an instant! Write "Mini-Math" at the top of a tagboard strip and laminate. Write in an operation, followed by a list of ten numbers, with a wipe-off marker (as shown). Students visit the center and record their answers in mini-math booklets. Each day, change only the operation on the strip to create ten new problems. At the end of the week, wipe the strip clean and reprogram. Provide supplies for booklet construction at the center each Monday. (Materials needed per child: five 2" x 8 1/2" paper strips, two 3" x 9" construction-paper strips for covers, and a stapler)

Beth Jones, Niagara Falls, Ontario, Canada

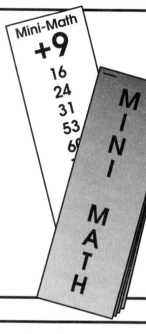

The Incredible Coffee Can

This portable center has endless programming possibilities! Cut a paper strip to cover the outside of a coffee can. Decorate and program the strip as desired. Cut out and program answer pieces. Laminate all parts. Tape the paper strip to the outside of the coffee can and attach answer pieces to magnetic strips. Store student directions, pieces, and an answer key inside the can. Programming suggestions include math facts, number words, abbreviations, synonyms, antonyms, contractions, and more.

Wendy Sondov
St. Louis, MO

The Surprise Center

Each week I place a surprise cooking, art, or hands-on activity at a large center table. Small groups of assigned students visit it daily. The children can hardly wait to find out what the surprise activity is for the week!

Sr. Mary Catherine Warehime
Emmitsburg, MD

Lace It Up

Cut out shoe shapes from poster board for a versatile center. Color and laminate before punching holes for eyelets. With a permanent marker, write words beside the eyelets on one side of the shoe and their antonyms beside the eyelets on the other side. Provide a shoelace for each cutout. Students lace a shoe by pulling the shoelace from one eyelet to the eyelet of the corresponding word. Wipe off and reprogram for homonyms and synonyms.

Debbie Crump
Centerville, OH

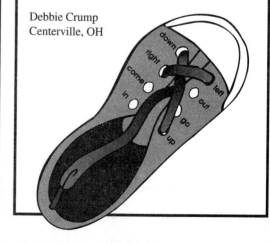

"Bounce" Into Soft Sounds

An empty fabric softener box can create a novel center for soft *C* or *G* practice. From white or pink construction paper, cut "fabric softener sheets." Write words for students to sort for soft sounds, and put them in the box. A small piece of real softener sheet can be glued behind "soft" words for self-checking.

Ann Fausnight
Canton, OH

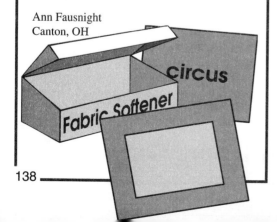

The Clubhouse Center

Cover a cardboard washer or dryer carton with flannel material. Cut a door in one side, and you have a perfect "time-out" area as well as a three-sided game area for flannel stories and flannel games. By using drapery hooks, straight pins, or tape, you can display manipulative games. The top of your clubhouse is a terrific book display area.

Maria D. Malone
Tulsa, OK

Unprogrammed Laminated Squares

Turn boring drills into instant fun! Laminate small, posterboard squares. Attach a piece of magnetic tape to the back of each card. Use a wipe-off marker to program the cards with vocabulary words, punctuation marks, math facts, or any other skill. Your students will love moving the cards around on any magnetic surface such as a chalkboard, filing cabinet, or cookie sheet.

Lisa Sulzberg
Portsmouth, VA

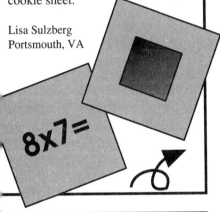

Easy-To-Make Holiday Centers

Look for two-sided decorations in discount department stores during holiday seasons. Use sticky dots to make a game trail on the front of the decoration. Glue on a holiday gift tag with the name of the game and directions. Laminate the decoration. Put a clear pocket on the back to hold question cards. Your holiday center is ready for use.

Mary Anne T. Haffner
Waynesboro, PA

Laminated Pocket

When assembling a file folder activity that requires a pocket, here's an inexpensive solution. Cut a piece of construction paper the desired width and twice the desired length. Fold the paper in half as shown and glue to the folder like a pocket. Laminate. Use a utility knife to carefully slit an opening. Slide in your activity pieces.

Terriann P. Bonfini
Bellaire, OH

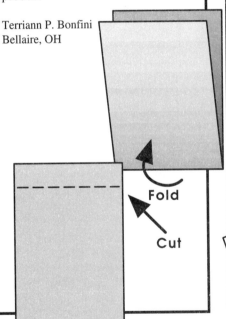

Fold

Cut

Cardboard Pencil Boxes

Children's cardboard pencil boxes make excellent centers. I've purchased ones with pictures of such things as children dressed in foreign costumes, U.S. presidents, and unicorns. I fill the boxes with related activity cards, story starters, flash cards, and laminated reading materials. Students can take these boxes to their desks and choose from a variety of free-time activities. The pencil boxes are also easily stored.

Theresa Angel
St. Louis, MO

Giving It The Edge

I make attractive file folder activities for centers by using the scalloped bulletin board borders from The Education Center. I glue a strip of border along the bottom edge of a file folder, add directions for the activity, and then laminate. Using colored folders makes the final product even more eye-catching!

Kathleen Geddes Darby
Cumberland, RI

Graphic News

Resourceful teachers are always looking for free or inexpensive items to aid them in creating original teaching materials. Newspapers, especially *USA Today,* are great sources of colorful graphs and charts. Cut out the desired graph. Type five questions about the graph on one side of a 4" x 6" index card. Write the answers on the back of the card. Attach the graph to the card, and laminate.

Janet Taylor, Rockport, TX

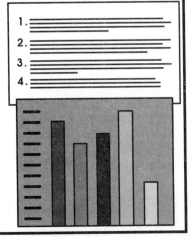

Quick Pocket

Lick an envelope and fold back the flap, attaching it to your paper, gameboard, or center activity. Now that's a speedy pocket!

Rebecca Gibson Calton
Auburn, AL

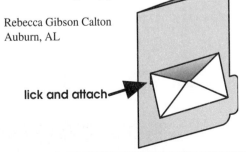

lick and attach

GAMES

Beep

Here is a noisy but very funny game to play when the weather keeps you indoors. Select one student to be IT and blindfold him. Write an *X* somewhere on the chalkboard. Hand IT a piece of chalk and turn him around a few times to disorient him. IT begins drawing a trail in the direction in which he thinks the *X* is located. The rest of the class starts chanting the word "Beep." The farther away IT is from the *X*, the slower the students chant. As IT comes closer, the chant becomes more intense. It is hysterical to see the chalk trail left by IT in his endeavor to touch the *X*.

Paper Toss

Here is a way to exercise and have fun at the same time. Have each student wad up a piece of scratch paper. Divide the class into two teams. Designate a center line on the floor in the room. At a signal, each person throws his paper to the other side. Time the paper throwing for one minute. The winner will be the team with the least amount of paper on its side. This activity really gets the students moving, and they get so tickled, they forget they are exercising as well!

Chief

Have children form a circle. Choose one person to be IT. This student leaves the room. Choose a CHIEF from the remaining children. At a signal, the chief begins a movement or makes a sound. All others follow his lead. IT is called back and goes into the center of the circle. He must figure out who the chief is. The object of the game is for the chief to lead the class in changing movements without being discovered. IT gets three guesses. If the chief is identified, he becomes IT. If the chief is not discovered, have him identify himself and choose a new IT and chief.

Milk Carton "Balls"

To minimize ball chasing, use empty milk cartons for tossing, catching, and kicking practice. The pint and half-pint sizes are great for tossing and catching. The quart size makes a super football for small hands, and the half-gallon works well for kicking.

Kay Wright
Spokane, WA

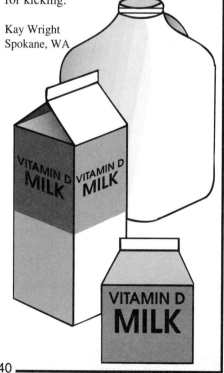

Chinese Crayons

Send one student out of the room. Select another student to be IT. The object of the game is for IT to use ten crayons to form a letter that is *not* in his own first name. Call the student who went outside back into the room. He has four chances to use deductive reasoning to determine who made the letter. If he is correct, he chooses a new IT to form a letter and another student to leave the room. If he is incorrect, he again goes outside, and play continues.

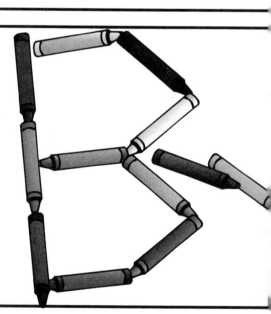

Recess Choice

Make a "recess choice" spinner to add variety to indoor recess. Pick a student to spin and determine what the class will do that day. Divide the spinner into four sections: toys and games, draw and color, group games, and listening centers. Or adapt to your particular situation.

City Of Boston

Divide the class into two teams. Players sit in a circle, and one of them begins, "I will sell you wool when you come to the city of Boston." The next player continues, "I will sell you wool and beans when you come to the city of Boston." Each player repeats what he has heard and adds an item of his own until a player misses. On a miss, a point is scored by the opposing team.

Make Him Take It

Divide students into pairs. Give each pair 15 small objects such as toothpicks or buttons. Players take turns removing objects from the pile. On any turn, a player may remove one, two, or three of the objects. Each player tries to force the other to remove the last object.

Bowling

Divide students into two teams. The first team stands. Each student tries to roll a playground ball through the legs of a student chair without touching any of the legs. The team scores one point for a correct roll. After all students have had one roll, the second team rolls the ball. Each team should have a total of two turns before totaling the score.

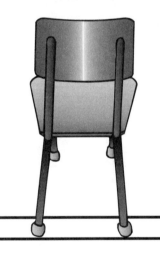

Under The Covers

Select one student to be IT and have him leave the room. While he is gone, one student is picked to hide under a sheet or other large piece of cloth. The remaining students switch seats. IT returns to the room and is given three tries or one minute, whichever comes first, to guess who is under the sheet. If IT guesses correctly, he picks someone else to be IT. If he is wrong, the teacher selects another IT.

Four Corners

This is a quiet game that involves the entire class! One student faces the chalkboard with his eyes closed. The remaining students each choose a corner of the room in which to stand. The student at the board calls out a corner number (1 to 4), and all the students in that corner must sit down. The remaining students change corners until only one student is left. That student becomes the new caller.

Electric Shock

Choose one student to be IT and have him leave the room. Select another student to be the ZAPPER. Have all the children sit or stand close together in a circle. IT returns to the room and stands in the center of the circle. The ZAPPER squeezes the hand of the person to his left or right. IT tries to catch someone giving a classmate a "shock" (squeeze). If a child is caught, IT returns to the circle and the person caught becomes the new IT. He leaves the room, and a new ZAPPER is chosen.

Pipeline

Have each student make a paper tube out of rolled construction paper. Secure both ends of each tube with a paper clip. Divide the class into two teams. Have each team line up side by side with paper tubes in hand. Have the first person in each line put a crumpled paper ball in his tube; then have a relay race to see which team can pass the paper ball through all the tubes on their team. No hands are allowed to touch the ball except the first person on the team.

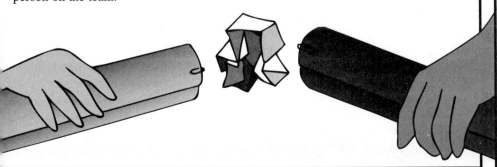

Bird, Beast, Fish

Choose one student to come to the front of the room. He throws a ball of crushed paper to another child in the room. As soon as the ball leaves his hands, he calls out one of the three categories—bird, beast, or fish—and counts to ten. Before the count reaches ten, the child who catches the ball must name a creature fitting into that category. If he succeeds, he throws the ball. If not, the child in front throws again. Try animal, vegetable, or mineral, too!

GAMES

Tennis Anyone?

If your school's budget is limited for physical education equipment or you'd just like to use something different, try making these racquets and balls with your class. The balls are made from yarn wrapped about 50 times around a four-inch square of cardboard. The yarn is tied in the middle and slipped off the cardboard. Clip the ends and "fuzz" the yarn to create the ball. Racquets are made from old panty hose and a wire coat hanger. The hanger is bent to form a diamond shape, and the leg cut from the panty hose is slipped over the hanger and tied at both ends. Use yarn to cover one end of the hanger for a handle. This makes an inexpensive indoor/outdoor game.

BessAnne McKnight
Memphis, TN

Bingo Markers

Add variety to bingo games with edible markers students can eat when the bingo's over. For a healthful snack, try popcorn, raisins, grapes, or peanuts. M & M's, candy corn, jelly beans, or conversation hearts make a sweet treat. With these fun markers, everyone's a winner!

Mary Anne T. Haffner
Waynesboro, PA

Snowball The Snowman

Set up this game for some winter cleanup fun! Draw a snowman on the board and label the point areas as shown. Place a trash can beneath the snowman. Place a length of masking tape on the floor about ten feet in front of the trash can. Instruct students to clean out their desks and wad up any papers that are headed for the trash. Collect these "snowballs" in another trash can and set it next to the masking tape line. Students line up single file behind the line and take turns snowballing the snowman! Points are collected for a hit and doubled if the ball lands in the trash can. This is a great team or individual game. Clean desks and clean fun will brighten a dreary winter day!

Cindy Newell
Durant, OK

Balloon Volleyball

Balloon volleyball is a favorite indoor recess game. Move the desks out of the way and place yarn on the floor to indicate where the net would be. Indicate in advance where the boundaries are. Children take their shoes off and play on their knees. You'll be surprised how much energy kids can burn off during this active game.

Annette Fiala
St. Louis, MO

Ribbon Sticks

These easy-to-make ribbon sticks encourage creative movement. To make a ribbon stick, use a stapler or tape to attach a 12"–18" ribbon length to a 10" length of a 1/4" dowel. Next time you have to have recess indoors, put on some music, pass out the ribbon sticks, and watch your students put rhythm in motion.

Kimberle Suzan Byrd
Wyoming, MI

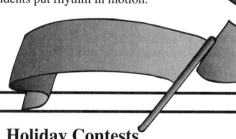

Holiday Contests

Channel holiday excitement into a skill-building contest. Print review questions or problems on holiday cutouts: Easter eggs, ghosts, hearts, Christmas trees. Write a point value on each cutout; then hide them around your room. Set a time limit for students to find the questions and give their answers. (No questions directed to teachers are allowed.) Total points at the end of the allotted time period, and award a prize to the winner.

Susie Frost, Effingham, KS

Laminated Game Pieces

When cutting out laminated learning centers, save the pieces that you would normally discard. These can be cut into squares or different shapes to be used as game cards, answer keys, or playing pieces.

Geraldine Fulton
Sedgewickville, MO

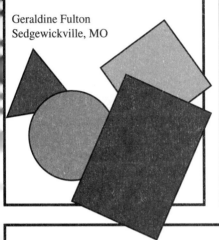

Candy Game Markers

Make games even more enticing by using colorful, wrapped candy pieces as game markers. Players will be delighted that they may eat their markers at the conclusion of the game.

Elizabeth Cole
Annapolis, MD

Skill Board Markers

Give a new look to old gameboard markers. Glue pom-poms and wiggly eyes to used colored-marker tops. Children will love steering the new critters across the gameboard.

Cherry Evans
Ormond Beach, FL

Game Dice

If your little ones have trouble handling standard-size dice, try this easy-to-make variation. Use a permanent marker to program the sides of one-inch blocks with numbers or dot sets. Even little hands can easily manipulate these durable dice.

Anne Manning
Vermillion, SD

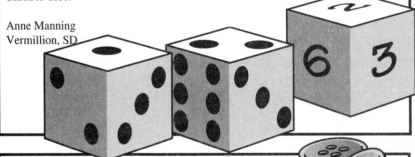

The Button Box

For inexpensive game markers, keep a basket of buttons handy for students to use.

Paula Holdren
Chalfont, PA

Adding Up Points

When playing classroom games in which points are given, I award 100 points (rather than 1 point) for a correct answer. As questions become more difficult, a correct answer receives more points. Scoring in this manner creates enthusiasm and maintains interest.

Bev Carlson
DePere, WI

Keeping Points

When playing a class game, you can keep track of team points by coordinating a season or theme. For example, at Easter time, laminate several small decorated eggs and attach magnetic tape to the back of each. Draw two Easter baskets on a magnetic chalkboard. When a team member gives a correct answer, he places an egg in his team's basket. When all the eggs are gone, the team with the most eggs in its basket wins. Variations of this idea include apples on apple trees and ornaments on Christmas trees.

Lona Hanner
Perryville, MO

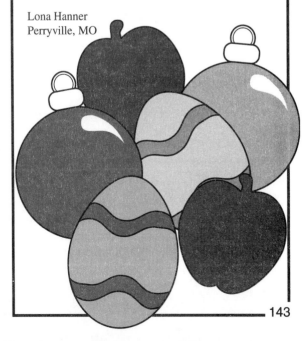

GAMES

Yes And No Cards

How about some class participation? Hand out "yes" and "no" cards to each child. After listening carefully to the question, students raise a card in response. At a glance you will see which students need reinforcement. Vary this idea by giving children vowel cards for auditory discrimination practice. As you say a word, students listen for the vowel sound they hear and raise the appropriate card.

Kaethe McGonigle
Curwensville, PA

Double Duty

Teach sight words and counting by tens with this fun flash card activity. Label a set of cards with reading words. Have students practice testing each other in pairs. Tell students that each card is worth $10. If a student reads a word correctly, he keeps the card, earning $10. If he misses, his opponent gets the card. When they've finished, students add their cards, counting by tens. Ten cards should be placed in a stack so students learn that "ten 10s equal 100."

Rebecca Gholston
Plano, TX

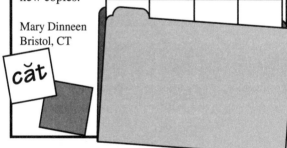

Let's Have A "Cater-bee"!

This fast-paced category game is played just like a spelling bee. Instead of spelling words, students name items in given categories. Students who repeat answers, or are unable to provide answers, sit down. As an additional challenge, have the final three contestants begin their answers with specific letters. Category suggestions: mammals, cities, things that come in boxes, snacks, ice cream flavors, careers, tools, parts of speech, insects, liquids.

Mary Anne T. Haffner
Waynesboro, PA

Instant Game Cards

Here's an easy way to replace worn-out game cards and directions. Each time you make a new game, visually divide a sheet of paper into spaces the size of game cards. Program each "card" with the desired words or information for the game. Write the directions for the game on another sheet of paper. Duplicate the game cards and directions on oaktag, and laminate if desired. Cut the game cards apart. File both originals. Now whenever your game cards or directions are misplaced or become worn out, simply pull the originals from your file and make new copies.

Mary Dinneen
Bristol, CT

Three-Finger Exercise

Students exercise their minds and fingers when playing this fun review game! Prepare a list of review questions. Use the numbers 1, 2, and 3 to assign each question a level of difficulty, making a three-point question the most difficult. Set a large bowl of wrapped candy at the front of the room. Each student chooses the level of question he would like to answer on his turn. For example, if a two-point question is answered correctly, the child goes to the candy bowl and gets one try to fish out as many candies as he can, using only two fingers. If a student misses a question, a classmate may try again; however, the value of the question decreases by one.

Sherry Ostroff
Lancaster, PA

Wipe-off Slates

Use lids of margarine and coffee containers as portable slates. Students write answers with crayons. After holding answers high for the teacher to check, they wipe them with a tissue and write again.

Glenda Lindsay, Boston, MA

Game Box Savers

Increase the durability of your game boxes with laminating film. Cover each corner of your game boxes with a piece of clear laminating film (available from The Education Center). The reinforced corners will prolong the life of the boxes.

Rebecca Gibson Calton
Auburn, AL

Test Review Game

Here's a great game for a test review. Place student names in a container. A name is drawn to answer each review question. A correct answer earns a coupon. Coupons can be traded in for prizes, additional test points, or free time. Encourage your students to submit review questions to be used.

Rose Rasmussen
Mountain City, TN

Reading Uno

Stimulate your students' interest in oral reading groups with this takeoff of the card game Uno. With students seated in a circle or around a table, have each one read one sentence at a time, beginning in a clockwise direction. At any time, the teacher can give a command to change directions or readers. Some possibilities for commands are:

1. Skip—maintain same direction but skip the next reader.
2. Reverse—change to counterclockwise.
3. Wild—reader gets to choose someone else to read; maintain same direction.
4. Take two, wild—next reader reads two sentences and gets to choose another reader; maintains same direction.
5. Take four, wild—next reader reads four sentences and gets to choose another reader; maintain same direction.

Bill Sterrett
Arvada, CO

File Folder Transparencies

Consider this alternative for playing class games: use a *Mailbox* Ready-To-Go File Folder. Make a transparency of the game for the overhead projector. Divide the class into two teams and use plastic bingo chips for game markers.

Sr. Margaret Ann Wooden
Martinsburg, WV

Money Words

This quick game is a good five-minute filler. Assign each letter of the alphabet a monetary value. (For example: A=1¢, B=2¢ . . . Z=26¢.) Challenge your students to come up with one-dollar words or 98-cent words. The value of the words may vary each time the game is played. Students will learn to add columns of numbers quickly with this game.

Beverly A. Strayer
Red Lion, PA

The Buzz Game

Sharpen skills quietly with The Buzz Game! Place a skill card on each desk. Each student needs a sheet of paper and a pencil to begin. Students write the answers to the cards on their desks. When a signal is given, they check their answers by turning over their skill cards. When the teacher says, "Buzz," students take their pencils and papers and move to another desk. Repeat this procedure seven times. Buzz your class with multiplication facts, division facts, fractions, parts of speech, states and capitals, and lots more!

Margaret S. Griffin
Stone Mountain, GA

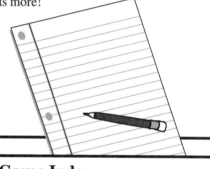

Game Index

I have devised an index to classify the games in my classroom according to skill. For example, synonym and antonym games might be A; sequencing games B; cause and effect games C. Each game within a category is numbered; for instance A-1, B-1, or C-1. I label each game with its letter and number. I also keep a file card for each game. The card shows the title of the game, number of players, grade level, and skill to be taught. The games for each subject are indexed on a different color of file card.

Kathy Horsley
Marshall, IL

Competitive Review

There's nothing like friendly competition to perk up review time. Label one box "Team A" and one box "Team B." Write each team member's name on a slip of paper and put the slips in the appropriate box. As you ask a content-oriented question, have your helper draw a name from a box. If the student whose name is drawn can answer the question correctly, he scores a point for his team. The team with the most points wins.

Sr. Mary Dorothea, RSM
Paducah, KY

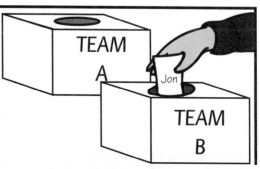

 # GAMES

Parts Of Speech Game

Organize your class for a group game by placing a card labeled with a part of speech under each student's chair. Designate an area in the room for each part of speech; then have students group themselves accordingly. When they're assembled, give each group a newspaper. Have the students cut out examples of their parts of speech; then give each group an assignment using their words. Try tasks such as the following:

— Paste your words to a poster in alphabetical order.
— Create a story or poem using your words.
— Use all of your words in one long sentence.

Sr. Ann Claire Rhoads, Greensboro, NC

Pop The Balloon

Keep your students alert by having them "pop balloons." Draw balloons on the chalkboard and fill each one with a vocabulary word or a math fact. Ask for a volunteer to read a word or solve a math fact. If the student gives the correct response, the other students "pop" the balloon by clapping once together. Erase that balloon before proceeding.

Sr. Margaret Ann Wooden
Martinsburg, WV

Classroom Jeopardy

Limitless numbers of topics can be reviewed while playing Classroom Jeopardy. Use a permanent marker to make a blank grid on an overhead transparency. With a wipe-off marker, fill in the categories and answers on the grid. Cover the answers with adhesive squares cut from Tacky Back Sheets (available from The Education Center) or sticky notes. Label these squares with cash amounts. Divide the class into two teams. A member of Team 1 selects a category and a cash amount. A correct response (given in question form just like the television version) earns his team the cash and allows another Team 1 member to make a selection. An incorrect response allows a Team 2 member a chance to respond. If he correctly responds, Team 2 earns the cash and makes the next selection. Play continues until the grid has been entirely uncovered or time has run out. The team with the highest cash amount wins.

Sr. Margaret Ann Wooden

Vocabulary Blockbusters

This vocabulary game is great to fill in five or ten extra minutes. Draw a large 4 x 4 grid on the chalkboard. Label each horizontal row with a familiar category. Instruct students to make their own chart on a piece of scrap paper. When everyone is ready, write a letter of the alphabet above each vertical row. Set a time limit of two to three minutes. At a signal, children fill in their boxes with words that begin with the letters at the top and fall into the categories on the left. When time is up, students exchange papers to check. Children who have filled in all of their boxes correctly choose the next categories and letters. Students will amaze themselves and others with their ever-expanding vocabularies.

Carol Savoldi
Plainfield, IN

	S	T	B	L
Color	sage	teal	blue	
Songs	Shiny Happy People	Thriller		
Boys' Names	Seth	Thomas	Bryon	
Cities			Bryson	Los Angeles

Cross Out

Paper and pencil are the only equipment needed to play Cross Out. Have each student write 15 numbers between 1 and 50 on his paper. After all students have finished their lists, call out numbers between 1 and 50 at random. Students cross out any numbers on their lists that are called. The first child to mark out all the numbers on his paper is the winner. Play Cross Out using other categories such as colors, holidays, flowers, cars, fruits, states, and names of classmates.

Rebecca Gibson Calton
Auburn, AL

No-Frills Drill

Slower students really enjoy making a game of review. Ask a content-area question that can be answered by reading a sentence from a page or section you're reviewing. The first person to spot the correct answer-sentence gets to ask the next question of the class. This is great encouragement for skimming.

Sr. Madeleine Gregg
Portsmouth, RI

Spelling "Monster"

To play "Monster," choose a word. On the chalkboard, draw a blank for each letter in the word. Draw five steps for each team. Add a monster to the base of each set of steps. In turn, team members guess letters to be put in the blanks (like "Wheel Of Fortune"). Each wrong guess causes a step to be erased. When the fifth step is erased, the monster "gets" the team, and the other team is awarded a point.

Spelling Bee Variation

Line students up for this spelling bee variation. When a child misspells a word, have him move to the end of the line. This allows all spellers to continue getting practice. Give small prizes to students who don't lose their places in line.

Poker Spelling

Use this game with small groups to provide spelling practice. With a permanent marker, write letters of the alphabet on poker chips or colored game chips. Give each child a set of consonants and vowels. As one student calls out the words for the week, children use their chips to spell them. The first student to spell a word correctly gets a point.

Cindy Ward
Rustburg, VA

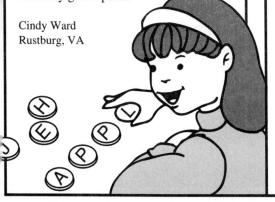

Spelling Ticklers

Here's a tactile approach to spelling your students will love. Write each spelling word on a slip of paper and place in a box. Divide the class into two teams. Call two members from a team to the front of the room. One student draws a slip from the box, and then traces the word on his partner's back. If that child can guess the word correctly, his team earns a point. Play continues until all the words have been drawn.

Spelling Baseball

When baseball fever strikes your classroom, don't sweat it! Set the bases up around your room and divide the class into two teams for this spelling game. While one team is up at bat, the other team remains seated. When a batter takes the plate, he tells the pitcher (his teacher) if he wants a single, double, or triple. A single is a word from a present or a past spelling list. A double is a word from a future spelling list. A triple is a word from the next grade's spelling list. If the player correctly spells the "pitched" word, he and any teammates on the bases advance the appropriate number of bases. A misspelled word constitutes an out. Each team is allowed three outs per inning. Play continues for nine innings or until time is called. You'll be amazed at the strategies this spelling game motivates!

Jan Drehmel, Chippewa Falls, WI

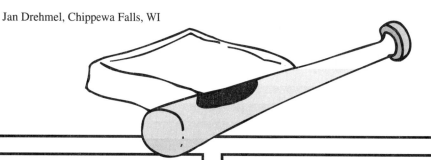

Spelling Challenge

Try this challenging spelling bee variation. When a student misses a word, have him sit down. Any sitting student may challenge a word spelled by another child. If the sitting student can spell the challenged word correctly, he replaces the child in the line. Since students know they can get back in line, they stay involved in the bee.

challe...

Spelling Bee Fun

Try these variations to add some zip to an old-fashioned spelling bee:
- Instead of naming the vowels in the word, have the student say "blip" for each vowel.
- Have the student write the word on the chalkboard with a wet paint brush.
- Set a timer for five or ten minutes. All students who are still in the bee at the end of the time limit are declared winners.

Mary Anne T. Haffner
Waynesboro, PA

GAMES

All Kinds Of Things

Spark creative thinking and provide extra credit with "quick lists." Write a topic or category on a 3" x 5" card. Each student selects a card and lists at least five items for that category. Give an award to the child who lists the most items for a specific category. Sample lists may include things found in the sky, kinds of tools, things with wheels, things you can do in winter, and types of buildings.

Lori Schmidt
Lima, OH

Things that live in the ocean.

Things you can do when it rains.

Spelling Jeopardy

Spelling drill won't be a drag when you play Spelling Jeopardy. List several definitions on the board. To the left of each definition, draw blanks to represent the number of letters in the word. Divide the class into two teams. Players take turns asking the teacher if specific letters are in a word. If a correct letter is guessed, the teacher writes it in the appropriate blank. A team may guess a word at any time. The team that guesses the most words correctly wins the game. Play Spelling Jeopardy to practice social studies and science terms as well.

Barbara Edmonds
Starkville, MS

Sentence Balloons

The entire class participates in this review game of telling, commanding, asking, and exclamatory sentences. Inflate three balloons and attach to three sticks. Label one balloon with a question mark, one with a period, and one with an exclamation mark. To play, students form a large circle. Beginning from different points, the balloons are passed around the circle, with one balloon traveling against the other two. When "stop" is called, the students holding the balloons say sentences about a picture. Their sentences must use the punctuation on their balloons. If an incorrect sentence is given, help the students form an appropriate sentence. Incorporate music as a variation. Pass the balloons until the music stops.

Pamela Huntington
Redington Shores, FL

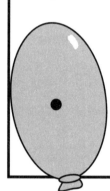

Verb Charades

Add dramatic flair to the classroom while reinforcing verb recognition. Divide the class into teams. Each child acts out a word he draws from a stack of verb cards. The opposite team has one minute to guess the verb. The team with the most points wins.

Cindy Ward
Rustburg, VA

Word Values

Need an idea for a rainy day or time filler? Using a place value chart, assign number values to letters. Display the chart and instruct children to figure the score for names, spelling words, or holiday terms.

Teri Butson
Lancaster, PA

SWAT

"Easy to make and fun to play" describes this open-ended review game for three players. Label game cards with sight words, spelling words, math problems, or other review skills. Program a piece of poster board with corresponding answers. One player reads the game cards. The two remaining players each hold a flyswatter with a square removed from its center. The first player to swat the correct answer earns a point. For versatility, laminate cards and poster board; then program with a wipe-off marker.

Kathy Horsley
Marshall, IL

Alphabet Jumping Rope

This active game promotes language development skills. While others say the alphabet, a student jumps rope. When he misses, he must give a word that begins with the last spoken letter. Another student uses that word in a declarative sentence or question. While learning vocabulary, the students also practice large motor skills.

Annette Mathias
Partridge, KS

GAMES

Shamrock Rock

Reinforce basic number concepts with this small-group game. Cut out and laminate a green construction-paper shamrock for each player. Write a different number on each cutout; then place the shamrocks facedown on a table. While Irish music is playing, have children march around the table. When the music stops, each player picks up a shamrock. The child with the lowest number is out. Continue playing until one child is left. For older students, write math facts on the shamrocks. The student with the lowest answer in each round is eliminated.

Sarah Horton, Fort Payne, AL

Alphabet Race

Race against the clock to review letter sequence. Give each child a large flash card labeled with a letter of the alphabet. (If necessary, give some students more than one card.) Obtain a stopwatch. Have the child with the letter *A* place it on the chalkboard ledge. Start the stopwatch. The student with the letter *B* places his card beside *A,* and so on until the letter *Z* is placed and the stopwatch is stopped. If the class beats its previous time, reward students with small prizes or extra recess time.

Kathy Mobbs
Southfield, MI

Telephone Trivia

Have your class create a telephone trivia game by making up reference questions using the phone book. Your students will enjoy creating and playing a new game as well as practicing a valuable life skill. Use last year's phone books or contact the phone company for possible current copies.

Susan Kenyon
Ettrick, WI

Art Gallery Game

Recycle old calendar pictures into a fun art gallery game. Mount each old calendar picture on a different sheet of tagboard or poster board. For reference, program each picture with a different letter of the alphabet and a "price tag," which features its "cost." Display the pictures in a prominent place; then have students use paper and pencils to calculate answers to problems relating to the prices of the pictures. When the game is over, place the names of the students who answer all of the problems correctly in a small container. Draw out one name, and allow the winning student to choose his favorite picture to take home.

Debbie Schneck
Schnecksville, PA

World Map Runoff

Save newspapers and newsmagazines until you have one for each member of the class. During a two-minute time period, have each student list as many place-names as he can find in his publication. Then, in a World Map Runoff, have students locate and put color-coded stickers on those locations atop duplicated maps. Have students check their maps using your class wall map.

Janice Scott
Rockport, TX

File Folder Transparencies

Turn your file folder activities into group games, using the overhead projector. Make a transparency of a file folder game and place it on the overhead. Put plastic bingo chips on the overhead to use as markers. Divide your class into two teams to play the game.

Sr. Margaret Ann Wooden
Martinsburg, WV

The Overhead Puzzle

Divide your class into two teams to play this language or math review game. Draw a picture on an overhead projector or use a plastic greeting-card overlay. Cover this with the pieces of a simple jigsaw puzzle. Read the class a question or problem. The first team to answer (through their team speaker) may remove one piece of the puzzle, revealing a portion of the hidden picture. Play continues until a team identifies the picture. A correct answer must be given before a guess can be made.

Sr. Ann Claire Rhoads
Greensboro, NC

Space Man

Are "finger spaces" between words likely to be forgotten by your students? Send Space Man to the rescue. Give each child a Popsicle stick and a smiley-face sticker to make his own Space Man. The student places Space Man on his paper to hold a space after each word. Your students will love using their Space Men, and you'll love their neatly spaced papers!

Nancy Weber
Lacey Township, NJ

Handwriting Houses

Teach handwriting placement as though letters lived in houses. Students will easily recognize and remember correct placement with this method.

Perry Stio, Piscataway, NJ

Table Writing

Quickly create a writing center your students will love to use. Tape sheets of chart paper on a table and cover with clear Con-Tact covering. Provide wipe-off markers for students to use.

Jane Dickert
Bath, SC

Rainbow Handwriting

Smiles shine when you announce handwriting practice with this simple technique. Encourage the children to bring colored pencils for handwriting practice. First, the students make "rainbow" names at the top of their papers. Next, the children choose a color to begin practice. After correctly forming a designated letter, a new color may be selected. Letter formation improves greatly while children create individual rainbows.

Dorothy P. Schenk
Sunderland, MD

Name-writing Practice

This desktop trick gives your students a personalized writing sample and practice surface in one. Write each student's name on a sentence strip and laminate it directly onto a table or desk. (The Education Center's laminating film is especially good for this, since it sticks so well and wipes clean.) Leave at least one inch of film around the edge so that the strips will stick. Several times each day, have children trace their names with their fingers or crayons on the strips. They'll be great writers in no time!

Jeanne Thomas
Cana, VA

Left To Right

Help students remember where to begin reading and writing. Put a friendly bear sticker on the left side of each desk. After a few days, students will remember to begin writing on the side of their papers closest to the bear.

Sr. Margaret Ann Wooden
Martinsburg, WV

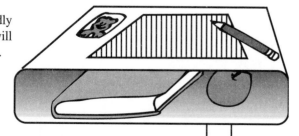

Penmanship Paper

When making a duplicating master that requires a dotted midline, use a dressmaker's wheel. Run the wheel along a ruler for a perfect dotted line.

Tina Palmer
Wolcott, CT

Slant Reminders

Have your students try this tip to remember the correct paper placement when writing in cursive. Have each child use his writing hand to loosely hold the top corner of his paper. (Right-handers hold the right-hand corner and vice versa.) Holding it in this manner will cause the opposite corner to point to his belly button. Have him draw a smiley face in this corner, and instruct him to keep the smiley face positioned so it's always smiling at his tummy. This technique ensures proper paper placement every time.

Mary Anne T. Haffner, Waynesboro, PA

Cursive Challenge

To make your beginning cursive drills more fun, challenge youngsters to determine the words they will practice in the lesson. Post each cursive letter that has been learned; then have each student determine several words that can be spelled using only those letters. After checking his words for correct spelling with a partner or in a dictionary, each student then practices writing his own words. Having a choice eliminates much of the drudgery of the daily handwriting drill.

Marilyn Borden
Bomoseen, VT

Skywriting

Have children practice correct letter formation in the air with their fingers before writing on paper. Verbalize each step as they skywrite. For capital *A* you might say, "Slant down left, slant down right, straight across the middle."

Rebecca Gibson Calton
Auburn, AL

Handwriting Practice

I combine handwriting drills with another subject area for a little "extra mileage." For example, if my class is practicing capital *C*s, I have them brainstorm to think of 25 states, cities, or countries that begin with that letter. After making this challenging list, I assign additional activities such as: circle those areas located in the United States; put a star beside the areas located in the Southern Hemisphere; put the list in alphabetical order; categorize the areas by state, city, or country. This activity may be adapted for individual or class work.

Sherry Ostroff
Lancaster, PA

The Three *P*s

Prepare your students for a handwriting lesson by reminding them of the three *P*s—posture, paper (should be slanted), and pencil (holding it correctly). After students get used to the ritual, simply say, "Get ready—three *P*s."

Mary Anne T. Haffner

Cursive Learner's Permit

As soon as we begin to learn cursive, some of the eager beavers start writing their names and doing their assignments in incorrect cursive. To head them off, I have a discussion about teenagers not being allowed to drive until they learn all about driving and have earned a learner's permit so they can practice. When the class has learned 15 or so lowercase letters, I outline the following training program in a letter to each student. When a student has received three *A*'s on directed lesson papers, he may apply for a cursive learner's permit. I will then give him a private lesson to help him write his name. After the class has learned all 26 lowercase letters and a student demonstrates his ability to write his name properly, I award him a learner's permit.

Carole Pippert
Bowie, MD

Cursive Learner's Permit

Issued to _____
on _____
by _____

You may now write your name in cursive on every paper you do as long as you continue to do it properly!

Handwriting Grade

I choose one assignment each week on which to evaluate handwriting progress. In the upper right corner of the student's paper, I put the subject's code (for example, SP for spelling) and the grade. Below it, I put the handwriting code (HW) and grade. It's an easy way to inform my students of their handwriting progress.

Mary Anne T. Haffner
Waynesboro, PA

Dial 911

Help youngsters learn what to do in an emergency with realistic telephone practice. Have each youngster practice calling either 911 or your local emergency numbers on both a touch tone and a rotary dial telephone. Stress the importance of speaking clearly. Be sure students give the details of the emergency situation and their complete addresses. For additional practice, select one student to be the caller and another to be the dispatcher. This is also a good time to have each child practice dialing his own phone number complete with the proper area code.

Mary Anne T. Haffner

Prerecorded Plays

When putting on a play for an audience, I have the children record the reading parts in advance. This allows time for expressive reading, eliminates mistakes, and frees the children to use more gestures when the final play is performed.

Nancy Lach
Mandan, ND

Recipe Writing

My class has a cooking activity at least twice a month. While we are waiting for the dish to cook, I have the children copy the recipe in their best handwriting. I collect the recipes for the children to bind in booklets called "From Your Little Cook." They make great Mother's Day gifts!

Kim Zimmerman
Tulsa, OK

Poetry Tree

"Plant" a poetry tree in your classroom to encourage new interest in poetry. Anchor a branch in a sturdy pot or can. Program die-cut shapes or index cards with seasonal poems; then laminate them if desired. Punch a hole in each one, and tie it to the poetry tree with a length of yarn or ribbon. Students remove poems from the tree to copy or memorize in their free time. Each day, set aside some time for volunteers to recite poems they've memorized; then reward each successful participant with a small prize. As speaking skills improve, stress intonation and expression, too. Tape-record students to monitor their progress.

Tonya Byrd
Shaw AFB, SC

Video Pen Pals

My third-grade class corresponds with another third grade from across the state each year. We exchange letters monthly and then end the year by making a video for each other. Our video program includes student and teacher introductions, hobby presentations, choral readings, plays, and even "lip synchs." Our classes are too far apart to meet, but it's a great way to get acquainted! Students from past years have continued to correspond with their third-grade pen pals.

Linda Piper
Waverly, KS

Graffiti Shapes

Before having students listen to a book or view a filmstrip, provide each one with his own graffiti shape. Duplicate a shape relating to the subject of the book or filmstrip for each child. As the child listens to the book or watches the filmstrip, he jots down new words and facts. After the book has been shared or the filmstrip viewed, provide time for a discussion so that students can clarify the meanings of new words and discuss facts they've learned.

Sr. Ann Claire Rhoads
Greensboro, NC

Wall Dictionary

Sharpen spelling, dictionary, and alphabetization skills with this idea. Duplicate a large supply of pencil patterns on poster board and have your students cut them out. Punch a hole in each. Once a week, write each new spelling word on a separate "pencil" and display them on a bulletin board. Attach 26 cup hooks, or adhesive hooks, to a cabinet door. Label the hooks *A* to *Z*. As you replace old spelling lists with new ones, students hang the old pencils on corresponding hooks to create a manipulative wall dictionary. Later in the year, use the dictionary to teach alphabetizing to the second and third letter.

Ruth Wehrly
Lake Jackson, TX

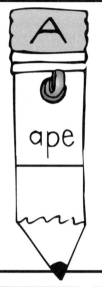

Heading Helper

To help my students learn to spell the days of the week and the months of the year, I have them include this information in their paper headings each day. By the end of the year, most are able to spell the school days and months correctly.

Mary Anne T. Haffner
Waynesboro, PA

Spelling Clues

Our spelling lists are usually done phonetically. For example, all words with the long *e* sounds are listed in the same lesson. On Monday, after introducing the long *e* words, I give the following directions: draw a red circle around all *ee* words; draw a green box around all *ea* words; with a blue crayon, underline all *e* words. It's an easy way to give spelling a colorful boost.

Susan M. Valenti
Emmitsburg, MD

Program Follow-up

Try this homework activity as a follow-up to a special program. Duplicate a copy of a letter form for each child, which features review questions about the program. After students have seen the special program, have each child use his form to copy a letter to his parent(s). Have each child take his letter home and discuss the questions with his parent(s). Instruct the parent to circle any questions his child is unable to answer and return the letter to school the next day. As a review, discuss any questions the parents circled with students again the next day.

Mary Dinneen
Bristol, CT

Spelling Workout

Combine spelling practice with an exercise session. Have students spell their words in movement, using their various body parts. New spelling words are practiced, and both the teacher and students get a good workout.

Mary Dinneen

Special Spelling Words

Spark interest in weekly spelling lists by adding a special word—one of your students' names. Depending on your grade level, you may want to include students' last names, too. This is an excellent way to emphasize unusual spellings of vowel sounds, blends, and digraphs as you build youngsters' self-esteem. The excitement is sure to build each week prior to the announcement of the featured name.

Sandra Anderson

Spelling List
room
farm
jump
<u>Tommy</u>
very
sure
some
chance

Storytime Props Packs

Reenacting stories is an excellent way for younger students to improve their oral language skills while practicing sequencing skills and recalling details. Enlist the help of older students or parents to help you make props packs for popular children's books. To make a props pack, fill a box with simple costumes and the props that are needed to reenact a children's story. Have a student illustrate a scene from each story; then glue it on the lid of the corresponding props pack. Cover the illustration with clear Con-Tact paper for durability. "Once upon a time..."

Julie Kleinberger
Bradford, PA

"Sparkle"

Try this variation of "Typewriter" (see below) called "Sparkle." Ask students to stand beside their desks. Call out a spelling word. Have the first person in the first row give the first letter of the word. Following the order in that row, each student says the next letter in the word. If the word is long enough, go on to the next row. When the word is completed, the next person in the row says, "Sparkle!" The child after that student must sit down. Continue spelling words in this manner. The last person to remain standing is the winner!

Spelling Takes Shape

Children have fun practicing their spelling words by creating word pictures. The pictures are drawn by using words instead of lines.

Jeanne Kuty
Austintown, OH

"Evaporation"

Play a round of "Evaporation." Pick a student to be IT. IT asks the other children to put their heads down, and then writes a spelling word on the chalkboard with a damp sponge. At IT's command, students look up at the word and write it on their papers as many times as possible before any part of the letters evaporate. As soon as the word begins to evaporate, IT calls out, "Stop." The student who has written the word *correctly* the most times on his paper becomes the new "sponge writer."

Stump The Teacher

What student doesn't love to "stump the teacher"? To sharpen spelling skills and learn new words, draw a student's name from a box. Have that child select any word he can pronounce from the dictionary and challenge you to spell it. If you spell the word correctly, write it on the board, discuss its meaning, and add it to a list of bonus-point words for the weekly test. If you misspell the word, the student is challenged by you to learn the word. If he spells it correctly on the weekly test (thus "beating the teacher"), he earns a sticker, ribbon, or other small treat.

Word Tap

To play "Word Tap," select a student to be the Tapper. The tapper calls out a spelling word and then taps a ruler, tapping once for each letter. He stops at a certain letter and calls on a classmate. That child must tell the tapper on which letter he stopped, then spell the word correctly. For example, the tapper calls out, "Rain," and taps twice. He then calls on a child who says, "You stopped at the letter *A* and the word is spelled R-A-I-N." If the child is correct, he becomes the new tapper.

Pasta Spelling

Give each student a generous handful of alphabet macaroni. As you call out words, have students spell them on their desks using the pasta letters. Be sure to store the macaroni in a container with a secure lid to avoid spills.

"Typewriter"

Improve listening and spelling skills by playing "Typewriter." Line up seven students and call out a spelling word. Beginning at the end of the line, each child gives one letter of the word in order. The student standing beside the child who gives the last letter spells the word completely. If a child forgets the next letter or gives an incorrect letter, he sits down and is replaced with another student.

Spelling Yarns

To give spelling practice words a twist, have children "write" a word in glue on heavy paper and press a yarn string into it. Then let the children trade papers and guess their neighbors' words by feeling the yarn with their fingertips—no peeking allowed!

Jo L. Farrimond
Broken Arrow, OK

Spell It Out

Make a set of alphabet cards for each student. Mark off three duplicating masters into 2 1/2-inch squares. On each square, print a lowercase letter of the alphabet. Duplicate on construction paper and laminate. Cut the squares apart, and store each alphabet set in a string-tie envelope. Students use the cards for lessons on letter recognition, letter sounds, ABC order, and word building.

Bonnie Marsh
Olathe, KS

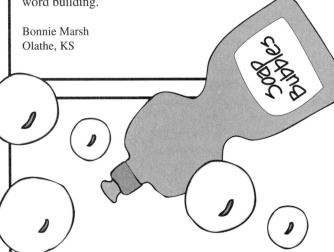

Bubble Up!

Turn a classroom cleanup into sudsy spelling practice. Fill a squirt bottle with water and a little detergent. Squirt a small amount on each child's desktop. Say a word and have each student "write" it in soap on his desk. Review math facts the same way.

Mary Dinneen
Bristol, CT

Colorful Sentences

Here's a colorful twist to using spelling words in sentences. Let students write each spelling word in the sentence with a colorful, fine-tipped marker.

Student Speller

After giving a spelling pretest, choose a different child to call out the correct spelling of each word. Children will listen more carefully, and each caller will love being the leader.

Mary Dinneen

Missing Words

Have each student create a sentence using a spelling word. The first student says his sentence, leaving out the spelling word, and then calls on a classmate to identify the missing word. The goal is to make the sentence so specific that only *one* word will fit in the blank. Continue until all students have had a chance to share a sentence and call on a classmate.

Sentence Challenge

For a real challenge, have students use the letters of their spelling words to make sentences. For example, "storm": **S**usan **t**asted **o**nly **r**ed **m**arshmallows.

Margin Markers

Since first graders have a hard time judging margins on written work, we use paper margin markers. Each student has a 2" x 9" strip of construction paper that has been folded in half lengthwise. He slips it over the left-hand edge of his paper and begins each line "right next to the marker."

Carol D. Dale
Omaha, NE

Typewriter Spelling

Put a typewriter in your classroom to motivate your students. After students have finished their assignments, give them opportunities to practice their spelling words using the typewriter. It's a great incentive!

Cindy Ward
Rustburg, VA

Spelling Signs

Here's a way to help your students improve their weekly spelling test scores. Display the spelling words on individual cards above the chalkboard where students can easily see them. Remove the cards on testing day. The extra exposure to the words really helps! Try it with math facts, and states and capitals, too.

Mary Anne T. Haffner
Waynesboro, PA

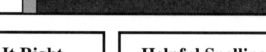

Spell It Backward

Have all the players sit in a circle. Call out fairly easy words for this game as the object is for the players to take turns trying to spell them backward. Players may be eliminated when they miss, but it is better to keep them all in the game and keep track of the score. This is not so much a game of spelling ability as it is recalling letters in an unusual order.

Write It Right

My students trade papers and grade each other's weekly spelling practice. If the words cannot be easily read, they are counted wrong. The children are tougher than I am, and the meaning of legibility becomes perfectly clear!

Cindy Newell
Durant, OK

Helpful Spelling Hint

After children copy their spelling words at the beginning of the week, staple each list to a scrap of brightly colored construction paper. This helps the children find their lists if they misplace them.

Cindy Ward

Spelling Practice

Add a little variety to spelling practice with game cards available from The Education Center. Prepare a deck of correctly and incorrectly spelled word cards and "yes" and "no" cards for each student. As you display a word card, each student holds up "yes" or "no" to signal whether the spelling is correct or incorrect.

Rebecca Gibson Calton
Auburn, AL

Spelling Study Aid

For a new method of studying his spelling words for the week, have each student cut a page in his composition book. Each student will write the list of words on the top half of a page and definitions on the bottom half and then make a horizontal cut between the sections. When studying, the student can flip over one page section (or the other) for easy, self-checking reference.

Sr. Ann Claire Rhoads
Greensboro, NC

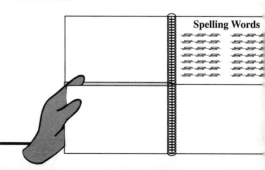

Specialized Spelling Folder

Is giving the dreaded spelling test a chore? Is more time spent on passing out paper than taking the actual test? If so, prepare a spelling folder for each student to eliminate pretest confusion. Staple blank spelling papers to the bottom half. Students use the spelling format shown on the outside cover. This takes work before school but reduces headaches later.

Marilyn Sánchez
Somerville, TX

Name _____ Date_____	
Spelling	
1. _____	6. _____
2. _____	7. _____
3. _____	8. _____
4. _____	9. _____
5. _____	10. _____

Sophie

Spelling Word Wall

A spelling word wall creates an instant dictionary for your students. To construct a word wall, label several strips of construction paper with a range of alphabet letters. Below each strip, post a sheet of paper. Then have your students help you identify the words they most frequently misspell. Write the words atop the appropriate posted sheets of paper. When proofreading students' work, simply circle each misspelled word and label it with an *sp*. This indicates that the student should use the word wall to check the spelling of the word. Add additional words as necessary, being careful not to ruin the simplicity of the word wall by adding too many words.

Marilyn Borden
Bomoseen, VT

Spelling Fun

When giving your weekly spelling test, let a child pick a topic to illustrate the spelling words. For instance, if he picks lunchtime as the topic, you would illustrate all the spelling words with sentences about lunch. This technique promotes careful listening.

Susan M. Valenti
Emmitsburg, MD

"Hole-y" Spelling

Put construction-paper scraps to good spelling use! Have each student use a sharpened pencil to poke holes in a paper scrap to spell a word. The student holds the paper up to a window or light to check the spelling.

Clay Spelling

Give each child a lump of modeling clay. After flattening the clay, have him use his pencil to "write" a spelling word in it. Smooth over the clay for the next word.

Colorful Spelling Perks

For fun, let students practice writing their words with colored chalk on black paper. Or use bright, watercolor paints on white paper.

Giant Spelling

Giant letters motivate students to practice spelling. Using construction paper or poster board, trace and cut out several sets of the alphabet letters. Laminate them for durability and store them in a large Ziploc bag. Instead of using paper and pencil, have students spread out on the floor and work cooperatively to spell their words. Students are sure to enjoy this spelling activity in a "big" way.

Donna Evert
Edina, MN

Chain-Gang Readers

Students link up for reading by joining this chain gang. Every time a student reads a book, he adds a construction-paper link to a paper chain that is suspended from the ceiling. Include his name and the book title on the link. Set a class goal, and measure the chain on the deadline.

Rebecca Gibson Calton
Auburn, AL

Reading Rafts

Inflatable water floats and tubes are ideal for silent reading corners. Even the most reluctant reader loves to curl up with a book and read.

Barbara Masiulis
Naugatuck, CT

An Author A Month

Spotlight an author each month, and watch as your students' interest in books escalates. In addition to reading books, have students locate information, pictures, and addresses of the author. Then have students write to him or her. When an author responds, students are delighted.

Pamela Myhowich
Selah, WA

Book Forum

Once a week I turn regular reading groups into "book forums." Students present brief reports on books checked out of the media center. They discuss plot, characters, and setting, followed by a short critique of the book. This method provides an alternative to individual conferences and exposes students to many good books.

Douglas Dillon
Cincinnati, OH

Read-aloud Book Jacket

Highlight the books you read aloud to your class with this unique book jacket. To make a book jacket, cut the center front of a sweatshirt from top to bottom. Sew on lengths of ribbon or seam binding to bind the raw edges. Each time you finish reading a book to your class, select a different student to use markers or fabric crayons and illustrate his favorite part of the story on a 5" x 7" piece of white fabric. Attach the illustration to the book jacket with fabric glue or Stitch Witchery. By the end of the year, you'll have a special momento of favorite books.

Janice L. Dodson
Columbus, OH

Reading Picnic

When the beautiful days of fall or spring cause interest in classwork to fade, try this reading booster. Pack a large basket with books of all kinds. Grab one or two old blankets and head outside with your class. Find a nice spot and read, read, read. Take turns reading to each other. The children really become excited about reading and look forward to the picnics!

Jeanne Thomas
Dugspur, VA

Follow-along Storytime

Next time you purchase a read-aloud book from a paperback book club, use your bonus points to purchase a few extra copies. Reward students by giving them the opportunity to follow along as you read the story aloud. When you've finished reading the book, put it in a special place along with the duplicate copies. Your students will be anxious to reread these popular stories themselves.

Mary Anne T. Haffner
Waynesboro, PA

Build Your Library

In need of more paperbacks for your library? Encourage students and parents to donate books ordered from student book clubs after they have been read. Inside each book, post a bookplate that tells who donated the book. Use a felt-tipped calligraphy pen to enhance your printing.

Mary Anne T. Haffner
Waynesboro, PA

Helpful Bookkeeping

I keep 4" x 6" alphabetized cards on my desk to help students and me keep track of book reports given during the year. Each child has a card. As the child gives a written or oral report, he records the title, author, number of pages, and date on his card.

Ginny Lichlyter
Hanover, IN

Book Cassettes

Provide an opportunity for your whole school to benefit from this activity. Divide your class into teams. Have each team select a book that would be appropriate for lower primary students and turn it into a creative oral-reading presentation. Students may decide to include background sounds, theme music, and different character voices. After the reading has been taped and enjoyed in your class, donate the finished project to the school library so that it can be borrowed by other classes.

Sue Ireland, Waynesboro, PA

Reading Nooks For Kids And Books

Instead of forcing children to read at their desks, which even most adults would not choose to do, make inviting arrangements to encourage independent reading in the classroom. For example, a pillow-lined clawfoot bathtub; a child's small, plastic (inflatable) swimming pool; a little pup tent; a colorful canopy; a miniparachute suspended from the ceiling; and even a plywood playhouse can be used for reading areas. I've seen lofts built out of lumber, large tires (thoroughly cleaned first) filled with pillows, and even a carpeted, hexagonal shape the children walk into and then curl up in to read. Use your imagination and make reading a private and personally satisfying way to spend quiet time along with a good book!

Florie Babcock
Webster, FL

Reading At Home

I ask my students to read aloud to their parents for 15 minutes every night. To keep them on track, I send home a monthly parent letter and bookmark (with a blank for each day of the month). Parents are asked to initial the bookmarks each night after their children read. Completed bookmarks are returned to school at the end of the month to earn small rewards.

Kay Jordan
Memphis, TN

Guest Readers

To promote good oral reading skills, each week several of my students are selected as "Guest Readers." Each reader must select a book he would like to share with the rest of the class and practice reading it. On Friday, each of the Guest Readers is asked to read about five to ten pages of his book to the class. The readers try to stir up interest in the books so that others will read them too. Each of the Guest Readers is given a certificate praising him for good oral reading skills. This is a real motivation for children to improve their oral reading skills and gain confidence in their reading ability.

Marilyn Borden
Bomoseen, VT

It's Transparent

For an added attraction to any book report, have your students try this simple yet great-looking way of making a book illustration. Place a transparency over a particular illustration. Using a straight pin, scratch out the design of the illustration. Remove the book, and carefully smear printing ink or paint on the scratched side of the transparency. Wipe it clean with a cloth. The etched places will retain the paint. Dry it, and it's ready for the overhead projector during a book talk or for display on your classroom windows.

Sr. Ann Claire Rhoads
Greensboro, NC

Book Exchange

Clean out those old paperback books and promote greater interest in "enjoyment reading" by initiating a book exchange. Students bring in used books and swap them for books they haven't read. All books are labeled by category as well as condition. Choose an interested student to be the librarian/recordkeeper to make sure the books are exchanged on an organized basis.

Marlene Rubin
Blackwood, NJ

Share A Book

I invited members of our community to read their favorite childhood books to my class. The response was terrific—we even had a state senator read to us! My students were exposed to a variety of books and reading styles, and they are learning that books are important to everyone.

Beverly A. Strayer
Brogue, PA

Share An Author

My fourth- and fifth-grade students did research on authors, such as Bill Peet, Ezra Jack Keats, and Beatrix Potter. After finding books by his chosen author, each student practiced reading the stories. He then told about the author and read the book(s) to kindergarten students. (First- through third-graders would enjoy being read to as well.) This gave the older students an opportunity to do research and practice reading orally. The younger students were provided with a story time and an introduction to new authors.

Dr. Rebecca Webster Graves
Burlington, NC

English For All Seasons

To add interest and music to my English lessons, I play a seasonal song that contains various parts of speech, such as "Frosty the Snowman." The children then write down the different parts of speech they hear on a drawing of Frosty. For example, all nouns are written on the bottom snowball and all the verbs on the middle snowball. The students can color the picture when they are finished.

Debra Cale
Niagara Falls, NY

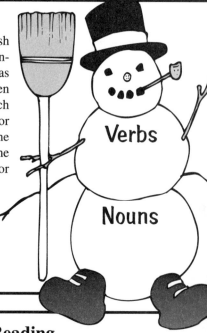

Bingo Reading

To encourage my students to read different types of books, I use a "bingo" approach. Each student receives a duplicated bingo card. In each space I have written a different book category. When a child completes a book report, I put a sticker on the appropriate space on his card. When the card is completely filled with stickers, I reward the student with a small prize such as a bookmark or paperback book from our book club.

Bonnie jo Kyles
Ennis, MT

B	O	O	K	S
SCIENCE FICTION	FANTASY	HIST. LIT.	FOLK TALES	GO
☺	FUN AND GAMES	SCIENCE FICTION	POETRY	SOCIAL STUDIES

Titles Of Books

To remind my students to underline book titles, I have them say "Put the book on the shelf" as they underline each example. As the children copy the title on their papers, I underline it on the board and draw a book on the "shelf."

The Cat In The Hat

Ellie Sulcer
Sandoval, IL

Microcassette Reporters

I encourage my students to share books they are reading by telling about them on my microcassette recorder. This helps eliminate stage fright, and students can be giving their reports while I'm working with other pupils. The children enjoy sharing books this way, and I get to listen at my convenience.

Evelyn Shaw
Tarrant, AL

Punctuation Marks

I use bright-yellow construction-paper-commas, periods, and so on with magnetic tape on the back when drilling punctuation marks. Students select the appropriate punctuation and place it at the correct spot in the sentence I've written on the board. I store the punctuation marks in a Ziploc bag and reuse them.

Joan Jackson
Biscoe, NC

Practicing Parts Of Speech

Have each child fold his paper into four columns, labeling them noun, verb, adjective, and adverb. Starting with the noun column, the students must write six nouns and then six verbs to go with the nouns. Next he writes six adjectives to describe the nouns and six adverbs to modify the verbs. When this is complete, the student must write six sentences using the words in his columns.

Cindy Ward
Rustburg, VA

Adjective Monsters

Have students brainstorm a list of adjectives that could be used to describe an imaginary monster. The students are to use the list to draw a monster. Display the monsters; then conduct a contest to decide which drawings best match the description. Award prizes to the three top vote-getters.

Cindy Murtaugh

ugly
big
hairy
short
toothy
horned
freckly

"Magic" Question Sticks

Help students write questions correctly with "magic" question sticks. To make a question stick, use a permanent marker to program a tongue depressor with a list of question words. A student can be sure his sentence is a question when he begins it with a word from a "magic" question stick.

Sara G. McGee
Evans, GA

Language Challenge

Make a game out of learning the parts of speech. Have students think of a noun, verb, and adjective that begin with the first letter of each class member's name.

O.J. Robertson
Russell Springs, KY

Joshua   jar   jumped   jolly
Nichlaus   note   needed   nice
Katie   kite
Janet   jet   kicked

Grammar Mistake Search

Before the students arrive in the morning, write the daily schedule or a story on the board, deliberately including capitalization, punctuation, and spelling errors. Keep this covered until everyone is seated, and then have the class correct your mistakes. An alternative would be to mimeograph a story full of errors and have each student correct them individually.

Robert Kinker
Bexley, OH

Subject-Predicate Switch

Create lots of silly sentences with this fun game. On a sentence strip, have each student write the subject of an original sentence in red. Then, on another sentence strip, have him write the predicate of his sentence in blue. When the sentence strips are complete, call "Subject Switch!" Each student then switches subject strips with a classmate. Have each child read his new sentence aloud. Continue repeating this procedure, alternating between switching subjects and predicates. Beware! These sentences are sure to tickle your students' funny bones.

Sr. Ann Claire Rhoads
Greensboro, NC

Alphabet Necklaces

String your class along for an all-day alphabet game! Cut out a large paper letter for each student's first initial. Attach each letter to a separate piece of yarn to make a necklace. When students wear their alphabet necklaces, they should be called by their letter sound rather than by name. If several students' names begin with the same sound, the entire names could be sounded out. Great for letter recognition and beginning sounds!

Kathleen Hess
Honaker, VA

Spelling Readiness

Vary reading readiness practice with a cut-and-paste activity. Duplicate mixed-up words written in large letters. Children cut out the letters and paste them on a second sheet in the correct order.

Claudia Wilcox
Vernon, CT

Sponge Letters

Turn letters and word practice into spongy fun! Cut upper- or lowercase letters out of foam rubber or thin sponges. Have your students moisten the letters with water, press them to the chalkboard or sidewalk, and then pull them off. Students will enjoy writing the letters with chalk after watching the pictures fade away. For an eye-catching art display, dip the letters in tempera paint, stamp them on underlined paper, and let dry.

Jo L. Farrimond
Broken Arrow, OK

Pancake Pandemonium

Cook up a delicious language experience with a griddle and a bowl of pancake batter. Ask a volunteer to write his initials on the cooking surface with batter. Or conduct phonics drills by having students spoon on batter in response to a question. You might ask, "What is the beginning sound in horse?" The marvelous thing about this drill is that students may eat their responses.

Tina Fogel
Emmitsburg, MD

Peekaboo Letters

The search is on for letters with this fun activity. To make a peekaboo letter finder, duplicate an animal or seasonal character on a 3 1/2" x 5" piece of tagboard for each child. Cut out the area around the character's eyes in an oval shape. Then color and laminate. Randomly program an 8 1/2" x 11" sheet of paper with the letters of the alphabet. Using construction paper, duplicate a copy for each child. To play peekaboo letters, call out a letter; then have students use their letter finders to locate the letter on their copies.

Elke DuPree
Alpharetta, GA

Red/Green Phonics

When your beginning readers practice identifying words on flash cards, color-code long and short vowels to assist them. Use green for long vowels and red for short vowels. The other letters should be in black.

Jo-Ann Hill
Clinton, MS

Glitter Worm Wall Display

When a student masters all of his alphabet letters, have him print his name on a paper plate and decorate it with glitter. Display the plates in a worm design on the wall and watch it grow! Add feet on the worm for mastering numbers 1–20, colors, and color words.

Carolyn Wojtera
West Monroe, LA

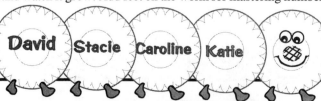

You Name It

What better way for your students to learn vowel sounds, syllables, and the schwa sound than to use their own names! List the names of your students vertically on a piece of tagboard and display it near your reading center. Use the names as a key-word list to review consonant digraphs and other reading skills. The roster comes in handy, also, for keeping track of assignments individuals need to complete.

Kathy Thompson
Nevis, MN

Our Vowel Song

Teach your students these lyrics to the tune of "BINGO" to make learning vowels a breeze.

There was a class that learned its vowels,
And this is what it sang—oh:
A,E,I,O,U; A,E,I,O,U; A,E,I,O,U;
And now we've learned our vowels—oh!
(Continue as in "BINGO.")

Susan Staats
Urbana, IL

Blue-Chip Reading

Rather than interrupt students during oral reading, I place a blue bingo chip in front of the student whose turn it is to read. This improves the flow of oral reading.

Francine Reinel
Sarasota, FL

Secret-Word Detectors

My third graders love using "secret-word detectors." Make tagboard magnifying glasses. Cut out the inner circle. Laminate front and back, and trim off excess film around edges. Leave laminating film in the center for the "lens." When searching for vowel sounds, prefixes, and suffixes, provide a secret-word detector for each student.

Pamela Aigner
Baltimore, MD

Reading Checkup

To provide extra oral reading practice, I give my students a special bookmark at the beginning of each reading unit. After reading a story in class, the students read the story again to a parent or older friend at home. The listener then initials the bookmark. I check the bookmarks the next day. I award a sticker to each student who has all but one story checked.

Kathryn Irwin
Lewisburg, PA

Reading Rebus

Children love to solve puzzles. This exercise will give them an opportunity to create puzzles as well. Attach a long strip of shelf paper to the blackboard. Ask each child to think of a word that can be illustrated with a rebus drawing. In his space, each student will draw and color rebus clues. Directly below, have him write the word he selected and cover it with a flap that can be lifted. Display the students' work in the hallway so that other classes can test their rebus reading skills as well.

Susan M. Valenti
Emmitsburg, MD

Worn-out Readers

Cut out illustrations and sentences from old reading texts. Have each student glue either a picture or the sentences on a sheet of paper. Each student may draw a picture to match the sentences, or write sentences to describe the picture.

Connie Connely
Tulsa, OK

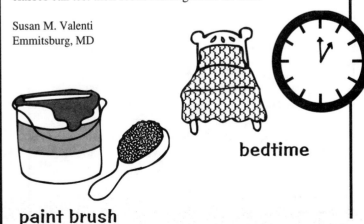

bedtime

paint brush

Sight-Word Shade

Refresh sight-word drills using a permanent marker and shade. Program a shade with appropriate words and spread it on the floor. One child will stand on the first word and advance after correctly reading it. When that student misses a word or finishes the list, another student takes a turn. To vary the practice, indicate a point value for each word. Students will enjoy tossing a beanbag on a word and collecting points for each correct answer.

Francine Reinel
Sarasota, FL

"Getting Off The Bus"

Here's a fun game to play that will prevent the hectic rush when students leave the reading circle. Students individually repeat and complete the sentence "As I was getting off the bus, I took a _____." Students, in turn, complete the sentence with thumb, thimble, thermos, and so on and quietly leave the reading circle. Responses can be correlated to the reading lesson.

Gail Cross
Bluff City, TN

Reading Aloud

Corral wandering minds when reading orally in the content areas. Have each student read one sentence instead of a complete paragraph. This forces students to follow closely, and it also lets the reluctant readers participate with greater confidence. Setting up a pattern for reading will allow the material to be read smoothly.

Sr. Madeleine Gregg
Portsmouth, RI

Color-coded Reading

Here's an idea that saves a lot of confusion in first- and second-grade classes. Assign each reading group a color. Then write the day's assignments on the board in the corresponding color of chalk. Have students place completed assignments in appropriately colored baskets.

Carole Pippert
Laurel, MD

Management Calendar

Each month I duplicate a calendar for students to help them keep track of reading seatwork assignments and special events. Students staple these calendars in their reading workbooks. This saves me time and helps students sharpen calendar skills.

Leticia A. Porter
Garden City, KS

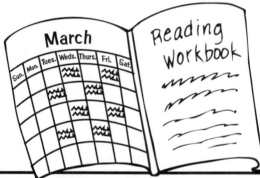

Reading Tip

To improve oral reading flow, have students try reading with their bookmarks above the line being read. This enables the student to see where the sentence ends and to adjust his voice inflections accordingly.

Kathleen Baily
Avon, CT

Word Recognition

When checking the word-recognition skills of my learning-disabled students, I use "highlighters" in a variety of colors. The first time the student reads the list, I mark correctly read words with a highlighter. At the bottom of the page, I indicate the date which that particular color represents. The next time I evaluate him, I repeat the procedure with a different color marker. Students love this colorful indication of how much they've learned.

Florie Babcock
Webster, FL

Vocabulary Necklaces

Parents are eager to help their children practice vocabulary words, but lists are boring and easily lost. Solve this problem with necklaces made from yarn and tagboard cards. Print, or have the students print, vocabulary words on cards. Punch a hole in the top of each card. Insert yarn through the holes and tie in a bow. When students need vocabulary practice, they wear their necklaces home to practice and wear them back to school the following day. As vocabulary needs change, replace the cards on the necklace. The necklaces may be unstrung to change the vocabulary list or for composition or alphabetization practice.

N. Jean Ellis
Dallas, TX

Accordion Lists

For individual skills practice, I make lists of special words (such as compounds, contractions, and long vowels) on accordion-pleated papers. Each paper is attached with a clothespin to a bulletin board. The student chooses a list, removes the clothespin, and unfolds the paper to practice skills.

Sr. Ann Claire Rhoads
Greensboro, NC

he'd
she's
isn't
here's
don't
can't

Collecting Sight Vocabulary

Write words on cards as children are introduced to them, punch holes in the cards, and hang them on a shower certain ring. This lets the pupils take the cards off to build sentences and provides a neat and easy way to keep the words together.

Mary Jane Farrar
Hamilton, Ontario
Canada

Key Word Comprehension

Key words often help children remember details of a story. Divide the class into two or three groups before reading a selection. Inform each group which key word they are to listen for (who, what, where, when, or why). After the reading, each child must ask a question that pertains to the key word. Upper levels can adapt this by doing a written assignment. Key words may be posted for a visual reminder.

Cindy Ward
Rustburg, VA

Vocabulary Practice

Each Monday I give my students ten new vocabulary words. I have each student write the words on the left side of his paper, and then write the definition of each word on the right side. After the definitions are written, each child cuts the words and definitions apart and stores them in an envelope. For review, I have my students match the words to their definitions each morning. Students can make an additional set for practice at home, too.

Cindy Ward

Vocabulary Cards

The student desk tags available from The Education Center make terrific theme-related vocabulary cards. Write vocabulary words on corresponding desk tags and laminate them. Display the cards around the classroom or in a writing center for student reference. Children will enjoy using these colorful word lists.

Kathleen Geddes Darby
Cumberland, RI

Using Basal Vocabulary

Here is a meaningful reading activity that's ready to use in a moment's notice. Using the word list in the back of the basal reader, have students use the words listed for a particular story in original sentences. More advanced students can use all of the words in the list to create stories. This is a good activity to suggest as a time filler for your next substitute.

Mary Dinneen
Bristol, CT

Main Idea And Details On TV

Try this activity to tie TV watching to class discussions. Send a letter to parents explaining that the class will choose one TV show to watch each week as a homework assignment. Then during class, discuss the show, emphasizing the main idea, plot, details, characters, and sequence. You'll find students eager to complete the homework so they can participate in the discussion.

Cindy Ward
Rustburg, VA

Story Sequence

Cut out an interesting story from an old reader for some fun with story sequence. Cover the page numbers and laminate each page. Challenge students to put the pages in order and read the story. Tie the pages together with a shoelace or notebook rings when the pages are in sequence. This also makes a nice "take-home" story to read with parents.

Connie Connely
Tulsa, OK

Following Directions On Newsprint

To build vocabulary and practice following directions, print sight words on a large sheet of newsprint. Have students follow oral directions such as: "Draw a purple circle around _____," "Draw an orange square around _____." This is also a good way to review shapes and colors.

Susie Frost
Effingham, KS

about   chop
reach   block
sell   rainy
grow   spring

Easy Alphabetizing

To cut time and avoid frustration in alphabetizing words, I have my students use this happy, hands-on solution. Each child writes the words on separate strips of paper. He then manipulates the strips on his desk. When they are in the correct order, he writes the words on his assignment sheet. No sneezing allowed until the job is done!

Terry Barton
Bristol, CT

Cutups

Try cutups in your reading class. After the children have read a story, run off a copy of it and cut it up. Each student has a part to read. After rereading the cutup, the student won't miss as many words when presenting the section orally. This helps reinforce comprehension as students deliver their cutups in the appropriate sequence.

Rebecca Gibson Calton
Auburn, AL

Alphabetical Order

Try this simple trick to help students "see" what letter comes next. Have the children trace the first letter in the words to be alphabetized with different colored pencils. These colorful letters immediately catch their attention. As they repeat the alphabet to themselves, they can easily locate the colored letters and put the words in the proper order. To reinforce this, have the class line up in alphabetical order. Each day, the previous day's leader goes to the end of the line. In no time, the children know the alphabetical order of the class—first with their bodies, then by verbalizing the order, and finally by being able to read and write each name in alphabetical order.

Judith Stechly
Wheeling, WV

Oral Reading Activity

My Chapter I students and I have come up with a fun way to read orally. I begin by reading orally. Next I call on an individual to read. Since the students don't know where in the story I will stop or on whom I will call, they must follow along carefully. Students also know that I may stop after one word, one sentence, or several sentences. I may even stop in the middle of a sentence! To keep some from dominating the activity and others from hardly participating, I ask that each child read more than two or three sentences, but not more than two paragraphs. Since stopping to look around defeats the purpose of the game, the reader should also know who he or she is going to call on next. And be sure to pay attention—you may be called on, too!

Connie DuBois
Montgomery, AL

Magic Slate Fun

Give each student an inexpensive magic slate to use during reading groups, spelling lessons, and activities involving any large group. It's easy to assess answers when the children hold the slates up in unison, and they love writing on them. I save paper, erasers, and chalk when I use one, too.

Connie Harper
Parishville, NY

Sight Vocabulary Perk

Keep student interest high during sight-word drills with this motivational perk. Intermingle flash cards featuring the names of singing groups, cereals, cars, or athletes with your sight-word vocabulary cards. This technique holds students' interest and works particularly well with reluctant readers in the upper grades who still lack an adequate sight vocabulary.

Isobel Livingstone
Rahway, NJ

Vocabulary Graffiti

Youngsters love to write on the wall, and they can when they write vocabulary graffiti. Mount a long length of bulletin board paper on a wall. Have students fill the paper with a specific type of vocabulary graffiti such as compound words or words with long vowel sounds. Display your graffiti in the hall for passersby to read, too.

Sr. Margaret Ann Wooden
Martinsburg, WV

Synonym Of The Day

I write a special word on the board each day for a "quickie" vocabulary booster. In their free time, children come to the board and write synonyms for the word underneath it. I encourage them to use the thesaurus, dictionary, glossary, and other sources to find the synonyms. At the end of the day, we review the list.

Nancy Lach
Mandan, ND

Suffix Surgery

Turn your students into surgeons to learn about base words and suffixes. Each word becomes a patient awaiting "suffix surgery." A surgeon must decide which letters need to be removed and if a reattachment is necessary. (Example: living—remove *ing*, reattach *e*.) After surgery, the surgeon must explain his operating procedure. With a little practice, the survival rate (number correct) will be very high!

Debbie Retzlaff
Elizabethtown, KY

Sight Vocabulary Drill

Use this flashy technique to add a little pizzazz to ordinary sight vocabulary drills. Write each vocabulary word on the chalkboard. Then darken the room and pull down the shades. Call on a student to read a word as you quickly flash it with a flashlight. If the child reads the word correctly, he becomes the "flasher."

Chava Shapiro
Monsey, NY

Comprehension Check

Here's a special method to check students' comprehension during silent reading. After assigning a silent reading selection to a reading group, write several questions about the selection on the chalkboard. After reading the selection, each child in the group uses chalk to write the answer to one of the questions on the chalkboard. He then signs his name after his answer. Students will be motivated to read more carefully when given the opportunity to write on the chalkboard.

Mary Dinneen
Bristol, CT

Creative Writing

Correction Corner

A corner of the room is set aside for a poster that displays a list of frequently misspelled words, which is updated daily. The children use this reference to help them with their writing assignments.

Cindy Ward
Rustburg, VA

ABC Word Board

Create a center that will help students spell words during the school year. Take a sheet of colored tagboard and glue 26 library card pockets on it. Each pocket is labeled with a letter of the alphabet. Whenever a student needs a word spelled, ask him to identify the first sound of the word and check the appropriate card pocket. If the word is not located, write it on a card. This can be a wonderful self-checking board for the class.

Danielle Lautensleger
Auburn, WA

Super Spellers

Encourage correct spelling without stifling creativity with this helpful bulletin board. Post strips programmed with five frequently misspelled and/or commonly used words on a bulletin board. As students master the words on a strip, replace it with a new one.

Kathleen Geddes Darby
Cumberland, RI

Bulletin Board Dictionary

Students can produce more creative stories as a result of this bulletin board dictionary. Label a library card pocket for each letter of the alphabet. Staple the pockets in order on a bulletin board. Cut 26 3" x 8" cards, and place one in each pocket. When a student needs help spelling a word, he brings the card from the appropriate pocket to the teacher, who writes the word on the card. The student copies the word on his paper and returns the card to the pocket. Students will soon find many words they need already on the cards. This may inspire them to try a different word instead.

Tami Johnson
Augusta, GA

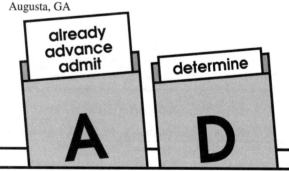

Hung Up On Said?

Are your students hung up on the word *said*? Attach a long strip of paper to a hanger. Suspend the hanger from a wall in your classroom. Challenge your students to list synonyms for *said* on the paper. When a student needs a synonym for *said,* he visits the hanger.

Pamela Ferguson
Lake View, IA

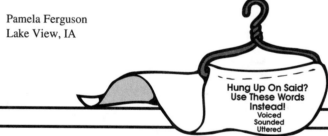

Personal Speller

Every year each of my students receives a "Personal Speller." This is a booklet of alphabetical pages in which the student can write down any new or misspelled words. The student can then check his personal speller first before asking for help. It also gets students into the practice of checking for spelling accuracy.

Eileen Lichtblau
St. Joseph, IL

Pictionary Of The Month

On the first day of every month, I ask each student to illustrate a word that goes along with that month. After the children complete their pictures, I place the words in alphabetical order, and then staple them on a bulletin board. I encourage students to refer to the board when trying to spell words or think of words for creative writing. After the month is over, I take the pictures down and make them into a book. Students look forward to changing the board each month and seeing the words illustrated with their own artwork!

Danielle Lautensleger
Auburn, WA

Creative Writing Notebook

Instruct each student to use a spiral notebook for creative writings. The student writes the first copy of a story on the back side of a page and the final, corrected copy on the front side of the next page in the notebook. This eliminates turning back and forth when editing the final copy. My students like this method of rewriting stories.

Bonnie jo Kyles
Ennis, MT

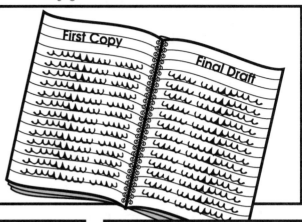

Self-Evaluation

A day or two before report cards are sent home, I give each student a list of the major subjects on which they are graded. I describe my decision-making process, for example, in reading. Do you pay attention? Do you correctly answer questions? Do you contribute to discussions? Are your assignments completed on time? Then the students are asked to determine their own grades individually and to comment on or explain their reasoning in the space provided. Sometimes I send these self-evaluations home with their report cards.

Carole Pippert
Laurel, MD

Story Covers

Using the Print Shop computer program, students can create story covers for their compositions. Using the *sign* maker, they create borders, pictures, and titles. Teachers can also create covers for students to select. Children love this way to enhance creative writing.

Mary Anne T. Haffner
Waynesboro, PA

The Year In Review

Take a cue from popular news periodicals by creating a class "Year In Review" magazine. As a class, list the most interesting events over the past school year. Let small groups of students illustrate each event on a large piece of art paper. (Don't forget to ask one group to design a cover.) Staple the finished drawings in chronological order to complete the giant magazine. Display the finished project in the school library or lobby.

Journal Writing

I have used journals to encourage my children to write. Our daily topics include ideas that are fun and require some quick thinking. Here are a few of my favorites: list cereal names; list the sounds you hear at this moment; list things you find in pairs; write things you should never do; write a list of rhyming words.

Sally Williams
Nashua, IA

Writing Dialogue

Use comic strips for a fun way to practice writing dialogue. Have each student choose a comic with at least two characters, preferably with each character speaking twice. Have the student copy the dialogue, remembering to indent each time a different character speaks. I've used this approach with great success.

Bonnie jo Kyles
Ennis, MT

Ancient Letters

Combine history facts and letter-writing skills with this activity. Have each student write a letter pretending he is an important historical person. The letter should mention important facts from this person's life and time period. Each student addresses his letter to an assigned classmate. Later in the year, pass the letters out. What a thrill to receive a letter from Ben Franklin! This activity could also be done with literary figures.

Robert Kinker
Bexley, OH

A New Middle

Many times we ask students to write a new beginning or ending to a story. Put a new twist in your creative writing assignments by asking students to write a new "middle" for a story. Extend the idea further by asking students to draw a large picture of the main character from the story. Then have them write the new version of the story on the character's middle.

Sr. Ann Claire Rhoads
Greensboro, NC

Classroom Books

Twice a week I bind my students' creative writing papers into books and place them in our reading corner. Because the books are written by classmates, they hold special meaning to my students and are read over and over again. At the end of the year, as a special surprise, each student is allowed to choose a book to take home for his very own.

Pamela Myhowich
Sela, WA

Big Book Success

My class loves to make and read big books! After writing individual poems or stories, the students glue their writing papers onto large sheets of drawing paper. When illustrations are added, completed projects are glued back-to-back, forming the pages of the book. Holes are punched, and the book is tied together with yarn. Big books can also provide a big boost to student self-esteem. As a special project, my class made and presented a big book of stories based on *The Gingerbread Man* to our kindergarten class. It was an instant success!

Janyce L. Dodson
Columbus, OH

Book Of Classmate Records

Encourage students to improve their writing skills while compiling a Book Of Classmate Records. Pose several questions for students to investigate and answer. Be sure to include categories that will spotlight every student in the class. Then have students work together to write a book about these records.

1. Who has been to the most countries?
2. Who's the shortest?
3. Who's the tallest?
4. Who has the most shoes?
5. Who has moved the most?
6. Who has read the most books this year?
7. Who has the fewest dental fillings?
8. Who has the most ink pens?
9. Who's the oldest?
10. Who's the youngest?

Robert Kinker
Bexley, OH

Hobo Booklets

Use fabric scraps to create unique hobo booklets. To make a hobo booklet, use pinking shears to cut several 8" x 10" rectangles of different fabrics. Stack the rectangles one atop the other; then sew or have students sew a seam down the center. Have students glue completed stories and illustrations atop the pages of the book. Make individual booklets for each child if desired, or publish several cooperatively as a class project.

Sandi Lewis
Ocala, FL

A Dinosaur Hunt

Capitalizing on the popularity of dinosaurs, I purchased a large, inflatable one at a local discount store. During the first week of school, I hid the dinosaur in a wooded area behind our school. Some large paper footprints led the way to the creature. After listening to a dinosaur story, we went outside on a dinosaur hunt. Not only did we find the dinosaur, but we also found the "egg" it had laid—a large watermelon. We returned to our classroom to write stories, complete with illustrations, about our adventure. After sharing our stories, we ate the "dinosaur egg"! The dinosaur became a permanent fixture in our reading corner. He is always a willing listener.

Deborah Marko
Lancaster, PA

Magic Glasses

Wild sunglasses can motivate creative writing. Enlarge the pattern. Trace one pair for each student on tagboard. Children can design, color, and cut their original sunglasses. Finally, tape colored cellophane over the holes. Magic glasses enable the wearer to use his imagination during creative writing.

Heidi Blomberg
Marathon, WI

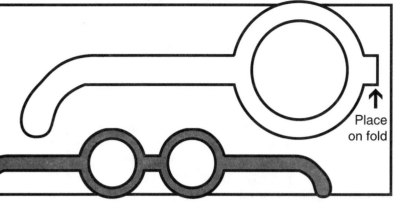

Place
on fold

In Their Own Words

Every Friday, send home a newsletter containing events of the week. This is accomplished by an open discussion each day with the class. A copy of each day's notes is summarized on a duplicating master. Leave room at the bottom for any notes, reminders, or seasonal decorations. This is a good method to keep parents informed and helps children recall daily events.

Susan Knell
Webb City, MO

Sticker Talk

On each paper, put two different stickers that illustrate a noun. Students create a ministory with the objects talking to one another in cartoon fashion. Have students "translate" cartoon talk into sentences with proper punctuation.

Mary Anne T. Haffner
Waynesboro, PA

Descriptive Paragraphs

I instruct each student to describe his physical characteristics in a paragraph and draw a picture to accompany it. I mount both of these on construction paper and write the child's name under a flap of paper at the bottom. I then display them on the wall for classmates to read. The children love to see if they can guess who has been described before lifting the flap.

Debbie Retzlaff
Ft. Knox, KY

Descriptive Snacks

To encourage descriptive writing, ask students to bring to school a secret snack in a bag. Have students think of many different adjectives to describe their secret snacks and write these words directly on the bags. Each student will then write a descriptive paragraph about his snack using the adjectives on the bag to help him. Now it is time for the fun to begin. The students exchange bags and paragraphs. Everyone takes turns sharing the paragraphs and guessing the snack in the bag. Finally the bags are opened and the snacks are eaten!

Carol Lindenfeld
Cranbury, NJ

Research Pyramid

Build a pyramid of research right in your classroom! After researching assigned topics, students complete duplicated research forms. Completed forms are cut apart and glued to the sides of boutique tissue boxes. Cover the tops and bottoms of the boxes with construction paper squares. Stack the boxes in a pyramid shape at a center. Students visit the display and learn from the research their classmates have done.

Wendy Sondov
St. Louis, MO

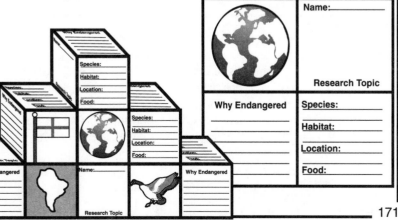

Fan Mail Fun

As you finish your unit on letter writing, post a list of NFL football teams and their addresses. (Check a current world almanac for a list of team addresses.) Have each student bring in a stamped envelope and write a fan letter to his favorite team. In a few weeks, your class will be buzzing with the news of surprise-filled letters from across the country. Bumper stickers, team pictures, and interesting schedules will motivate students to write more letters. Check the most current issue of *Free Stuff For Kids* (Meadowbrook Press) for additional addresses.

Cindy Newell
Durant, OK

Good Fortune

Here's a sweet treat of a writing idea! To begin, the student writes a brief fortune predicting good luck for someone else. He then cuts off the corner of an envelope and colors it yellow or orange to make a paper fortune cookie. (The size of the corner will depend on the length of the fortune.) After placing his fortune inside the "cookie," the students tapes the open end shut and fold the cookie slightly in half. Store the cookies in a cookie jar. On the next rainy day, pass the jar around and enjoy a little good fortune!

Jeffrey Kuntz
Punxsutawney, PA

Today is your lucky day!

"What's Up, Doc?"

Scenes from coloring books made into transparencies perk up flagging interest in creative writing. Choose a picture that is full of action and contains several familiar characters, such as Bugs Bunny and Elmer Fudd. Display the picture and ask students to write about what they see on the screen. Set a five-minute time limit and instruct students to write quickly, paying no attention to spelling and punctuation. When the time is up, ask some of the students to share what they wrote. Complete the activity by having each student produce a finished piece about the picture, including a title and good form. Variation: Ask the students to write about what happened before or after the scene you are projecting.

Janice Scott
Rockport, TX

Journaling

At the beginning of each year, my students make journals by binding loose-leaf paper in wallpaper covers. At least twice a week, I have the children write about something that happened and how it made them feel. A journal is a wonderful avenue for self-expression.

Sr. Joanne Francis
Watertown, NY

Color-coded Research Papers

My class begins a research paper by formulating an outline. I assign a different color to each subtopic. The students gather notes, skipping a line between each note. When note taking is completed, I teach students to color-code each note by underlining it with the color of one of the subtopics. After students have used crayons to underline each note, they can group all notes of the same color into a paragraph. Each paragraph is then written, putting the notes in the proper sequential order. Even my slower students surpass my two-page minimum using this method!

Chris Christensen
Las Vegas, NV

Story Starters

Put the beginning of a sentence on the board and set a timer for three to four minutes. Encourage students to complete the sentence and formulate stories using their imagination. Emphasize that these will not be checked for mistakes since the activity is to help students see writing as fun and easy. At the end of the time period, ask for volunteers to read their short stories to the class. Collect and date these, and place them in the students' folders so that throughout the year they'll be able to see their progress.

Linda Ferkinhoff
White Mountain, AK

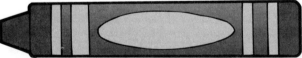

It was a rainy day when...

Free For All

As part of a letter-writing center, provide addresses where students can write for interesting free materials. These addresses can be collected from magazines or from books devoted to providing freebies for kids. To complete the letter-writing assignment, students must bring examples of the free things they've received for classroom display.

Janice Scott
Rockport, TX

Card Stories

Let students use card-game characters as story characters! Give students a card from a deck of Old Maid or Slap Jack. Encourage students to write stories or poems using the character on the card as the main character. Put the creative writing and cards on a bulletin board or display them in booklet form.

Dr. Rebecca Webster Graves
Burlington, NC

Mini Information Books

Research can be exciting for students due to their natural curiosity and the opportunity to work in the library. After approving student-chosen topics, provide each child with several small, blank pages. After consulting a variety of sources, the student writes one important fact, in his own words, on each page. He then adds an illustration to each page and designs an original cover with a title. Ambitious students may include a bibliography, copyright information, a preface, or a dedication. The finished books are then stapled or bound with glue and wide strips of clear tape. The students are often inspired to create more books in their spare time. They have also learned to choose pertinent information, avoid plagiarism, and use a variety of resources.

Pamela Barni
Sunbury, PA

Changing Old To New

Student-created filmstrips make great aids for book reports. Old filmstrips or 35mm film comes clean when soaked in a solution of chlorine bleach and water. The clean film can then be marked off into filmstrip frames and drawn or written on with thin-line markers.

Janice Scott

Show-And-Tell Update

In upper grades, turn show-and-tell into a writing activity. Have each pupil bring something to show, but instead of telling about it, the student must write about it. During show-and-tell, the students present their objects as they read their papers to the class.

Isobel Livingstone
Rahway, NJ

Sticky Business

Let students stretch their imaginations while having a firsthand experience with bubble gum. List several of the following activities on the chalkboard. Give each child a piece of sugarless bubble gum. He chews the gum while he completes an activity; then the bubble gum is rewrapped and thrown away.

Janice Scott

STICKY BUSINESS

- Write a descriptive paragraph about bubble gum. Tell how it looks, smells, feels, tastes, and sounds.
- Think of as many story starters as you can that are about bubble gum. Choose one and write a bubble gum story.
- Count and record how many chews you get from your bubble gum before the taste is gone. Write a letter to Mr. Stick E. Business, of Bubble Power, telling him how to improve the lasting taste of his bubble gum.
- Write down all the ways you can use bubble gum. Be creative!
- Write the directions for blowing a bubble.
- Write a letter to your principal telling him or her why you think bubble gum should be allowed in school.
- List ten reasons why bubble gum cannot be chewed at school on a normal basis. Choose one reason and make a poster to support it.

Picture This!

Provide great writing motivation and put an end to the often-repeated phrase "I don't know what to write about!" with this easy-to-make center. Keep a camera close at hand and snap candid photographs of special classroom and school activities. Color, cut out, and glue a construction paper camera to the front of a file folder. Inside the folder draw a picture frame slightly larger than your photograph and write student directions and guidelines. Laminate the folder; then tape a photograph inside the frame. When desired, just replace the existing photograph and you have a brand-new writing center!

Kathy Quinlan
Lithia Springs, GA

Article Analysis

This activity teaches a skill that will prepare students for all kinds of reading. Choose articles from magazines for children to read. Select three of the articles and answer these questions together as a class.

1. Why did the author write this article?
2. How did the author gather his or her information?
3. What did the author find out?
4. Do you agree or disagree with the author?

Then turn kids loose to read whatever they like and do their own article analysis. Many of the average and above-average students can handle this assignment on their own and will enjoy hearing what their classmates have read about.

Dr. Rebecca Webster Graves
Burlington, NC

Demonstration Speeches

Children in my third-grade class enjoy demonstrating how to do or make something for the class. This activity gives students a chance to develop oral skills, understand order and sequence, and learn how to follow and give directions. It's as much fun to watch as it is to do!

Pamela M. Hartley
Twin Falls, ID

Invite A Columnist

Invite a columnist from your local newspaper to your class when students are studying the writing process. By sharing some of his or her work in the middle of revisions, as well as finished work, the speaker may help students realize that rewrites can be worthwhile. This activity has also encouraged some of my students to read the newspaper on a more regular basis.

Diane Richwine
York Springs, PA

Star Quality

Set up a fan mail center for letter writing. Let students choose from a list of favorite rock and movie stars and their addresses. Current addresses can be obtained from fan magazines from the supermarket. Have students request pictures or information about their stars. My students got gratifying responses in almost every instance.

Janice Scott, Rockport, TX

Bonus Boxes

Challenge centers can be made in a matter of minutes using pencil boxes decorated with theme pictures such as dinosaurs, sports, or wildlife. Using the theme, write bonus research questions on index cards. Store the cards inside the box. Indicate the difficulty of the questions by placing colored sticky dots on the cards. Be sure to encourage students to contribute questions to the bonus boxes, too!

Mary Anne T. Haffner
Waynesboro, PA

Opposites Booklet

Draw lines dividing several papers in half and label halves with corresponding antonyms. Have each student choose a page to illustrate. Collect the pages and staple them into a booklet for the class to enjoy.

Cynthia Albright
Tyrone, PA

Memorizing Math Facts

For students having difficulty with math facts, have them try some of these "home remedies":

- Choose a difficult fact and "write it" on the bathroom mirror in soap. You can concentrate on the fact while brushing your teeth.
- Put flash cards with math facts on your dresser. Facts can be recited while you're getting dressed.
- Play a cassette tape of math facts while riding to school.

Sr. Ann Claire Rhoads
Greensboro, NC

Roll Call Math Drill

To brush up on basic math skills, I made seasonal cards and printed an addition or subtraction fact on each one. I gave one card to each child to memorize as his own special fact for the day. The next morning, each student answered roll call with his special fact. After lunch, the students passed their cards on and received a new fact to learn.

Nettie Brandt
Gretna, MB
Canada

Counting Caterpillar

To help students learn to count to 100, use Buster the Counting Caterpillar. To make Buster, cut out a head and tail from poster board. Use markers to add details. Cut ten 4-inch circles from each of ten different colors of construction paper. Cut one 4-inch circle from aluminum foil. Program the colored circles (20s one color, 30s another color, and so on) with the numbers 0 through 99; then program the foil circle with the number 100. Store the circles in a pail. Have each child randomly draw several circles from the pail. Place Buster's head on the floor; then have children place their circles in numerical order behind Buster's head to form his body. When all numbers are in place, complete Buster by adding his tail.

Sandra Anderson
Montevideo, MN

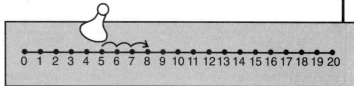

Making Math Facts Fun

Purchase slide frames from a photography store to create a fun math drill. Insert pieces of acetate into the frames and write math facts on them with a permanent marker. Place the slides in a carousel that attaches to your slide projector. This works well with vocabulary words, too.

Pat Miller
St. Petersburg, FL

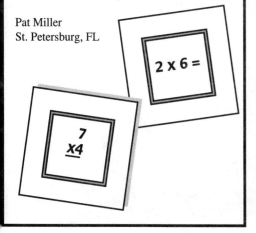

Laminated Number Lines

To reinforce the basic concepts of addition and subtraction, have students use individually laminated number lines marked 0 to 20 as gameboards. Have students place game markers on the number lines to show the first number in a number sentence. Students add the second number by moving right, or subtract it by moving left. Basic facts can be practiced by the entire class, in small groups, or individually.

Karen Morrell
Beavercreek, OH

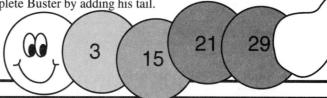

Hopping Along With Math Facts

This giant number line will have your students hopping to learn their math facts. Program poster board lily-pad cutouts with the numbers 0–18, and laminate them. At equal intervals, attach the cutouts to the floor along a length of yarn or rope. Students hop forward along the number line to add, and backward to subtract.

Ann Chiodi
Barnegat, NJ

Math

Pencil Lists

Make pencil lists for your students who need extra practice with math facts. Duplicate small lists that can be attached to pencils. When students have a spare moment, the lists are available for immediate practice.

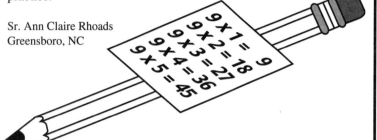

Sr. Ann Claire Rhoads
Greensboro, NC

The Chair Game

Here's a math review game that will keep your children interested in sitting down! One child is selected to sit in a chair facing the class, while a second student stands behind him. A flash card is shown. When the seated child correctly responds first, he remains seated and another child takes a turn behind the chair. When the standing child correctly responds first, he sits in the chair and another classmate stands behind the chair. Continue play until everyone has had a chance to sit in "the chair"!

Sister Mary Dorothea, RSM
Paducah, KY

Facts Certification Test

To help students master math facts, give a certification test for each operation. To pass the test, students must complete 100 facts in five minutes or less with 100 percent accuracy. (Vary the number of facts and the time limit to meet the needs of your students.) Students sign up for a test when they feel they are ready. When a student passes a test, have the principal present him with a special certificate; then take his picture and display it on a bulletin board or in the hall.

Mary Anne T. Haffner
Waynesboro, PA

Deal For Division

Make a big deal of division practice! Use a deck of cards labeled with division facts. The dealer deals one card to each player. Each player must say the correct answer. The player with the highest quotient in each round gets a point. The player with the most points after all cards have been dealt is the winner.

Anne Runyon
Littleton, CO

Musical Math Facts

This musical twist makes practicing math facts fun. Have students form a large circle; then place a flash card on the floor in front of each student. Start the music and have students march around the circle. When the music stops, each student picks up the flash card that is on the floor in front of him. If a student can correctly solve the problem on his flash card, he remains in the game. If he can't, he is out. Play continues until only a few students remain standing. These remaining students are declared the winners.

Ann Chiodi
Barnegat, NJ

Place Value On The Overhead

Inexpensive plastic needlepoint canvas is great for place-value practice. Cut canvas into grids of 100 squares, columns of 10 squares, and single ones. Place on the overhead projector and project onto the screen.

Mary B. Hines
Kingston, TN

Concentration Math

Improving memory skills is a bonus in this math game. Write math facts on one color of cards and the answers on another color of cards. Prepare an answer key. Shuffle the cards and lay them facedown on a table. A student turns over a card of each color. If the student has selected a matching fact and answer, he may keep the cards. If the cards aren't a matching pair, he turns them facedown again. Players take turns and check with the answer key. The student who has the most cards wins.

Cindy Ward
Rustburg, VA

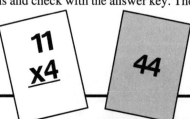

Place-Value Helpers

To help students remember to write zeros as place holders in larger numbers, use these place-value helpers. Have each student use a marker to visually divide a Popsicle stick into five sections; then label each section with its place value (ones through ten thousands). Students use their helpers to help them check to make sure they've written the correct number of digits for a particular number.

Sr. Ann Claire Rhoads
Greensboro, NC

Holiday Place Value

Use these holiday treats as place-value manipulatives:

Holiday	Denotes Tens	Denotes Ones
Valentine's Day	candy kisses	cinnamon hearts
Easter	back jelly beans	pastel jelly beans
Halloween	candy pumpkins	candy corn
Thanksgiving	candy corn	popcorn
Christmas	peppermint candy	gumdrops

Mary Anne T. Haffner
Waynesboro, PA

Place-Value Practice

Place value takes on a new look with this easy-to-make activity. You will need the single-digit playing cards from an old deck. Program the back of each card with a four-digit number that includes the numeral from the front of the card. Next, write *O, T, H,* or *TH* (ones, tens, hundreds, or thousands) to correspond with the placement of this numeral in the four-digit number. The student decides which numeral is in the programmed place (O, T, H, TH), and then turns the card to check.

Geraldine Fulton
Sedgewickville, MO

Pom-Pom Place Value

Pom-poms make wonderful manipulatives for teaching place value. Use the smaller ones to represent ones and the larger ones to represent tens. Attach a small piece of magnetic tape to each pom-pom for easy display on a magnetic chalkboard. Students love these colorful, fuzzy manipulatives.

Mary Anne T. Haffner

Sideways Math

Help your students achieve straight columns while calculating math problems with this little math twist. Instruct students to turn their papers sideways and use the lines as column dividers. A new angle can make all the difference in the world!

Cindy Newell
Durant, OK

Number Board

Reinforce whole number and decimal place value with this easy-to-make chart. Use heavy paper (12 inches wide) and fold as shown. Tape or staple the edges to make the chart stand alone. Cut several 1" x 3" strips of construction paper for digit cards, commas, and decimal points. Each student should have three comma cards, one decimal-point card, and several digit cards. As you read out a whole number or decimal number, each student will display the number on his chart.

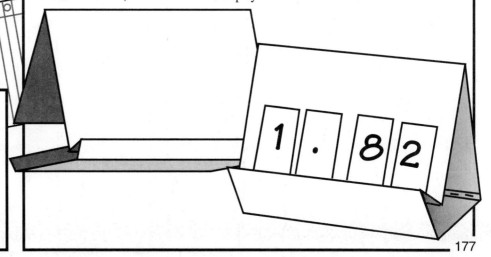

Tens And Ones

Having trouble getting your students to remember that the tens are on the left, and the ones are on the right? Have them write "to" above the number and then draw a line down the middle.

Gretchen Lewis
Boone, NC

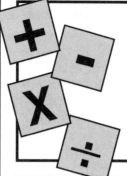

Math

Graph Cards

Graphing is quick and easy with graph cards. Have each child label a 3" x 5" index card with his name, and then decorate his card as desired. Store the cards in a Ziploc bag. Whenever you wish to graph students' preferences or opinions, distribute the cards. Have each child display his card in the appropriate place on the graph. The information is ready for instant interpretation and discussion.

June Assenheimer
Baldwinsville, NY

What's Your Sign?

Drill the whole class in one-step problem solving. Give each student a light-colored piece of construction paper to cut into fourths. On each fourth, have the student draw a different math sign, large enough to be read from anywhere in the room. When you read a one-step word problem, each student holds up the card with the correct sign.

Janice Scott
Rockport, TX

Graphs

To help reinforce the concept of graphs, use them to tally scores in class games or elections. Either bar graphs or line graphs can be utilized. This really helps students understand the concepts used in making and reading graphs.

Mary Dinneen
Bristol, CT

Consumers Can Be Producers, Too

As a class, decide to provide a product or service at your school. Create a school logo to have imprinted on T-shirts or tie-dye shirts to sell as class fund-raisers. Older students may set up a school supply store to sell pencils, paper, and erasers to other grades as well. Your class will benefit by experiencing the laws of supply and demand. Have students keep track of sales on a daily basis to discover which items are in demand and which should go on sale.

Operation Determination

Selecting the correct operation can often be the most challenging step in solving word problems. Supply four sets of cards in different colors. Give each student a card of each color. List the four operations and the color that represents each operation on the board. Read or display a word problem for the class. The student holds up the card that corresponds to the correct operation. At a glance, you can determine whether instruction is necessary before continuing.

Jewel Harmon
Mountain City, TN

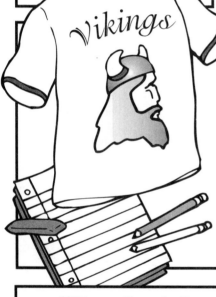

"Photo-Graphs"

Personalize class graphs with student photos. Xerox each child's school photo; then trim it to the desired size and laminate it. If desired, back each one with felt for display on a flannelboard. Use the photos to indicate each child's preference when graphing information. The photos can also be used to personalize word problems. Students get more involved with math when these photos are used.

Sherry Kay
Stoughton, WI

thousands	hundreds	tens	ones

Playing The Numbers

Play this game of chance for a quick review of place value. Have each student draw and label a thousands, hundreds, tens, and ones column on his paper. Remove all face cards and tens from a deck of playing cards. To play, draw a total of four cards, one at a time. Students strategically write each number in a column in hopes of making the largest possible number. Numbers may not be moved once they have been written. Players may also play to make the smallest possible number. Challenge students further by increasing the number of place-value columns.

Marie Brost
Gladstone, ND

Time Cards

Help your students learn how to tell time with grandfather clock flash cards. Stamp clock faces onto blank cards shaped like grandfather clocks. Program times on the clock faces and write the answers on the back.

Kathy Graham
Twin Falls, ID

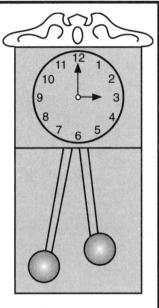

A Balancing Act

Take a hands-on approach to weight measurement with this teacher-made balance scale. You will need one wire coat hanger, two aluminum tart pans, four 8-inch wire lengths, and two 10-inch wire lengths. Punch two holes in each pan rim. Thread an 8-inch wire length through each hole. Twist the wire ends, securing the wires to the pans. Bring the wire pieces together above the pans and twist. Using the 10-inch wire lengths, attach the pans to the hanger. Cover wire ends with tape and your balance is ready to hang. Challenge students to compare the weights of various items placed at the center; then make estimations based on their findings.

Vita Campanella-Feldstein
Brooklyn, NY

Temperature Update

On a large line graph, chart the daily temperature of your city and an ocean-front city. Use a daily newspaper to gather needed information, or arrange for a daily call to a weather station in your area. As a class, compare and contrast the temperatures. Then have students create word problems using the information from the graph.

Velcro Time Telling

Students will think telling time in five-minute intervals is "cinchy" with this class-size clock! Draw a large clock face on poster paper. Cut it out, leaving a wide border. Using a contrasting color, cut out 12 construction paper circles. Number the circles by fives to 60. Attach Velcro to the circle backs. In the clock border next to the hour numbers, attach Velcro dots. Fasten the numbered circles in place and the clock is ready to use. Or remove the circles from the clock, and have students replace them in their correct positions.

Dartha J. Williamson
Athens, GA

Economical Practice Clocks

Make clocks for time-telling practice from common classroom supplies. On construction paper rectangles, paste clock faces without hands, or use a clock-face stamp. Laminate the cards. Provide a card, tissue, and wipe-off crayon for each student. Call out a time. Students respond by drawing hands on their clocks to indicate times. Have students erase using tissue, and continue practicing.

Dartha J. Williamson

Pillow Time

Start the clock for time-telling practice, and improve motor skills. Sew felt numbers onto a round pillow to make a clock face. Attach felt clock hands in the center of the pillow with a button. Add a button beside each number on the clock's face. Cut a slit in each clock hand for a buttonhole. Program tagboard cards with times, and draw a clock on the back of each card to show the correct answer. A child picks a card, buttons the pillow hands to the correct time, and checks his answer on the back of the card.

Debbie Giamber
Falls Church, VA

Timely Idea

Ever have trouble getting the hands to stay put as you demonstrate with a cut-out clock? Eliminate this problem by making a transparency with a brad. Place on your overhead projector for easy viewing by the whole class. The clock hands will stay put while your hands are free to teach.

LaVaughn Gooch
Denver City, TX

Math

Inequality Shoot-out

Students have no trouble remembering correct usage of inequality symbols (>, <) with this catchy reminder. I tell students that "the big guy shoots arrows at the little guy." In an inequality, it's easy for students to see that the arrow is pointed at the little number.

Mary Hemp
Hill City, KS

Clear Measures

To teach students about angles, I use a clear plastic protractor on the overhead projector. The projector enlarges the numbers, making it easy to demonstrate how to draw and measure angles.

Dr. Rebecca Webster Graves
Burlington, NC

Worms

This measurement activity is appealing to students and simple for you to prepare. You will need varying lengths of ribbon in different colors, decorative adhesive covering, and a coffee can with a lid. Cover the can with adhesive covering, and place the ribbons inside. Attach an answer key to the bottom of the can to make this activity self-checking. Students remove each ribbon, write its color and measurement in inches and centimeters on their papers, and check the answers using the answer key.

Betty Brooks
Filer, ID

Flavorful Fractions

Here's an instructional technique for teaching fractions that's guaranteed to hold your students' attention. When introducing fractions, explain that there are two types of fractions—Hershey bar fractions (parts of a whole) and M & Ms fractions (parts of a set). Using both types of candy as visual aids, divide them into fractional parts and sets. When your students have internalized the lesson mentally, divide the candies into fractional parts and internalize them physically. Now that's a "tasteful" math lesson!

Hannah Means
Cheshire, CT

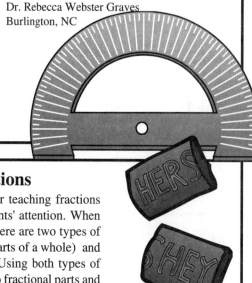

Count In Time

Combine counting, listening, and observation skills with this activity. Arrange your students in three rows. Row 1 begins counting aloud in unison as Rows 2 and 3 listen and watch the teacher. When the teacher raises his hand, Row 1 stops counting and Row 2 continues. Row 3 will begin to count when the teacher raises his hand again. The students will be tuned in and ready to count!

Sr. Margaret Ann Wooden
Martinsburg, WV

Geometric Scavenger Hunt

Here's a fun approach to reviewing geometric terms. Challenge your students to locate a list of shapes somewhere in your classroom, in your school, or on your school grounds. Provide students with duplicated lists, instructing them to record where they find each shape beside its name. Set a time limit before the hunt begins. After the game, let students share the locations of various shapes and award themselves five points for each shape they located.

Paula K. Holdren
Chalfont, PA

Money Cups

Before beginning a unit on money, I prepare a large drinking cup with appropriate play-money coins for each child. The cups are placed on a plastic serving tray until the lesson begins. This gives each student his own supply of money for the lessons and keeps the coins from getting lost.

Carol D. Dale
Omaha, NE

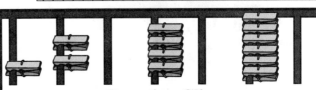
Counter Collectors

Corral manipulatives with these counter collectors. To make a counter collector, line the lid of a one-gallon ice cream pail with felt. Have each student use a counter collector when working with small manipulatives such as beans. Students will have neat, quiet spaces for counting, and fewer manipulatives will end up on the floor.

Bonnie jo Kyles
Ennis, MT

Flannelboard Math Fun

Individual 9" x 12" flannelboards work wonders in my math class. I use them to teach number concepts, review sets, practice addition and subtraction facts, and play math games. "Match Me" is a favorite math game using felt shapes and the flannelboards. Students try to make the same design on their flannelboards that I make on mine.

Judy Lee
Letcher, SD

Putting It All Together

To help teach number sets, use interlocking building blocks. Children snap together blocks into groups to show different sets. Use the blocks to reinforce addition and subtraction facts, also. Two blocks snapped to three blocks shows 2 + 3 = 5. Reverse the process for subtraction.

Myrna Kokales
Aberdeen, SD

Personal Chalkboards

Keep children on task during math class with personal chalkboards. Give each child a small slate and a piece of chalk. Write a problem on the board or overhead projector, and have the children work the problem on their slates. When all students have finished, ask them to hold up their slates. At a glance, you'll be able to identify students who are having difficulty with the concept. Let each child use an old, clean sock to wipe off his slate. Children can store their pieces of chalk in their socks after the math period is over.

Brenda H. McGee
Plano, TX

Counting Clips

To catch up on counting skills, put large paper numerals on the bulletin board. Under each numeral, hang a heavy piece of rug yarn. Students clip the correct number of clothespins under each numeral.

Sue Guenther, Waterloo, IA

Clothespin Math

Your students will enjoy number recognition practice when you use this manipulative approach. Have each student bring in 20 clothespins. To begin the activity, ask students to turn their chairs around and sit facing the backs of their chairs. Hold up a number card and direct students to clip the corresponding number of clothespins on the backs of their chairs. This activity is also great for beginning addition and subtraction practice.

Susan M. Valenti
Emmitsburg, MD

Mathematically Inclined Cereal

Kellogg's two-toned cereal, Crispix, is a great manipulative when teaching number combinations. The first time I used Crispix, students were learning the facts for 8. Each child tossed eight pieces of Crispix out of a cup. He then wrote the corresponding addition equation to show how many yellow and brown sides were exposed. For subtraction practice, students recorded the total number of Crispix and subtracted the number of brown ones from the total.

Julie Mitchell
Louisville, KY

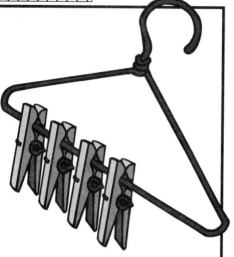

Visual Math Aid

Teach the commutative property of addition using a wire hanger and colored, plastic clothespins. Show a number sentence by displaying two sets of different colored clothespins on the hanger. When students respond with the answer, flip the hanger around to show the number sentence in the reverse order. Children quickly see that the answer is the same for both problems.

Tiny Stamps

Tiny Stamps (available from The Education Center) and minibooks provide students with hands-on addition-facts practice. To make a minibook, staple several 3" x 5" pieces of newsprint between construction-paper covers. Program each page with a different addition fact. To use the minibook, a student stamps a Tiny Stamp (the appropriate number of times) below each number in the equation. He then counts the total number of stamps and records the sum.

Kathleen Geddes Darby
Cumberland, RI

Musical Math

To teach averaging, try the "American Bandstand" method. Play a recording for 15–20 seconds. Pick two students to rate the record on a scale of 10 to 90, and a third student to compute the average. Repeat the exercise several times.

Rebecca Gibson Calton
Auburn, AL

Sponge Math Practice

Liven up your math fact review with this race against time. Wet a sponge and use it to write a number on the board. Students write as many corresponding math facts as possible before the number disappears. Before going on to the next number, discuss the correct answers.

Janet Boyd
Chandler, OK

Individual Flannelboards

I make individual flannelboards for my math class. With boards in their laps, children can match a design, make sets to match a numeral, or add and subtract.

Judy Lee
Letcher, SD

Keeping Track Of Beads

Here's a great device for keeping track of plastic bead counters. Provide seven-inch bicycle spokes for first graders and ten-inch spokes for second and third graders. Have students slide beads onto spokes for counting, or have students create interesting bead patterns on spokes. Spokes are bent at one end and have a screw at the other end, so beads won't fall off.

Mary Jane Farrar
Hamilton, Ontario
Canada

Math Tool Bag

I organized my math manipulatives into individual math tool bags and saved precious time. Inside each bag (a handy bag available from The Education Center) I placed a small clock, a 35mm film can filled with buttons, a ruler, a small piece of cardboard, clothespins, a Ziploc bag of money, and a Ziploc bag with fraction pieces. Then I attached a teddy bear shape labeled "Math Tool Bag" to the bag front. At math time, we quickly pass out the bags and begin. My students eagerly await a chance to use their "tools" and look forward to math each day.

Dorothy P. Schenk
Sunderland, MD

Calculator Check Center

There are times during the year when teachers don't need grades for the grade book, yet the students need to continue practicing math skills. At these times, set up a "Calculator Check Center" in the classroom. Students go to the center with finished math assignments to check them with the calculator. No pencils are allowed at the center, and incorrect problems must be reworked at the student's desk. This is a terrific way to teach calculator proficiency and let students check their own work!

Cindy Newell
Durant, OK

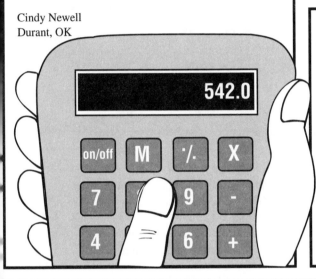

Math Management

Create subject folders for math to minimize planning time. Select colored file folders for each unit. Classify all supplemental books, worksheets, and tests by subject. Include photos of bulletin boards, games, and learning centers.

Carole Pippert
Laurel, MD

addition with one regrouping

multiplication tables

addition with two regroupings

division with no remainder

Mini Math Sheets

For an instant math review, cut old drill sheets or leftover workbook pages in half. Half a sheet doesn't seem as much to a child and makes skills practice a breeze!

Geraldine Fulton
Sedgewickville, MO

Let's Get Warmed Up!

My students, like athletes, don't begin math class until they've warmed up. I put five review problems on the board. Students work the problems on their papers. We correct the problems after five minutes. Students with a perfect warm-up earn a drink of water or some other small reward. This is a great way to settle children down, especially if they change rooms for math class.

Patricia Weinand
Sioux Falls, SD

Musical Math

Spice up a worksheet drill by playing musical math. Each child receives a worksheet, completes the first row, and raises his pencil. After everyone has finished, check the row and start the music. Children walk around the room until the music stops. Then everyone finds a seat and solves the problems in the next row. This breaks up the class routine and makes skill mastery musical fun!

Susan Staats
Chicago, IL

Calculator Week

The week before Christmas vacation makes a great "Calculator Week." Children bring calculators from home. Each day we learn about a calculator function and play a calculator game or complete a worksheet designed for a calculator. The children think they are "getting out of work," and I have no math papers to grade.

Cindy Newell

Tear Into Math

Watch students tear into math practice with this creative approach! Trim off the metal-tooth edge from a box of foil or plastic wrap to fit the top and bottom inside edges of a recipe card box. Glue in place. Write math problems on a roll of adding machine tape to put inside the file box. Students tear off problems to solve for extra math practice.

Elizabeth Cole
Annapolis, MD

The Checkbook Challenge

Practice addition, subtraction, and writing numbers with this math activity. Each child has a "checkbook," which includes several copies of a blank check and a record-keeping form stapled inside a construction paper cover. After sufficient instruction on check writing and record keeping, $100 is deposited into each child's account. Each day several transactions are listed on the board. At the end of the week, checkbook totals are compared and corrections are made.

Pamela M. Hartley
Twin Falls, ID

Math Spirals

Have each student buy a spiral notebook at the beginning of the year to use for math assignments. The notebook is used to keep all work together; it is also a record of student progress that can be used for parent conferences.

Paula K. Holdren
Chalfont, PA

"Buy" The Day

To reinforce the value of coins, have students "buy" the day. Duplicate a large supply of paper coins, and store them in a Ziploc bag. Each day, as the day's calendar number is added to your calendar, help students determine various combinations of coins that are equal in value to the day's number. Then have a student select corresponding paper coins from the bag and tape them onto the calendar. This daily reinforcement will help your students master counting money in no time.

Pamela A. Wert
Webb City, MO

Mighty Math

For students who continually finish their math before anyone else, I make a book called "Mighty Math." It has 15 to 20 pages of math problems that require more thinking than regular assignments. Students use Mighty Math only when their regular math assignments are finished. They work at their own pace. When the book is completed and corrected, students receive good-work certificates and may go on to Mighty Math II. On the cover of the book is a drawing of a hero for students to color.

Ruth Thomann
Noble, IL

Book Club Math Posters

Several children's book clubs offer posters for the children to sign when they place an order. I laminate the posters and program them with math problems. The students write the answers on the poster and look at the back to check.

Barbara Bosshardt
Hawthorne, CA

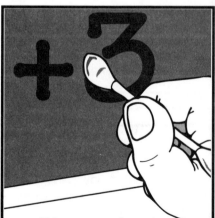

Disappearing Act

Using a Q-tip dipped in water, write a math problem on the blackboard. Then challenge your students to provide the answer before the problem evaporates.

Sr. Ann Claire Rhoads

Playground Mathematics

For a change of pace, teach a math lesson on the playground, using the painted game lines and equipment for materials. Example: Add the numbers in the hopscotch area to the number of circles drawn on the blacktop.

Sr. Ann Claire Rhoads
Greensboro, NC

Social Studies & Science

Social Studies Sneak Preview

Before each social studies quiz, I write the questions on the blackboard. Students may then pair up to reread their notes and/or consult their textbooks. When quiz time rolls around, students are more confident. Their thinking and writing skills have also improved due to the previous discussion of material.

Mary Anne T. Haffner
Waynesboro, PA

This Week's Challenge Assignment

During Monday's social studies and science classes, I ask a challenge question, such as "What state in the southeast region is the leading producer of peanuts?" or "What is the total of the planets' moons?" Students use reference materials to find the answer by Friday. Or I might present a creative challenge, such as to design five new products from peanuts. Students who complete the assignment are rewarded.

Mary Anne T. Haffner

Around The U.S.A.

Students demonstrate their knowledge of the 50 states with this question-and-answer game. Play begins with one student standing behind a seated classmate in his row. The teacher calls out the name of a state and the type of fact desired (capital, abbreviation, nickname, products). The first of these two students to answer correctly stands behind the next seated classmate in his row. The other student sits down. The winner is the first student to return to his original seat after traveling to all other desks in his row. (If no student makes it all the way back to his seat, the winner is the student who travels to the most desks.)

Mary Anne T. Haffner

1-800 It's Free!

Many states will send a good selection of maps and pictures for your use in regional studies of the United States. The phone numbers can be found in travel guides available at supermarkets or bookstores. Even calls that aren't toll-free don't cost much more than a stamp and envelope.

Janice Scott
Rockport, TX

Product Puzzles

Divide the class into small groups and assign each group a state. Have each group make a list of the products and resources of its state. The group then collects pictures of these items and glues them onto a large outline of the state drawn on poster board. The state-shaped collage is then cut out and jigsaw-puzzle lines are drawn on the back. Laminate the state and display it. When display time is over, each group cuts its state into pieces and stores them in a large Ziploc bag labeled with the state's name. Putting the puzzles together is a good free-time activity.

Janice Scott

Letter Test

To test social studies skills in a different way, I tell my students to pretend that they work for the chamber of commerce. Their job is to write me a letter providing information about a specific state: largest cities, climate, products that provide job opportunities, places of interest, reasons why this state is a good place to live. Students enjoy this type of test, and it also provides great practice in writing business letters.

Mary Anne T. Haffner

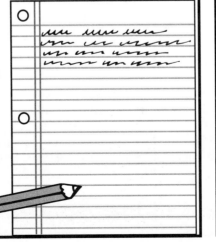

Grid Seating

Make changing seats fun and educational. Mark the front desk of each row with a letter. Put numbers on the desks in the far right row. When a student enters the classroom, give him an index card with his desk's location, such as "C-3." As students get better at this, begin labeling the rows with degrees of latitude and longitude. Give children cards with names of countries. Each student must go to the map, find his country, determine its latitude and longitude, and then find the corresponding seat. This activity helps review these skills throughout the year.

Linda M. Fonner
New Martinsville, WV

Social Studies & Science

Munchable Maps

Turn a field trip to the zoo into a munchable map skills lesson. Prior to the field trip, duplicate a simplified version of a map of the zoo for each child. Discuss the location of each type of animal, incorporating the use of the four cardinal directions. After visiting the zoo, have youngsters use animal crackers to design their own original zoo maps. Additional animal crackers may be used in the map key, too. When the maps are finished, munch on the leftover animal crackers.

Paula Metzgar
Circleville, OH

In The News

Spark interest in newsmakers with an "In The News" display. Cut out magazine and newspaper pictures of people in the news. Mount them and display them for students to identify. Include a variety of people from all walks of life who are making a difference in the world. In no time at all, even little ones will recognize political figures, movie stars, musicians, and other celebrities. This activity provides positive role models for today's children to emulate.

Becky Thompson
Cyril, OK

Mystery Trip

Introduce your students to new places and develop listening skills by taking a five-minute trip! With fingers ready, students listen to directional clues and trace the route on their own maps. (For example: Start in California, go north to the next state, and so on.) When the trip is over, students guess where they are. Encourage the children to write their own mystery trip directions to read to the class.

Mary Anne T. Haffner
Waynesboro, PA

Content-Area Management

Content areas are often the first to be cut when the school day is shortened or interrupted. To cover these subjects on days when the schedule has to be adjusted, write several sentences or questions pertaining to a content-area lesson on the chalkboard; then have students copy them. Have them read the corresponding lesson in their textbooks for homework, and complete the assignment. This activity helps make students more familiar with the lesson before it is discussed in class.

Mary Dinneen
Bristol, CT

Laminated Maps

These durable United States maps last all year. At the beginning of the year, duplicate a copy of a United States map for each child and laminate each copy. Have each student store his copy in his desk. Whenever a state is mentioned during one of our lessons, students quickly pull out their maps and race to see who can find it first. At the end of the year, students may take their maps home and continue using them.

Jolene Vereecke
Higginsville, MO

Weather Maps

Use weather maps to incorporate social studies skills into your science lessons. When unusual weather conditions (blizzards, thunderstorms, hurricanes, and so on) are forecast for your area, keep your radio tuned to a local station for weather updates. Have students track the storm or condition using maps of your state. This is a great way to enhance learning when students' minds are preoccupied with the weather.

Rebecca Gibson Calton
Auburn, AL

Globe Trotters

Add an element of chance to your geography lesson. Have each student spin the globe, and then use a finger to stop it. Wherever his finger lands becomes his "vacation spot" for a week. Have students research their vacation spots in encyclopedias, atlases, and resource books and at travel agencies. Their research should include information about the area's climate, tourist attractions, and government.

Cindy Newell
Durant, OK

As Free As Air

Who says only the air is free? There are sources of free materials for your classroom right in your community. Some places may charge a nominal fee as a matter of policy, but either way, most are glad to find someone who can use what is of no use to them.

Restaurants: colorful place mats and menus
Discount stores: card and magazine displays, pegboard and hangers, foam packing, small and large boxes
Video stores: posters that advertise movies (examine for suitability)
TV stations: weather maps, hurricane-tracking maps
Chamber of commerce: city maps, brochures
Police department: pamphlets on safety
Health department: pamphlets on drugs, etc.
Furniture stores: carpet and wallpaper samples
Card shops: holiday store decorations

Janice Scott
Rockport, TX

Beautify The School Grounds

Does your school have an unsightly planter or other neglected outside area filled with weeds instead of flowers? Combine a science activity with a good citizens' project to remove weeds, prepare the soil, and plant flowering bulbs. Your students will be proud of their efforts with the blooming of spring flowers.

Phyllis Marcus
Olean, NY

Shoe Box Show-offs

For an interesting end-of-a-unit project, I have my students make shoe box floats. Each child brings a shoe box (without the lid) to school. After turning the box over, the student decorates the top and sides with crepe paper, tissue, or construction paper. Our floats are then displayed "on parade" in the library for everyone else to enjoy.

Joyce Newman

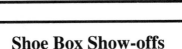

Let's Make A Rainbow

To make a rainbow in the classroom, simply put water in a glass pie plate and place the pie plate on top of a lit overhead projector. Hold a prism horizontally above the pie plate. The light rays will refract and shine a beautifully colored rainbow on the ceiling!

Chris Christensen
Las Vegas, NV

For A Good Cause

To raise money to adopt a whale, my students made wildlife bookmarks. After laminating the bookmarks, we sold them for ten cents each. The students really enjoyed designing, making, and selling the bookmarks to earn money for wildlife conservation. This project can be used to raise money for any wildlife organization or good cause.

Marsha Hood
Hampton, GA

Starry, Starry Night

My students really enjoy making constellations on black construction paper using minimarshmallows and toothpicks. They learn the shapes of the constellations and eat what is left!

Marsha Hood

Deciduous Tree Watchers

This yearlong science activity is a fun family project. At the beginning of the school year, send a note home with each child asking his parent(s) to help him find a deciduous tree to observe all year long. To make identifying the tree easier, attach a length of yellow ribbon to each note for the child and his parent to tie around the special tree. Select and mark a tree on the school grounds to observe as well. Have students photograph their special trees throughout the year as the seasons change. Culminate the activity by planting a tree on the school grounds in celebration of Earth Day.

Sara G. McGee
Evans, GA

Student Teachers & Substitutes

Fire Drill Reminder

I converted a bulletin board figure (from *Bulletin Boards Your Kids Can Make*) into a fire drill aid that is especially helpful for substitute teachers. I post the fire drill route on the cutout, along with a press-on pocket. I place a class roster in the pocket before mounting the cutout near the exit. As I (or the substitute) leave(s) the room, I grab the roster so that I can call roll.

Marilyn Borden
Bromoseen, VT

Emergency Worksheets

Label a large, brown envelope "Substitute Emergency Worksheets." Place plenty of puzzle sheets and worksheets to review skills in it. Also include a list of time-filler activities and a package of weekly student newspapers.

Name Cards

It's crucial that a substitute quickly become familiar with students' names. Seating charts require continual updating, and it's often difficult to make a quick determination of a child's name by looking at a chart. Early in the school year, have each student fold a 5" x 7" index card in half lengthwise and label it with his name. Store these name cards with other materials for a substitute. On days when you're absent, students stand their name cards on their desks.

Substitute Saver

This little idea can save your next substitute teacher a lot of headaches. In your plans, suggest that he or she offer 15 extra minutes of recess at the end of the day if students maintain good behavior. Students are usually motivated by this proposition and will work hard for the opportunity to spend more time outside.

Robert Kinker
Bexley, OH

Clean-up Cards

Ensure that your room will be in order when you return by leaving the substitute a deck of clean-up cards. Write a classroom job on each of several tagboard cards. Number and laminate the cards. Your sub can pass them out at the end of the day for a quick and easy cleanup. Since they're numbered, the sub can quickly collect the cards by calling for them in numerical order.

SUBSTITUTE First Aid Kit

Substitute First Aid Kit

Cover a cigar box or other container with bright Con-Tact paper. Label it "Substitute First Aid Kit" and place it by your teacher's guides. Fill the box with the following items:

1. A list of basic information about your classroom procedures
2. Nonperishable munchies, such as granola bars, a box of juice, and a candy bar (Sometimes a sub is called on such short notice that he or she doesn't have time to eat breakfast or make a lunch.)
3. Stickers and behavior awards
4. An explanation of your discipline system
5. A bag of small candies to distribute at day's end
6. A list of reliable students
7. A list of favorite class games.

"Quiet, Please!"

Here's a discipline tip to share with your substitute. Print the word "QUIET" on the board. Explain that each time you must remind an individual or the class to cooperate, you will erase a letter. If you must erase the entire word, students will lose time at recess (whatever amount you believe is appropriate). After one or two letters are erased, students usually settle down on their own.

Getting Off On The Right Foot

Help your student teacher get off to a good start by welcoming him or her into your classroom. The week before a new student teacher arrives, prepare a folder of information including daily schedules, a teacher's handbook, a building floor plan, a list of faculty and staff members, and a letter of welcome from each student and yourself. Invite your student teacher to visit your classroom and pick up the folder before he or she is to begin working with your class.

Cheri Richardson
Columbia, MO

Substitute Helper

Help your substitute teacher by keeping a small notebook of math problems and word lists. The notebook will be an instant guide for math and alphabetization practice. It's also handy for filling in five or ten minutes of free time.

Ametra Terry
Ft. Meade, MD

Welcome Mug

Welcome a new teacher or student teacher with a mug full of goodies: tea bags, pens, pencils, small Post-it™ notes, a sample bottle of hand lotion, change for the soda machine, and instant broth mix. This cup of kindness will make a new colleague feel like a part of the family.

Mary Anne T. Haffner
Waynesboro, PA

Guest Teacher

Use the term "guest" instead of "substitute" for a teacher who fills in when you are absent. Students will cooperate better and be more helpful for a guest in the room. Your "subs" will feel extra special, too!

Barbara Hosek
Canoga Park, CA

Substitute Saver

Your next substitute will enjoy using this technique to reward your class for good behavior. Ask the substitute to begin the day by introducing himself and drawing a smiley face on the board. Have him tell the students that he will add another part of the face to create a man each time they demonstrate desired behaviors. Students will be motivated to do their best and anxious for you to return and see their creation.

Brenda Terry
State College, PA

Student Teacher Strokes

Each month, I try to have something special on my student teacher's desk. At the beginning of the year, I include a folder with stickers, a magazine, a catalog, and one idea book. Then, each month I pass on a teaching tip or aid from a magazine, including catalogs and gifts. What a great way to encourage new teachers!

Sr. Ann Claire Rhoads
Greensboro, NC

Student Intern Gift

Every spring my class enjoys a student teacher for several months, and by the time the internship is ending, the students have become quite attached. As a gift from the students, I take a class photo; put it in a clear, plastic frame; and let each child help create a border by autographing the edges of the frame with paint markers. This is a wonderful keepsake for the student teacher and would make a great gift for a parent volunteer as well.

Kim Zimmerman
Tulsa, OK

Puppet Productions

Two to three weeks before the end of the school year, I begin this puppet project for last-week performances. First I show the class examples of different kinds of puppets made from paper bags or socks, paper plates on sticks, or finger puppets. Then I divide the class into groups of three to four students. They decide what kind of puppets to make. Then each group writes a play for their puppets to perform. Students usually find it easier to write scripts after their puppet characters have been created. After the plays are written, have a dress rehearsal for each group to perform for the rest of the class. During the last week of school, I allow groups to perform "on the road" for neighboring classes.

Kerrie L. Good
Sumter, SC

Game Day

For something different at the end of the year, the children bring in their favorite games to share in a morning activity. After breaking into small groups, they take turns teaching each other how to play the games. This not only holds their interest, but also reinforces the skill of following directions.

Cindy Ward
Rustburg, VA

Student-made Games

As an end-of-the-year activity, I have my students make gameboards to take home and play during summer vacation. I give each child the following materials: one file folder or piece of construction paper, 20 sticky dots, game cards cut from construction paper, a library card pocket, and a penny. Each child uses markers, crayons, and original drawings or magazine pictures to decorate his gameboard. The sticky dots are used to make the game trail. The student labels his game cards with a skill and stores them in the library pocket attached to the back of the game. Have students copy directions from the board on the backs of their games. Explain to children that the penny will determine the number of spaces for each move: heads = one space, tails = two spaces.

Kay Brickley
Houston, TX

"Choose Your Own Assignment" Week

With the "Choose Your Own Adventure" stories so popular, try this idea. During the last week of the grading period or school year, allow the class to choose their assignments in math, language, spelling, reading, and other subjects. After you select the unit for the day, the class has two minutes to scan the unit for their favorite page. Four nominations for favorite page are taken from the class; then one is chosen by a vote. The length of the assignment is also chosen by class vote (even-numbered problems only, first half of page, last half of page, and so on). Naturally the class will choose the easiest page, but when a review grade is needed, this type of assignment pleases everyone. I allow them 15 or 20 minutes to complete the assignment in class, so students have no homework that week!

Cindy Newell
Durant, OK

End-Of-Year Crossword

For the last day of school, make up a class crossword puzzle. The answers to the puzzle are your students' names. Puzzle clues should be positive comments about or characteristics of the individual students. You may need to fill in a few random spaces with the correct letters for added assistance. This makes a fun farewell.

K. M'Gonigle
Pittsburgh, PA

Leftover Lifesaver

Put restless students and leftover supplies to work for you! Mount white background paper on a bulletin board. Place half-used markers, pens, stickers, and other leftover materials in a box. When students finish their work, let them use the supplies to decorate the board. You'll finish the year with a creative bulletin board and fewer "leftovers" to pack away.

Our School Family

For an end-of-the-year activity, have each child draw a self-portrait on a stencil. Duplicate enough copies of each drawing for every student. (To save stencils and paper, divide each stencil into four parts.) Have each child staple his copies of the self-portraits together to make a booklet. Your children will have fun autographing their pictures in their classmates' booklets. The booklets will also be great reminders of the school year.

Susan Boyles
Winston-Salem, NC

Summer Letters

During the last week of school, I take a class picture of my students. In the summer, I have copies made and include them with letters I write to all the students. I tell them how much I enjoyed having them in my classroom and give encouragement for a great time next year. The students love getting these letters!

Michael C. Zeidler
Wausau, WI

Ready For Fall

Plan now to minimize your work next fall. As you take down your displays for summer break, place items that will be displayed again at the beginning of the year in a special box. Also include display materials such as tape, pushpins, and clips. You'll be organized and ready for action when you return in the fall!

Nancy Dunaway
Forrest City, AR

May-To-September Bulletin Board

My first bulletin board in September is made during the last week of school in May. My second graders write letters to the first graders telling them all the things they think they should know about second grade so they will have a good year. Writing on story paper, the students also draw a picture at the top, showing what they liked best about second grade. I always read them to the new second graders, and then make them into a book.

Betty Ann Morris
Houston, TX

Last Day Of School

On the last day of school, I ask each student to write a letter to the person who will be sitting at his desk next year. Each child fills out a form letter telling about such topics as his favorite subject, the best thing about the class, the funniest moment, and so on. Just before my new students arrive on that all-important first day of school, I slip each letter inside a desk with a "Welcome To School" pencil from The Education Center. The students' eyes really light up as they open their new desks. Parents always tell me how excited their children were that day.

Sharon Hayden
Perryville, MO

Ice Cream In A Can

Have students contribute the following ingredients and materials to make this tasty end-of-the-year treat.

1 egg	dash of vanilla
1/2 cup sugar	rock salt
1 tablespoon vanilla instant pudding	crushed ice
1 cup milk	plastic wrap
1 cup half-and-half	

Put all ingredients, except ice and salt, in a bowl and beat. Pour the mixture into a one-pound coffee can. Cover with plastic wrap and then the plastic lid. Place the container in a three-pound coffee can. (One-pound and three-pound coffee cans may be substituted with 13-ounce and 39-ounce sizes.) Add ice and salt around the smaller can and cover with the plastic lid. Roll the can on the floor for about 20 minutes. If the center of the ice cream is still soft, place the container in a freezer to harden. Since one recipe makes about four servings, divide your class into groups of four.

Tonya Cogan
El Dorado, KS

Story-Starter Send-off

On the last day of school, give the students story starters or writing ideas for each week of summer. Some suggestions may be to write the teacher a note, start a diary, or begin a travel journal.

Carole Pippert
Laurel, MD

Snapshot Surprise

With your final report cards, enclose snapshots of the entire class. The picture can be taken of a class activity and copies made for treasured momentos.

K. M'Gonigle
Pittsburgh, PA

End Of The Year

Appreciation Cards

The last week of school, my class makes appreciation cards for someone in our school other than students and teachers: the principal, secretary, custodian, a cafeteria worker, or the librarian. It's a good lesson in consideration and ends our school year on a positive note. I let each child deliver his card sometime during that day. A little kindness goes a long way!

Debbie Wiggins
Myrtle Beach, SC

To: Cafeteria Staff

This week's lunch menu has been one of the best ever. Miss Thomas's class of second graders thanks you. Have a nice day!

Worksheet Workout

This easy end-of-the-year subject review challenges your students' creativity, too! Ask students to pick any chapter out of a certain textbook that has been covered during the year. Have them create a worksheet, puzzle page, or question/answer exercise on that unit. Duplicate the activities for the entire class to do. Keep the sheets for a quick overview next year.

Debbie Wiggins

Student Summer Books

When spring rolls around, I'm busy preparing summer workbooks for my students. I provide practice sheets in areas where improvement is needed for each student. I also include fun activity pages featuring the students' favorite characters: Ninja Turtles, Care Bears, or My Little Pony. A construction-paper cover completes the booklet along with a smelly sticker for a surprise. It's a special treat for the last day of school!

Pamela Myhowich
Selah, WA

Awards Day

Because my young students go unrecognized during our school's final awards ceremony, we have our very own "Awards Day" during the last week of school. The children are given certificates decorated with stickers in recognition of outstanding achievements in reading library books, being super math students, exhibiting helpfulness in class, and other noteworthy accomplishments. We enjoy a super day together, and each child ends the year with several awards.

Claudia Nisbett
Greenville, MS

Thank-You Postcards

When children give me end-of-the-year presents, I always send them thank-you notes in the form of postcards. I send them from a vacation spot where I always go after school is out. It's more exciting for the students, especially if the postcard is from a different country.

Kathleen Baily
Avon, CT

Summer Teacher Meeting

Some of the teachers at our school meet during the summer to work on centers and prepare bulletin boards for the new school year. It's an easy way to get ahead on time-consuming projects and have a good time. At the beginning of the school year, our rooms look great—much to the surprise of the other teachers!

Rebecca Gibson Calton
Auburn, AL

Autograph Turtle

This last-day-of-school activity will delight your students and their friends. Make a large turtle pattern that children can trace on 12" x 18" pieces of construction paper. Each child traces and cuts out two turtles. He decorates one side of one turtle and passes his other turtle cutout to be autographed. Afterward, staple each turtle pair almost all the way around. Stuff two pieces of tissue paper inside, and finish stapling.

Judy Bone
Belgrade, MT